Ruta's CLOSET

BY KEITH MORGAN
WITH RUTH KRON SIGAL

UNITY PRESS
AN IMPRINT OF UNICORN PRESS LTD.

ABOUT THE AUTHORS

Keith Morgan was born in January 1954, in Blackpool, England. He began his career as a reporter for his hometown newspaper in Blackpool in 1975, moving to Vancouver, British Columbia, in 1980, where he is currently the Driving Editor for The Province and Vancouver Sun newspapers.

Ruth Kron Sigal was born in Lithuania in July 1936. After the Second World War, she moved to Canada with her family, where she died in December 2008, shortly after the completion of Ruta's Closet. A more detailed account of her life in Canada is at the end of this book.

ISBN 978 1 906509 26 2
EBOOK ISBN - MOBI: 978 1 906509 27 9
EBOOK ISBN - EPUB: 978 1 906509 32 3

First published in UK in 2013 by Unity Press,
an imprint of Unicorn Press Ltd
66 Charlotte Street
London
W1T 4QE

This book is typeset in Minion Pro
Design and illustration: Frank Myrskog.

Printed in India by Imprint Digital Limited.

~

Dedicated to Tamara Kron

~

Much was hidden in the darkest corners of Ruta's Closet – her own mind.

After decades of silence, Ruth Kron Sigal emerged from its mental confines to shine a light on the horrors locked within.

The Holocaust survivor recalled her most painful memories, hoping the lessons they teach will ensure no child will feel the need to hide in such a dark place again.

Contents

Acknowledgements

Ruta's Closet would not have been possible without the assistance of many people around the world, who generously gave of their time.

Deep gratitude is extended to Ruta's rescuer Ona Ragauskas, now deceased; the Right Honourable Sir Martin Gilbert, the noted Holocaust historian and Winston Churchill's official biographer; Saul Issroff, a Jewish genealogist; the late Leiba Lipshitz, Shavl ghetto's unofficial historian; and Regina Kopilevich, our guide and interpreter in Lithuania.

The following people also contributed significantly: Sheila Barkusky, Christer Bergström, Giedre Beconyte, Aaron Breitbart, Simcha Brudno*, Ellen Cassidy, Coby Chorin, Rose Lerer Cohen, Mike Constandy, Michael Cooke, Bernhard Göepfrich, Ben Gotz, Masha Greenbaum, Curt & Inga Haase, Art Hister, Don Hunter, Saul Kahn & family, Riva Kahn-Kibaasky, Nathan Katz*, Rachel Kostanian, Dr. Robert Krell, Rachel Lapidus, formerly Peisachowitz, née Rauzuk *, William Levin*, Gene Luntz, Mike Miller, Shaya Moser*, Bella Pace, née Peisachowitz, Jack Perlov, Jacob Reuveny, Anne Segall, Dr. Piotr Setkiewicz, David Schaffer, Craig Scott, Lorne Segal & family, Zev Shafran & family, Dov Shilanski, Cecil Sigal, Gerry Staley, Knut Stang, Saulius Suziedelis, Polina Toker, Yankl* & Ester Ton, formerly Ziv, Dominicus Valiunas, Paula Verbalinsky*, Fioretta Wilinofsky, Father Bill Wolkovich*, Ken Wosk, Sonia Zilberman-Wasserman, Markas Zingeris.

Shortly after this manuscript was completed, co-author Ruth (Ruta) Kron Sigal died after a long fight with cancer. Her enthusiasm for the project was boundless and she passed away, thrilled to know that her important story would be told far and wide.

* Deceased

FOREWORD

I have watched the evolution of this book with considerable fascination. Keith Morgan's work over several years has created one of the finest Holocaust memoirs.

It has not been an easy task: memories of so long ago can be fragile and uncertain. But Ruth Kron Sigal – Ruta – was determined that the story should be told, and Keith Morgan worked exceptionally hard to ensure that it was told – to the highest possible standards of readability and accuracy.

We are familiar with many of the great Jewish communities of the pre-war years and of their fate when they were turned into ghettos and became the scenes of mass murder and deportation. One such place that is less familiar is the Lithuanian town of Siauliai, known in Yiddish as Shavl. The few survivors of that once vibrant Jewish community have often expressed to me their sadness that it does not figure as prominently as it ought in most accounts of the Holocaust. This book redresses that balance.

There is another strength to this book that gives it particular importance today. On a recent visit to Lithuania, I was shocked by the unpleasant resurgence of anti-Semitism that belittled the Jewish suffering and denials of the direct participation of Lithuanians in the mass murder have become quite rampant. Yet this Lithuanian participation during the Holocaust was fully documented by a Lithuanian Commission set up ten years ago when Lithuania was seeking entry into the European Union. Lithuanians today need to know the story that is told so movingly and so powerfully in these pages. They also need to give honour – as Ruta and Keith Morgan do – to those Lithuanians who, facing the hostility and enmity of their neighbours, risked their own lives to save Jews. Among the rescuers whose stories are told in this book was a Catholic priest, Father Adolfas Kleiba, 'rescuer of Jews'.

These Righteous Among the Nations, of whom more than 760 Lithuanians have been recognised by Yad Vashem in Jerusalem, redeem the grim reality of Lithuanian participation in Nazi crimes, while at the same time enabling us to recognize Lithuanian Christian courage and life-saving achievements at a time when Christian values were being so terribly subverted.

Even as this book tells a harrowing story, shafts of light – of Jewish courage and Christian righteousness – shine through its pages, instructing and inspiring.

The Rt. Hon. Sir Martin Gilbert
19 July 2009

PREFACE

Ruta's Closet is the true story of how a Lithuanian Jewish family sought to escape the deadly clutches of Hitler's Final Solution.

Meyer and Gita Kron's determination to survive grew stronger and they became more resourceful as family members and good friends perished at the hands of the Nazis and marauding armed collaborators.

A series of narrow escapes in their hometown of Shavl - Siauliai in the Lithuanian language – and threats of betrayal by formerly friendly non-Jewish neighbours failed to extinguish the family's spirit.

This story takes place in a tiny Baltic country that even today wrestles with its collective conscience. It does so not because so many of its population stood by and watched their Jewish neighbours perish but because too many among them played a significant role in the annihilation of more than 200,000 Jews – 96 percent of the pre-war Jewish population.

Today's Lithuanians are reminded constantly about the complicity of many of their forebears. The blood of murdered Jews, who lie in shallow mass graves on the edge of town, stain virtually every community. Simple memorial stones are all that reveal the approximate numbers of Jews buried there are all that identify these locations.

To date, the telling of the story of mass murders and collaboration in Lithuania has been largely confined to academic publications and limited distribution Holocaust survivor memoirs, which are rarely read outside of the Jewish community at large.

Ruta's Closet explores that dark side of recent history but it also celebrates the few who risked their lives to save their Jewish brethren. Outside the high barbed wire fence of each ghetto, there were Catholic priests, who practiced what they preached. They ignored the entreaties of the church hierarchy not to become involved in rescuing Jews. They also decried brother priests who played an active role in the wholesale murder of the Jews.

The righteous clergy members were aided by members of their mainly rural flocks, whose faith moved them to save Jewish lives. It is only the selflessness and bravery of such ordinary folks all those years ago that have made it possible today to share the Krons' inspirational story of the triumph of good over the jackbooted evil that rampaged through the Baltic lands in the 1940s.

Many rescuers of Jews remain unheralded today because their surviving kin still fear retribution even in the 21st century, more than 65 years after the last shot was fired. Years under the Russians, following the departure of the Nazis, has left many unsure of their newfound freedom in the now independent and democratic Lithuania.

Nevertheless, in Ruta's Closet you will encounter some of those saintly folks, whom the Jews call Righteous Gentiles, and read of their bravery. It is the authors' hope that the telling of this story will lead to the recognition of more heroes.

This book is not fiction but written in a fictional style to make it more accessible to all. The late Meyer Kron left behind a substantive unpublished memoir entitled "Through the Eye of the Needle" from which the basic story outline was drawn. Similarly, members of the Peisachowitz, Gotz-Ton, Luntz and Perlov families graciously provided unfettered access to unpublished memoirs and personal documents, enabling a better description of events and even the inclusion of near contemporaneously recorded conversations.

While the story focuses on the Krons and their extended family, it also tells of others who touched the lives of the family. Descriptions of important events in the ghetto are based on material gleaned from traditional academic sources such as books authored by learned and respected historians, documentary film, archived contemporaneously written material and survivor memoirs, extensive interviews with survivors and review of their personal diaries and papers. A bibliography cites the published books used in research and recommends further reading.

The conversations and event reconstructions derive largely from memoirs and survivor interviews. Where no accounts of conversations exist, the authors created them in keeping with the nature of the occasion and in line with how the subjects typically spoke at the time.

As Saul Issroff, a London-based genealogist, said, "They did not necessarily have calendars in the ghetto." Dates and times have been hard to nail down in some cases, especially those concerning the experiences of individual ghetto residents recalled many years after the fact.

Contemporaneous records of meetings and ghetto events kept for the Shavl Judenrat – Jewish Council – greatly assisted but they are not foolproof. However, we are confident the dates and times are close enough. A great deal of the material used to describe the debate and activities of the Judenrat was gleaned from a volume published in Hebrew only, called Pinkas Shavli: A diary from a Lithuanian ghetto (1941-1944), written by the council scribe Eliezer Yerushalmi.

The Lithuanian language poses a challenge for English readers and writers in that surnames are gender specific. There is a common stem but the ending changes depending on the gender and relationship of the person within the family unit. For ease of understanding, we have used only the male adult form of surnames for all family members.

Lithuanian given names retain their original form. German names and army ranks used reflect the records of the day. The authors attempted to obtain all chosen names but documentation is lacking in some instances. In the case of the latter, a surname alone is used. Individual Jews are identified by their Jewish names rather than Lithuanian versions found in documentation.

Throughout the book, some people describe non-Jews as 'Lithuanians' to denote their ethnicity rather than identify their citizenship as would be the case today. Its use also distinguishes them from the Jews, who were, of course, also Lithuanian citizens. Soviets are often referred to as 'Russians', which while technically not always accurate is in more common usage among Western readers.

Communities within Lithuania take Yiddish names with some minor exceptions, generally in quoted conversations involving Lithuanians or Germans.

In conclusion, Ruta's Closet is not an academic paper or strict documentary but it is an honest attempt to share the experiences of one family and tell the broader story of the Shavl ghetto and the tragedy of the Holocaust in Lithuania.

Keith Morgan, April 2011.

Website: www.rutascloset.com

 facebook.com/RutasCloset

 twitter.com/rutascloset

Contact: rutascloset@hotmail.com

SIGNIFICANT PEOPLE IN RUTA'S CLOSET

The Krons and Family

Meyer and Gita Kron, and their daughters Ruta and Tamara.
Shana Kron – Meyer's mother.
Mendel and Joseph Leibovich — Gita's cousins
(chairman and member of the Judenrat, respectively).
Dr. Wulf Peisachowitz – Gita's cousin and head of ghetto
medical affairs.
Chaim and Rachel Peisachowitz, née Rauzuk – Gita's cousin
and wife.
Abraham and Tzilia Schatz, and their children Betty and Nathan
(Meyer's sister and husband).
Moshe and Lina Shifman – Gita's parents.
Iudite and Bluma Shifman – Gita's sisters.
Aharon 'Ore' and Hoda Shifman, and their son Yosef (Gita's uncle)

Friends and Neighbours

Berta and Simcha Brudno – mother and son
(close friends of the Krons).
Zava and Riva Gotz – Ghetto police official and his wife –
whose son Ben was born secretly in the ghetto.
Aaron Katz – Judenrat secretary
Nathan Katz – assigned to the German administration, smuggled
in medications (no relation to Judenrat secretary Aaron).
Dr. Joseph Luntz and Berta (Barbara) Nurok Luntz –
ghetto gynaecologist and his wife.
Dr Juozas Pasvaleckis – medical doctor hidden
by Father Adolfas Kleiba.
Polina Toker – dentist
Yankl Ton and Ester Ziv – Brother of Riva Gotz and companion.
Eliezer Yerushalmi – Judenrat scribe.
Joseph and Felya Zilberman – work colleagues of Meyer Kron.

The Rescuers and the Righteous

Pranas and Barbora Jakubaitis – pre-war neighbours
of the Shifmans.
Dr. Domas Jasaitis and Sofija – medical doctor and his wife.
Jonas Jocius – black marketeer.
Father Vincas Byla – Shavl priest.
Father Adolfas Kleiba – friend of the Ragauskas family.
Father Justinus Lapis – the Ragauskas family priest.
Antanas and Ona Ragauskas – school teacher and his wife.

The Germans and their Lithuanian cohorts

Ewald Bub – senior regional administration official.
SS Hauptsturmführer Heinrich Forster –
Einsatzkommando and senior SS officer.
Gebietskommissar Hans Gewecke –
head of regional administration.
Albinas Grebliunas – Siauliai (Shavl) deputy police chief
Petras Linkevicius – German appointed Mayor of Siauliai (Shavl)
SS Oberscharführer Hermann Schlöf –
Kommandant of Shavl concentration camp.
Antanas Stankus –
Head of Jewish Affairs for the Siauliai (Shavl) city government

CHAPTER ONE

Barbarians at the gate

A rural road, northern Lithuania –
Monday, June 23, 1941.

THE KRONS WERE REMARKABLY calm considering they were fleeing a hellhound in the shape of a massive Nazi invasion, bent on taking the ultimate prize for Hitler – Soviet Russia.

The Jewish family was trying to outrun the 3.5 million-strong force, which crossed the border at precisely 3:15 a.m. the previous day on foot, by bike, inside 3,350 tanks, riding in 600,000 motor vehicles and astride 750,000 horses, along a 1,080-mile frontier. Its aim was to subjugate Moscow quickly, create Lebensraum – living space for the expanding German peoples – and draw upon its vast natural resources to finish off the Allies.

If Meyer and Gita Kron had known of the overwhelming numbers involved in what was dubbed Operation Barbarossa, perhaps they would have taken their chances and stayed at home in Shavl, especially as their only choice of transportation was a horse and cart. This was a desperate attempt to steal a march on Hitler's henchmen, many of which would have a strong appetite for eliminating members of the Krons' ancient faith. Latvia would provide a temporary haven. However, it was Russia beyond that offered the most hope for their continued security, undesirable though its communist regime might be and despite its leader's anti-Semitic tendencies.

Meyer and his wife Gita walked, while their children, four-year-old Ruta, her two-year-old sister Tamara, and his widowed mother Shana clung uncomfortably to their spots on the rickety wagon. It was over laden with household goods and far too many personal belongings for there to be any speedier progress along the rural highway north to the Latvian border.

They were not alone on the road, which also made anything more than a snail's pace impossible. Hundreds of other Jews from their hometown and farther afield were making the same trek alongside, ahead and behind them as far as the eye could see. Fragments of the retreating Red Army, who moved somewhat more quickly, were also heading in the same direction to regroup and plan a counterattack against the tank-driven invasion.

Less than 50 miles away, there was frantic activity, the cacophony of the battlefront deafening all within earshot. Shells soared skyward, their eardrum piercing whistles providing an auditory account of their progress, soon swiftly silenced by earth shaking explosions and the screams of human beings torn apart by the fiery munitions.

In contrast, the Krons' journey so far had been quiet and uneventful, disturbed only by the barely audible murmur of anxious conversation from others on the road and the low hum of military vehicles, passing by.

Few words had passed between them, as they picked their way past the potholes on the poorly paved highway to the land of their Baltic neighbours. By the late afternoon, they were so lost in their own private thoughts that they let the bickering between their oldest daughter Ruta and her younger sister Tamara to continue longer than normally would be tolerated in the Kron household.

As the girls' shrill voices rose to a crescendo from the back of the cart, provided by their maternal grandfather Moshe Shifman, both parents snapped out of their individual dazes. Shana looked on as her son admonished the children.

In the quiet that followed the last of his sharp words, the couple simultaneously noticed the absence of Soviet soldiers. Their heads swivelled in opposite directions, turning back to face each other with questioning stares that conveyed their meaning without words.

Fleetingly, Meyer wondered why he had not noticed sooner. Surely, they had not vanished in the short time that the girls had distracted him. They stopped in their tracks and each surveyed the scene again, methodically panning like movie cameras producing mental pictures of what was around them. Their uniformed escorts had abandoned their vehicles and disappeared. The first signs of anxiety began to show in the Krons' faces as they turned their heads more quickly and cast searching glances towards the ditches. As their focus sharpened, they saw the occasional helmet bobbing about.

Meyer reckoned comrades elsewhere had radioed the soldiers to tell them that danger from above was approaching fast. It was intelligence not shared with their fellow travellers. Meyer's thoughts were interrupted by the muffled sound of what quickly he figured were artillery shells or bombs exploding in the distance.

People scattered in all directions, bumping into each other, tripping and falling headlong into the ditches. Startled horses whinnied noisily and kicked for their flared nostrils also smelled the danger. Carts overturned as the beasts attempted to take off to safety, their contents falling with a clatter to the road below. The old horse pulling the Kron cart remained remarkably calm. It was too old to follow the example of its younger brethren.

Meyer remained calm and steered his entourage off the main road, negotiating the cart's passage between artillery strewn across the road, abandoned by half a dozen soldiers, now hidden in a nearby ditch. Their young, fear-filled eyes met Meyer's steely, determined stare as he passed; he doubted any of them had lived much more than half of his 36 years, few of their fresh faces showed any sign of whiskers.

The Krons parked the cart by a barn a short distance away from the soldiers. No sooner had the cart's rubber wheels made an impression on the spiky grass than the Krons and all about them got their first sight of the dreaded Junkers 87 dive-bomber – Sturzkampfflugzeug – better known as the Stuka. A formation of three of the distinctive planes, with the inverted gull-wings and fixed-undercarriage, was hurtling in their direction at high speed.

Meyer pushed Gita and their daughters, with uncharacteristic roughness, beneath the cart alongside his mother, who had already taken up her place there without need of encouragement. His rough handling scared the girls, who began to sob. They could not comprehend what danger specifically threatened but they sensed it must be bad for their normally gentle father to act in such a way. He barked orders to those in his care to lie flat and keep their heads down. He too sank to the ground without the cover of the cart's underside but he ignored his own advice and could not resist raising his head to follow the progress of the fast approaching planes.

The Stuka fixed in Meyer's stare was the last to roll into an almost vertical dive towards him. The eerie wailing of the so-called

Jericho-Trompeten sirens affixed to the landing gear drowned the sounds of distant shelling.

Meyer whipped his head back to the point where he was staring directly up at the nose of the screaming Stuka. His brain failed to register the sharp pain in his neck caused by this sudden move. Meyer's youthful heart did not know whether to stop or continue pounding. He did not blink, for he could not afford to close his eyes for an instant. They both watered and his eyelids twitched. Through the blur, he saw the bombs released above him.

Now it was the turn of his ears to register pain as they rang with the high-pitched piercing sound emitted by the whistles fitted to the fins of the descending bombs, which grew louder and shriller as they closed in on their target.

"These will be the last moments of my life," a whisper, matter-of-factly, announced in his head. He silently prayed for his life but begged that if the bomb should take him it spare the nearby cart that hid his loved ones.

Meyer, an engineer specializing in leather production, would later joke that if he had been an aviation engineer he would have known his end was not near and not have wasted a prayer, as though there were finite limit on such calls to God. Even though the bombardier had released the bombs directly above him, the dive-bomber was pulling out of its rapid descent by then and the bombs flew by design, not vertically, but at a steep angle towards its intended target some distance from Meyer. They hit the discarded artillery on the road as desired by the pilot.

The barn nearby was in flames as was a cart on the road the family had left just minutes before. When the smoke from the nearby explosions cleared, they revealed the bodies of the young soldiers, who had sought protection in the ditch. Shattered and mangled bodies covered the road. The screaming of the wounded all around was as chilling to listen to as the deafening sirens that heralded the fateful attack.

As MEYER SURVEYED the scene of death and destruction, he considered his family fortunate to be still drawing breath. He wondered if he should push their luck any more. Would it be long, he asked himself, before he and his family would lay dead or dying at the roadside, maybe just a few miles farther along the road.

It seemed the only alternative was to return to Shavl and await the arrival of the German invading forces. Gita, always a voice of calm and reason, squeezed the hand of the man she affectionately called Mara and spoke reassuringly.

"Mara, we don't have a choice but to return. Surely, we will be killed if we continue along this road," she said, her last remarks echoing those that had occupied his mind only moments before.

She continued, releasing her grip and shaking her free hand to emphasize her point: "At least back in Shavl you have the factory and whoever is in charge will need you."

Meyer was not so certain of that. He coaxed the shell-shocked horse into action. Gita brushed off the dirt and grass from the children, as mothers habitually do, and they both lifted their most precious cargo back onto the cart.

AFTER A FURTHER brief exchange, in which the shocked Shana remained quiet, the family and most of the remaining stunned human caravan gave up their escape attempt and headed homewards. What none realized was those that reached the border would be turned away by the Soviets unless they could produce a communist party membership card. Not one of the Krons held such a piece of paper and they would have cause to celebrate that in the months ahead.

The weary travellers scanned the skies constantly for signs of more danger from aloft. A couple of hours later a welcoming darkness enveloped them. There would be no more visitations by the Luftwaffe that day. Gradually the numbers of those continuing their journeys decreased as one by one families sought places to rest their heads for the night.

When the Krons arrived in the small town of Ligum, it was already teeming with refugees. The gregarious Meyer soon struck up a conversation with a Jewish farmer, who was standing by the roadside as he had done for most of the day observing the flight and return. The older man invited the young family to spend the night in his barn. He had extended the same hospitality to a dozen or so others, the Krons soon discovered. Nevertheless, they were grateful for the opportunity to rest and perhaps even sleep when their minds ceased racing.

Exhausted though they were, Meyer and Gita talked for hours about what had befallen them. Only a week ago, they had a good life. He was highly placed at Frenkel's leather factory. The Soviets had nationalized it shortly after they had marched in to 'protect' the Lithuanians but his job had not really changed. It was not long after this peaceful entry that the new, questionably elected communist government had asked Moscow to make Lithuania a full Soviet republic.

Gita, ten years his junior, who was fluent in Russian, worked as a translator at the court. She was extremely bright. If she had finished the legal training that she had begun, she would have been a lawyer by now. However, these were unsettled times; maybe in a few years she would realize her ambition, she had rationalized to herself many times.

All of the family doted upon their daughters. Ruta was a bright, inquisitive child. Tamara might have added 'bossy' to that description, if she had known the word, to describe her big sister's attentiveness. Tamara was still very much the baby of the family. She was cute and put a sparkle in the eyes of all, except Ruta who was perturbed by the loss of her position as the only child and thus the centre of attention. Their family life was almost idyllic.

The decision to make a run for it was no spur of the moment decision. Meyer and Gita had witnessed how the Nazis treated Jews in 1935, while honeymooning in Germany. They were visiting the places where Meyer had trained as a chemical engineer, spending a particularly disturbing two weeks in Frankfurt.

In between touring galleries and attending concerts, the couple walked the streets and witnessed the early outrages of the Nazi regime. They were stunned to see bearded religious Jews roughly jostled in broad daylight, their assailants showering them with venomous insults. Occasionally they caught a glimpse of the hate-filled attackers pushing their victims into alleys, barely out of public sight, where they would no doubt suffer a vicious beating.

At any sign of trouble, the Krons would retreat into a store, often a quiet bookstore where they made themselves inconspicuous, thumbing through the pages of their favourite authors' contributions to literary history. Sadly, Frankfurt's bookstore shelves no longer heaved with the masterworks of past and present civilizations. Exactly two years earlier the first of what became commonplace public book burnings had taken place. Any work that represented what the Nazis perceived as promoting decadent western, liberal values was kindling for those with the gasoline and matches.

The Krons choice of restaurants was also severely limited, as patronage by 'their kind' was frequently unwelcome. Owners posted notices to that effect in their windows.

The Krons had not suffered any overt personal discrimination, though truthfully they never tested their luck by trying to go anywhere where it was clear they were not welcome. Maybe Gita's blonde hair saved them, a feature that certainly would help in the years to come.

Meyer was not sure the nature of the conversation was helping either of them. It reaffirmed the wisdom of their choice to leave but now they were going back to face uncertainty.

Eventually, Gita drifted off to sleep but Meyer lay awake worrying about what fate held for them. Seeking the protection of Joseph Stalin was the right one. Yes, his own family had suffered at the hands of Tsarist and Soviet Russia in the recent and distant past but it still seemed the lesser of two evils.

If only they had heeded the advice of family and friends, thought Meyer, he would not be tossing and turning now fearing what tomorrow might bring, but observing from the safety of the West. Meyer recalled how horrified they were to hear on the radio about the events of November 9, 1938 – *Kristallnacht*, the Night of Broken Glass. In one night, 91 Jews were murdered, 200 German synagogues destroyed and thousands of Jewish businesses were ransacked in a pogrom coordinated by the Nazis. Subsequent news of the advance of Hitler and his bloodless takeover of Austria raised more than an eyebrow but still it seemed so far away.

Later in the summer, his cousin Milton Shufro visited the family from Chicago, before heading home via Prague where he witnessed the German takeover of the Sudetenland region of Czechoslovakia. After he had returned to the States, the astute young man wrote pleading with them to flee to North America. The Krons had even begun the immigration process but then decided to stay put when Gita discovered she was pregnant with Tamara.

There were so many other warnings the couple had ignored. The rise of nationalism in Lithuania in the early 1930s was also a sign of things to come. Ruta's birth in July 1936 had pushed those threats to the back of their minds.

The meek surrender in 1939 of the German ethnic region on the Baltic coast known as Memelland – Klaipeda in Lithuanian – to the Reich should have been the final straw. That was just a couple of hours' drive away.

"How could we have been so blind?" Meyer tortured himself. He dozed off with that unfathomable question echoing in his mind.

Ligum, Tuesday, June 24, 1941.

THE SUN ROSE again on the Tuesday and shone brightly on the rural village of Ligum, just as it had the previous day. Somehow, that did not seem right given the dark events of the day before.

The Krons rose with the sun also, if somewhat gingerly. They gently awakened their offspring and Gita tapped her still slumbering mother-in-law on the shoulder. Shana awoke with a start and then surveyed the depressing scene before greeting her protectors. Meyer broke up some stale bread and passed it around. Ruta grimaced as she took her first mouthful but knew better than to complain. Tamara was less astute and spat it out. Ruta was surprised, and perhaps a little disappointed, that this act did not bring admonishment. The fact is both parents were too tired and worried about what lay ahead to take umbrage.

They were ready to continue their journey back to territory that was familiar but to a future that was unknown. They began to retrace their steps along the 20 miles of road between Ligum and Shavl. They had no protection this time, not that the Russian soldiers had offered much in the end. Their calmness of exactly 24 hours ago when they set out was replaced by high anxiety. In their minds, every rumble from the not so distant fighting heralded the imminent arrival of another aerial assault.

Some passers-by, heading in the opposite direction, heightened their anxiety with stories about partisans with white armbands, who were reportedly seizing and shooting every Jew and suspected communist they encountered. How bizarre, Meyer thought, that these fanatical anti-Semitic partisans could call him a communist, especially after what had befallen other family members a week earlier.

CHAPTER TWO

The enemy within

One week earlier, Shavl Railway Station –
Saturday, June 14, 1941.

GITA'S UNCLE AHARON SHIFMAN and his young wife Hoda shivered as they shuffled with the crowd towards the cattle wagons waiting in the blackness ahead of them.

The chill of the hour and the inadequacy of the clothing they had hastily donned before leaving home could have caused the tremors that shook them. More likely, it was a combination of the cool air of the late spring night and the fear that took a firm grip of them from the moment Russian soldiers roused them a few hours earlier.

They had both been deep asleep when the loud banging on their front door began, but they stirred quickly as the rapid rat-a-tat ripped through their dreams. Minutes later, the soldiers ordered them to dress swiftly and fill a bag with clothes. Obediently, they grabbed what they thought they might need; not that they had any idea where they were going. They did so meekly and without question for they intuitively knew that querying the instruction would result in them being assaulted or even killed.

While hundreds screamed and shouted around them in the station, the couple just glanced at each other, trying to make sense of what was happening to them. They wanted to say so much but they kept their exchanges to a minimum to avoid drawing attention. Their youngest son Yosef was quiet. He had asked them what was happening but, despite the absence of a definitive answer, he did not ask again.

They were Jews and therefore no strangers to the outrages committed by their Soviet masters. The Russians were not the only ones who abused the Jews. During his 60-plus years on earth, Ore, as Aharon was better known, had also witnessed much suffering at the hands of his more nationalistic neighbours, who periodically sought to blame the ills of this Baltic state on the Jews. In fact, from the mid-1920s to the arrival of the Soviets, Lithuania was becoming much less of a desirable place for Jews to live. Government authorities introduced anti-Semitic measures that made it harder for them to go about their daily business.

Hoda was only in her 30s but she too had learned to keep her own counsel and avoid the authorities, be they Lithuanian or Soviet. Ore tried to reassure his young wife but she was wise beyond her years and though she smiled bravely, she was not reassured. She turned away to attend to their son. Ore was lost in thought. It did not seem so many years ago that he had bounced this sweet young woman on his knee when she was a baby.

She was the granddaughter of his older sister Pearl and though they were second cousins, she had always called him Uncle. When they fell in love and married there were many raised eyebrows. That was soon forgotten, though, when the first of their four children came along. Peretz, their first son was safe in South Africa and, as far as they knew, their daughters Sarah and Hadassa were beyond the reach of the Nazis. What now would become of Yosef? – Ore did not want to ponder that any further so he turned his attention to the swelling numbers on the platform.

Ore noted with no surprise that Jews were well represented on the passenger list. The former mill owner had no doubt his capitalistic tendencies had earned him his ticket. However, he was surprised to see such a significant number of ethnic Lithuanians manhandled into the wagons parked in the rail yards. This action was not some manifestation of anti-Semitism because he was sharing the platform with some homegrown persecutors of his fellow Jews.

No, the common thread was that all those arrested were potential troublemakers, according to the Soviet regime. However, they offered no public explanations or justifications and none were expected.

The mass arrests and deportations were happening simultaneously in Lithuania and neighbouring Estonia and Latvia. The Shifmans' story had a similar ending as others forced to make the same journey. An early death for some in Siberia met by means unknown, likely starvation or diseases contracted while enduring the arduous demands of slave labour. Others survived – barely - and lived out their lives in the most inhospitable parts of the vast country that professed to treat all as equals.

ACROSS TOWN, HOURS after the late night arrests, Meyer Kron rose early to go to work. He was hovering by the door as Gita was finishing her morning makeup ritual. The phone rang.

"Let it ring. We are going to be late," he demanded impatiently, his hand already having gripped and turned the door handle.

She ignored him. The darkening of Gita's facial expression persuaded him not to press her to hang up. The rapid-fire chatter he could hear on the other end of the line suggested they were not going anywhere soon. He loosened his grip and dropped his arm slowly to his side.

Gita was white when she dropped the handset into the cradle.

"Mara, it was Uncle Ore's neighbour. They came in the night and took them," Gita's voice tailed off as the shock of what she had just heard penetrated.

"Who is 'they'?" queried Meyer, although it was more of a nervous response than a real question as he knew there could be only one answer.

Her brow furrowed as she began to explain: "The secret police did the door knocking and the soldiers dragged them off in a truck. The rumour is they went to the train station but nobody knows why."

For a few moments, they stared at each other in the same way as Ore and his wife had hours earlier as they tried to make sense of their arrest. What would the secret police want with Uncle Ore?

The early morning call stirred Meyer's mother, Shana, who had lived with them since the passing of his father Leibe, back in 1937.

"They don't need a reason," she responded. "Well, at least not one that makes sense to the rest of us."

Shana had seen it all before in her long life. This was not the first time the Soviet authorities had arrived on the doorsteps of family and friends in the dead of night. In the past, they had periodically carried out pogroms against their resident Jewry. She prayed that the Shifmans would be transported to a labour camp rather than face execution. Father Joe, Stalin's nickname in some quarters, answered her prayers. They all perished in Siberia on dates unknown.

Meyer opened the door for his wife and she brushed by saying not a further word. Gita must tell her father, Moshe, of his brother's fate, if he did not already know. When the youngest of his three daughters arrived on his doorstep at the family home on Basanaviciaus Street, one look at the senior Shifman told her he knew already.

When Moshe had heard about the arrests, he called his brother Ore to see if he had any insight into the reasons for the action. With each unanswered ring of the phone, his fear increased. He made his way quickly on foot to his brother's home. Before he was able to knock on the door a neighbour was at his side, breaking the bad news. He had only returned home minutes before Gita arrived. Once she stepped through the door, he returned to consoling his wife Lina.

As MEYER WALKED through town, he passed many tearful people, some sobbing quietly outside the homes of loved ones who had disappeared in the night. Others talked excitedly, asking anybody and everybody if they could shed any light on what had happened.

During frequent stops to chat to friends and acquaintances, Meyer learned the Russians had awakened hundreds from their sleep – later estimates put the total at 700 in Shavl alone, including 200 Jews.

The captives apparently came from all occupations: there were rich men, working people, doctors, engineers and even prostitutes. Generally, there seemed neither rhyme nor reason to most of the arrests. Meyer's childhood friend Chaim Hirshovitz and his family were among those taken. Fortunately, the Building Trust, where Chaim worked, decided it simply could not function without him and successfully secured his release. It would not be the last time that a job would save the life of a Jew.

The consensus of the gossip on the street was that the Russians wanted to eliminate subversive elements from the population, fearing the Molotov-Ribbentrop non-aggression pact might not hold much longer, which would mean war. People questioned the Soviet choices as to who they considered subversive, though not too loudly.

The pact had held since its signing on August 23, 1939, when the Soviets and the Nazis had agreed not to invade each other's territory. A series of secret protocols carved up Poland and the

Baltic states between the two powers. On June 15, 1940, Red Army soldiers arrived in Lithuania at government invitation and subsequently a dubiously elected communist government asked to become a part of the USSR.

Meyer felt helpless. Rather fatalistically, he decided they might as well have their suitcases ready. Maybe his job would save him; he thought more optimistically.

The insecurity and anxiety in the Kron household grew a few days later. The phone rang. This time it was Meyer's turn to answer. In recent days, there was much apprehension about performing that simple act. During a short call, he learned a man he was supposed to meet in Vilna had also been deported. Meyer sighed and drew a line through that appointment in his work calendar.

Meyer later confided to his diary: "There's a feeling in the air that war is imminent, but no one has any idea when it will start. The Russian radio and newspapers are very quiet about it but the whole world around us is heating up under the pressure of the aggressive policies of the Nazis."

It was a fear often expressed in writing but spoken about only in whispers. There was no point in unsettling Ruta and Tamara. They would not understand the words spoken but they would notice the tone of their delivery, especially Ruta.

The number of Russian troops in the area had grown steadily in the year since the signing of the pact. Meyer further noted that camouflaged tanks were everywhere and it seemed a great catastrophe was about to befall Shavl.

Each night, after the girls were soundly asleep, the Krons would listen to the war news from the BBC in London. Just a week after the deportations began they heard the news they dreaded. The Germans were building up their troop strength just beyond Russian controlled territory, which included Lithuania. Tanks, artillery and armoured vehicles were within sight of the borders.

Still, the Krons thought, rather optimistically, that nothing would happen, at least for a while longer. On Sunday, June 22, Meyer slept in as usual but Gita got up to get ready for an afternoon picnic she had planned with her colleagues from the courthouse, where she worked as a translator.

Meyer came round slowly as his wife shook him vigorously. It was only ten; he wondered what was so important to warrant such a rude awakening. He reached for his glasses.

"The radio," said Gita, who was not her normal calm self and seemed to be fighting for the right words.

"Mara, they say the war has started. The Germans have attacked."
The words were barely out of her mouth before she left the room.
Meyer fell asleep again, doubting this short announcement was
more than a bad dream.

He slept soundly until a bomb exploded a couple of blocks away.
Never mind bad dreams, he was about to share a nightmare from
which six million Jews would never awaken.

Meyer thought it remarkable that none of the build-up to the
war was even in the Russian newspapers or on the radio, not
something that would surprise Russian watchers in future years.

The first bombs had dropped on Shavl before the Russians
deigned to acknowledge events. It was not a big bombardment
– only two or three bombs – but enough to make everybody
realize this was for real. Belatedly, at noon, Molotov himself, the
Soviet Minister of Foreign Affairs, broadcast his message that the
Germans had invaded at 3:15 a.m. that day. There were already
some refugees from Taurage, which is about 65 miles south-west
of the border with the Kenigsberg region (now Kalingrad).

In Shavl's streets, people were running about like headless
chickens. Some people tried to buy medications while others were
lining up at the bakeries. Meyer passed the bread line-up and
instead took his place in the queue at the drugstore. The dapper
man bought an old-style cutthroat razor figuring there would be
a shortage of blades for his safety razor, which never transpired.
However, the second item on his short shopping list was not in
the least superficial: diphtheria serum for the girls.

He recalled the earlier 'peaceful' arrival of the Russians when
there were similar scenes. That day he ran into a man called Heller
who was the director of the Bank of Commerce. While discussing
the events of the day, Meyer mentioned he had two safety deposit
boxes in his bank. It was late in the evening but the two men
decided to go to the bank immediately and empty the boxes. It
was a lucky stroke because by the next morning, the Germans
had already taken the banks, seizing all the cash and negotiable
financial instruments. The valuables and cash helped the Krons
survive the rigours of the Moscow imposed regime and have the
spare cash to buy such things as the serum now safely tucked in
the pocket of Meyer's light jacket.

"I DON'T THINK we should stay here tonight," announced Meyer before he had even taken off the jacket and removed the medical contents from one of its pockets.

"The bombardment of the city is only going to get worse."

He got no argument from his wife. She suggested, "We should stay at Violka, Mara" referring to her parents' rural farm, which was only a couple of miles outside of the city. The idea of staying with grandpa was very appealing to young Ruta, who was soon packing a little bag.

"No, Ruta, we're only staying the night so you don't need to worry about packing a bag."

The youngster complained but one look from her father persuaded her not to pursue the matter any further.

It was a very warm and beautiful night with no signs of war. The family slept in an open field staring at the night sky for any evidence of the expected aerial bombardment, which never came. Maybe the advancing Germans figured they had softened up the Russians enough. Maybe they had other more worthwhile targets on which to dump their munitions.

Meyer used the opportunity to teach Ruta about the stars above. For hours, he pointed out the different constellations to her. Ruta loved the attention.

The Krons returned home Monday morning to go to work. It was a strange time. Were they at war or not? Most chose to look on the brighter side of life.

By the time the clock struck ten, no optimism remained; neither did any of the Communist Party officials stationed at the factory. They were conspicuous by their absence. Above the deafening din of the clattering machinery, workers shouted the latest rumour. A delivery boy or somebody else with business outside of the walls had returned with news that the communists were evacuating the city centre headquarters. For most ears, it did not matter what the source of this rumour was but for Meyer it did. He made an excuse to leave and walked at a fast pace towards the headquarters where he encountered prominent officials walking at a similar pace in opposite directions.

"They seemed very nervous," he told Gita, who was already home when he arrived minutes after witnessing the exodus.

"It's obvious the brass is moving out very quickly. They're abandoning Shavl."

Gita likely heard the news first, as the courthouse was closer to the action and the communist judiciary had ended their day's proceedings before they had barely commenced.

"I don't think many people, and especially our people, are ready to leave. After the events of this past week and the last year I'm sure many Lithuanians would even prefer a German occupation."

Many politically active Lithuanians saw the possibility of a return to their own government with the arrival of the 'liberating' Nazis. Fanatical nationalist groups had also put great effort into distributing propaganda that accused the Jewish Community as being communist and Soviet collaborators. The fact that a disproportionate number of Jews were deported in the Siberian transport seemed to escape them.

From the safety of Berlin, the exiled members of the Lithuanian Activists' Front (LAF) fanned the flames of existing resentment and prejudice by turning out propaganda designed to incite and heighten the level of hatred. The LAF was virulently anti-Semitic, urging likeminded Lithuanians to take violent retribution and warning Jews their day of reckoning was nigh.

Meyer was not encouraged either to hear on a radio broadcast that Archbishop Juozas Skvireckas and Kaunas Bishop Vincentas Brizgys had wired messages to Hitler welcoming the Nazis for driving out the Russians. Brizgys would later appear on radio to encourage young Lithuanians to volunteer their labour for German-led construction battalions.

The Jews of Lithuania now faced the same fate as their kin in neighbouring Poland and all points west. So began the Krons' voluntary departure for Russia, short lived though it was. A little more than 24 hours later they were back, shaken from their near death experience with a Stuka but otherwise physically unscathed.

On Tuesday, June 24, when the Krons arrived home the town was dead and there was no movement at all. Police patrols stationed at the intersections would not let anybody through. Fortunately, Meyer still had his papers and when the police officers realized he was the head of the tannery no less, the way cleared.

The Krons expected the Germans to march in within hours of their return but Russian tanks held the advancing Panzer division at bay about seven miles south of Shavl. Some optimistically figured the Red Army success would push the Germans into full retreat.

On Wednesday, Meyer went to the headquarters of the Building Trust hoping to see Chaim. When he arrived, his childhood friend was loading his family, as well as other workers who wanted to move, onto a truck.

Meyer was offered passage but the rest of the entourage was not prepared to wait until he had gathered his family. Where would they go anyway?

The two men shook hands and wished each other well. Meyer went home to consider their next move. The cannonade seemed louder and to Meyer it was evident that it was dangerous not only to be outside, but also to stay in the house.

On the Thursday afternoon, the Krons made their way to the house occupied by Gita's cousins, where they took refuge with the Peisachowitz family in their cellar. Joining them were Chaim Peisachowitz, his wife–to-be Rachel Rauzuk and an assortment of neighbours and family friends. In an act of bravado, Mama Taube Peisachowitz stayed above ground, baking as though there was nothing unusual unfolding beyond the four walls of the family home.

The Germans outmanoeuvred the stubborn Russian resistance and were now within shelling distance of Shavl. All around the explosions sounded and through the walls, they could hear the screams of wounded soldiers, some burning while trapped in their tanks. Their moans would haunt Meyer for the rest of his life. The tension in the cellar was palpable. Nervous chatter alternated with absolute silence within, shattered by the explosions without.

"How can you go to the bathroom with all this going on outside," asked one neighbour, perturbed by a signal from her own nervous bladder.

"It's easy, I've been three times already, without moving from this spot," Gita retorted, breaking the tension and even prompting a little laughter around the room.

◞◟

THE ENTRY OF the all-conquering Wehrmacht to Shavl was less than awe-inspiring. Gita's favourite cousin Dr. Wulf Peisachowitz watched the arrival of Hitler's mighty land army in the early evening from the safety of the city hospital. There were some tanks and trucks but many of the conquerors pedalled bicycles. The sight of a breathless red-faced soldier, puffing away as his legs powered his two-wheel mount was certainly the more abiding image.

Wulf decided to chance returning home once he was certain he had done all he could to make his patients comfortable. He made his way ducking down the alleys to avoid coming face to face with the enemy.

At home, he was not surprised to see his cousin Gita and family among those holed up in the cellar. Before descending the stairs, he checked on his recently widowed mother Taube, to make sure she did not join her late husband Benzion prematurely. The plucky woman was still baking and complaining how difficult the cows were that day during "all that pandemonium."

Noticeably absent were the Shifmans, who decided to remain on their farm across town during the hostilities. Gita had heard nothing from her stubborn parents, not that she was expecting to until matters had settled down. Nevertheless, Gita desperately hoped for some news to reassure her that they were out of harm's reach.

CHAPTER THREE

First blood

*Violka Farm, near Shavl – Late afternoon,
Thursday, June 26, 1941.*

THE SHIFMANS COULD HEAR the crackling sound of gunfire all around the Shifman farm but it did not deter Lina from going about her chores.

It was during one of those ill-advised brief forays into the yard that she found herself caught in a rapid exchange of fire between the advancing German forces and the Russians trying to make a last stand. She screeched as the bullet pierced her skin and she fell beneath a sapling birch tree in the corner of the yard. Instinctively, Lina pulled her hands to her chest, though the warm pain that spread across her upper body masked the exact location of the bullet wound.

She passed out but began to stir when she heard what sounded like a hammer banging against wood. It was a neighbour banging loudly on the back door, calling to Moshe to come quickly. "It's your wife, it's your wife . . . see, by the tree," were the only words he heard as he stepped out.

Moshe was so transfixed by the sight of Lina collapsed in a heap he brushed silently by the messenger. At first, he worried that his sickly wife had suffered a heart attack or stroke. Despite the aural evidence of the battle raging close by, it did not occur to him that she had fallen victim to a stray bullet. The blood that trickled from beneath her prostrate frame clarified quickly his understanding of what had occurred.

Moshe knelt down, his knee sinking into the soft earth shaded by the leafy tree. She whimpered. He whispered some words of comfort. He decided he must try to get her into the house away from further harm. His mind was awhirl as he tried to assess the extent of her wound. He dashed back into the kitchen and grabbed a damp towel to help make his amateur diagnosis easier. As he gently dabbed away the blood, she yelped as the coarse edge of the fabric brushed the bullet entry point. The wound seemed quite small and closer to her shoulder than her heart. There was just an awful lot of blood.

Moshe crouched motionless for an eternal moment, contemplating what to do next. Suddenly, a man's yell in a foreign tongue shattered his concentration. In an instant, a sweaty, dirty uniformed man was at his side and Moshe was looking up the barrel of his gun. His nose twitched and he jerked his head away as the acrid aroma of the still smoking barrel filled his nostrils. As he did so, the angry officer raised the weapon to fire it again, this time at the crouched figure of Moshe. The sight of the bleeding woman had convinced him they were both fair game.

He had the old man's head in his gun's sight but before his twitchy finger could do its worst, a second officer arrived at his side. Moshe's heart was pounding as he watched helplessly. His fate and that of his wife seemed sealed until the second soldier's arrival. The older German, clearly the first soldier's superior, let go with a rapid-fire order:

"He's no threat. Don't shoot him. Save your bullets for a Russian."

The order did not find a receptive pair of ears. Its issuer sought to cool the situation with a rationale he figured the young hot head would accept and provide him with a chance to save face.

"Let him go to take care of his wife. He is just an old Jew. He'll die soon enough."

The young man was not ready to make a complete retreat.

"Then let's arrest him and check out where his sympathies lie later."

"I'll take care of that. Now go."

Although the second soldier remained, Moshe returned to the business of tending to his wife. He was shocked to hear his name spoken by the battle weary German at his side. He looked up and as the man wiped the mud from his face, a familiar smile shone through.

The Shifmans' saviour once owned a farm close by. He was a Volkdeutscher – an ethnic German living in another country. With the rise of Hitler, he believed his place was in das Reich – or, to use a term popularized among the Allies, the Fatherland. He moved there a few years earlier and subsequently obtained full German citizenship. That enabled him to join the Wehrmacht and fight for Hitler's dream, part of which was ridding the world of Jews.

However, in this case, the returning Shavler recognized Shifman as a good neighbour, who had helped him during his leaner years of farming. The German owed this old Jew at least one favour.

Lina had drifted in and out of consciousness during the earlier heated exchange. Their old neighbour knelt down with Moshe. The friendly soldier ripped away Lina's blouse to get at the wound. Moshe thought better of defending his wife's honour.

"She's only been winged . . . it's more shock than anything," he said dismissively. He stood up. "Now stay here and get help later or else you may be the next to fall. We will take Schaulen (Shavl) tonight but there will be stragglers from both sides behind our lines. They will shoot first and ask questions later."

It was a silly cliché oft heard in the Hollywood action movies shown in the Shavl cinema in peaceful times before the arrival of the Russians. Nevertheless, the meaning was clear and Moshe nodded his assent. With that said, he left abruptly without offering any farewell, leaving the older man to manhandle his wife back into the house. Moshe said a silent prayer as he pulled the kitchen door closed behind him.

He helped Lina to the sofa, bearing her weight, and gently laid her down, pushing a cushion beneath her head, which jerked as she sobbed. Moshe grabbed a towel and carried on with the cleanup, calming her with carefully chosen words of reassurance.

The towel was the damp cloth his wife had earlier used to mould the bread dough. Scraps dropped onto her shoulder as he dabbed but that was the least of his concerns. He marvelled at how she had shown her determination to continue her life as normal. She had paid painfully for such bravado, unlike Mama Peisachowitz across town, who had shown the same unwillingness to buckle to the invaders.

The wound was now no longer gushing blood. He began to move away to look for other cloths from around the kitchen to make a bandage. He was sure there must be some real bandages somewhere but he did not ask and she was in no condition to offer any guidance. No matter.

She was calmer now. Moshe decided to wait for just an hour not the four or five hours the officer had advised. He would carefully load her onto the wagon Meyer and Gita had used in their ill-fated attempt to flee the advancing German army. He would take her to the hospital on Pagyziu Street where he would seek out Dr. Wulf Peisachowitz, confident that she would then be in the best of medical hands.

Half an hour later Lina was a little too quiet for his liking. She had passed out. No neighbour in his right mind would come to his aid. As he carried her out to the barn she revived, much to his relief and she summoned the strength to climb aboard the buggy. By the time they reached the hospital, Wulf had left.

Not long after daylight on Friday, there was a rapid series of knocks on the door of the Peisachowitz home. Gita answered it rather than leave it to the residents of record; intuitively she knew the person outside was looking for her.

A red-faced young man, still panting from what must have been a dangerous run across town looked straight at her. He knew her but Gita only vaguely recognized him as somebody who occasionally helped on her parents' farm. He stepped in and breathlessly delivered the news of her mother's condition and her current location.

As she let the messenger out by the door he entered, she got her first sight of the results of the previous night's battle on their doorstep. There were dead Russian soldiers on the streets. The administration had fled days earlier and left few behind to fight for Shavl. There was little further opposition after the Germans' arrival.

Wulf escorted them to the hospital, taking a similar circuitous route to the one he had used the night before. The streets were deserted and the pungent smell of smoke from small smouldering fires filled the air. As they approached the surprisingly undamaged hospital, Wulf cursed that he had not been there when Lina arrived.

Mama Shifman was sitting upright in her bed, suggesting he need not have worried about her care and protection. He felt a little guilty for harbouring any doubts as he scanned her chart and noted the name of the doctor who had treated her. It was a doctor he greatly respected, as did all who knew Dr. Domas Jasaitis.

It was not just that he was an accomplished physician; his kindly demeanour endeared him to his colleagues and patients. He was a stocky, broad shouldered man, whose clothes were always crumpled and his straight greying hair in sore need of attention from a comb.

People invariably heard him before they saw him. The jovial man with the warm blue-grey eyes frequently announced his imminent arrival with a rendition of a famous operatic aria, which currently enchanted him. Once he caught sight of his audience, he would pause mid-stanza and greet them with a bear hug and a kind word. He refused to allow what was happening around him to dampen his exuberant behaviour and all who heard him were grateful for that.

There was also a serious, quieter side to the doctor that few people knew about at the time. Quietly and without fanfare, he often came to the aid of Shavl's Jews. In fact, he would play a significant role in the future well-being of the Kron family.

THE KRONS GATHERED the children and Shana from the Peisachowitz place and returned to their city centre home. All was quiet and clearly, the Germans were now in charge. They rationalized that at least now, there would be some semblance of law and order and they would therefore not likely come to any harm in their own home.

The new occupiers had set about the business of governing. Already large publicly displayed notices ordered all residents to remain quiet and to proceed with their daily work. The literature viewed on their walk home could have caused them to question their optimism but they pressed on to familiar territory.

WITHIN HOURS OF the German entry to Shavl, LAF members began to victimize Jews, robbing some and beating others. Two days later the same groups started to arrest Jewish men, housing them in deplorable conditions in the local jail. After the weekend, when no more could be crammed in, the LAF selected those arrested earlier and took them to the nearby Luponiai woods to execute them. During the next week, 1,200 more Jewish men were murdered. At the commencement of hostilities, 25 percent of the town's 32,000-strong population was Jewish. The armed anti-Semites were making a concerted effort to change those statistics rapidly. Was this pogrom motivated by their zeal or instigated by German secret agents, who had arrived in their midst prior to the military invasion? It was an open question, never answered satisfactorily.

On the Saturday at noon, the LAF arrested more than two dozen of the Jewish community's most prominent citizens. Among the captives were business people, lawyers, and religious leaders including Chief Rabbi Aaron Baksht. Their captors made it known that should Jews take any action against the occupying authorities they would execute their new hostages.

THE BANGING ON the door of the Kron household on the Sunday morning drew a slower response than would normally be the case. They were leery of answering, given the stories circulating about surprise arrests and disappearances. However, Gita braced herself and got up to answer. She was relieved to see it was not an LAF volunteer there to arrest Meyer.

Nevertheless, Gita was surprised to see her father at the door, thinking he would still be at her mother's hospital bedside. It was probably the safest place in town. The weary man hugged his daughter. That said it all and tears welled up in Gita's eyes. Her mother had cancer of the bladder and, even though the injury she sustained seemed small, her poor state of health and the shock had contributed to her demise.

The kindly Dr. Jasaitis arranged delivery of the body to the family so they could arrange for a burial within 24 hours, as is the Jewish tradition. It was a magnificent gesture but it also posed a significant problem for the Krons who must now plan a funeral in very difficult conditions. Meyer could not take the chance to go out on the streets to seek out those who might help.

Unexpectedly, a neighbour of the Shifmans offered his services and the use of his *drozhki* – a small, open cart he used to make deliveries. He placed the deceased woman in a simple pine box then loaded it into a rickety wagon.

The grieving Gita walked alone behind the casket as the family's sole representative. A large group of mourners would attract unwanted attention and thus threaten the lives of the rest of the family. Her sisters Iudite and Bluma could not have been there even if they had wished. Iudite then lived quietly in Italy and Bluma had left Lithuania just before the war to move with her husband Daniel to what is now modern day Israel.

"Mama, mama," she cried out, "we are alone today but we are not alone. Papa, Iudite, Bluma and all the family may not be here to mourn you but they all follow you here in spirit."

Just minutes later, Lina Shifman was buried without formal ceremony in the Jewish cemetery. There were no Rabbis available to officiate as they were all in the city jail. Gita was never able to recall exactly where her mother's body was interred. It would not have been much comfort because the Russian occupiers of a future era uprooted the Jewish cemetery, using the headstones to build walls and sidewalks.

MEYER'S MIND TURNED to thinking about a return to work. He figured the Germans would need the factory to continue operating and a Jew with a job would survive but how could he get back in, safely?

He was right. It was to play a vital role in ensuring those unfortunates fighting on the Eastern Front would continue to go into battle well shod.

When Meyer showed up at the factory on Monday, the Russian appointed workers' committee was still in charge. That situation changed rather quickly with the arrival of Müller, a wounded Luftwaffe pilot appointed director by the new occupying authority.

The idea was for non-Jews to replace the Jewish workers but Müller quickly figured out he was not going to get the production out of such untrained workers. Müller immediately recalled the Jews but some of the specialists he needed were among those arrested in recent days.

Meyer listed 100 staff that he said must return and handed it to the new German director. Many were awaiting their fate at the hands of the LAF. Meyer had learned their identities by some means and made sure they were on the list. Although some did not possess the needed skills, all would be quite capable of performing simple labour tasks to look busy during their shifts. Meyer smiled as he jotted down the last name. Each one of those listed had families of five or six so the whole family would enjoy the protection of their employment.

Müller appeased the local authorities by assuring them that the Lithuanians employed would learn from the freed Jews and eventually be able to take over key positions.

Many workers, including Meyer, ingratiated themselves with Müller, making him leather suitcases, handbags and the boots so treasured by the invaders. Müller thus became a powerful person in the city because he in turn was able to ingratiate himself by supplying such desired goods to high-ranking Nazis and German officials.

Later that same week, the Krons became hosts to the enemy. Two young German officers took over mama's suite in the house and helped themselves to some furniture, including the radio and the piano. At least they did offer a nominal payment. A pair of soldiers billeted with them during the most recent Russian occupation turned out to be a blessing, as they became their protectors. Perhaps the same benefit would apply.

Within days, their new tenants' worth to them as unofficial bodyguards became evident. The Krons heard of the arrest by persons unknown of their downstairs neighbours, Grozdienski and his two sons. They never determined whether the captors were partisans or Germans, though they thought it more likely the former.

When the unexpected visitors started up the stairs to the Kron suite, one of the Krons' non-paying German guests shouted: "Don't go up there. He is a good Jew." The Krons never saw the Grozdienski family again.

A DAY RARELY passed without some members of the Jewish community suffering an atrocity. One of the worst days was Friday, July 11. The LAF sent out dozens of small squads to arrest still more Jews and help themselves to their most desirable personal property. They began door knocking at 9 a.m. and searched every home for many hours until they had seized everything of value that they could find. Terrified families stood by as their former neighbours ransacked their homes and left with family jewellery, gold, cash and anything else that caught their eyes. The aggressors then arrested the men of each victimized family and forced them to carry the belongings to the police station.

This was the final straw for the German military police. If anybody was going to steal from the Jews, it should be members of the Master Race, as the Nazis liked to consider themselves. The occupiers' representatives confronted the LAF with their prisoners outside the People's Home movie theatre. The humiliated LAF members were disarmed, searched and the Jews were sent home with their belongings. Well, not all of their possessions: the military police kept the gold and cash.

LAF power, perceived or real, would soon be gone. In early August, the Germans dissolved the provisional Lithuanian government nationally and took complete control.

At noon that day, the prominent Jewish citizenry, arrested almost two weeks earlier, journeyed by truck to a nearby forest, where they were murdered. The ruse was that they were paying for the sins of their brethren, who had allegedly taken pot shots at German soldiers in some recent incident. The other version doing the rounds was that the shootout was in fact no more than the hijinks of drunken soldiers letting off steam.

THE SHOOTINGS OF other Jews continued that summer in the woods around the city, mainly under the supervision of Hitler's emissaries. Ona and Antanas Ragauskas flinched as shots rang out a short distance away. Each night they would sit outside their little schoolhouse home in Amaliai trying to forget the war and enjoy the light, warm summer nights. The first night they heard the gunfire was at the end of June. They shook with fear. At first, they wondered if the Russians had returned and a counter offensive was underway. The shooting began in the mid afternoon and went on until dusk.

They quickly realized there was only one set of people with guns. There was no return fire. The devout Roman Catholic couple was horrified when they heard accounts from neighbours about the summary execution of Jews in the nearby Kužiai forest. Some talked with glee, rationalizing that the Jews were getting their just reward for what they had done to good Lithuanians during the Russian occupation. This gossip confirmed their worst fears about their new Germanic occupiers and a disturbing number of their old Lithuanian neighbours.

"If I have a chance to help, I must do so," thought the compassionate young woman, squeezing her husband's hand tightly as each shot shattered the stillness of the warm summer night.

CHAPTER FOUR

Where death stalks

Ponevezh – August 23, 1941

MEYER KRON'S OLDER SISTER Tzilia Schatz often rambled along the country roads outside of Ponevezh in the summer, admiring the beauty of fields full of ripening crops as she strolled.

This time her thoughts were not in the least carefree as she walked slowly alongside her teenage daughter Betty. She guessed what awaited them somewhere down the road, probably in the Pajuris forest on the near horizon.

Tzilia would not share such doom-laden thoughts with her daughter and, judging by the quietness of the other 200 or so in the same column, other mothers had also decided to remain silent. She wondered if the girl and her brother Nathan had heard her quietly discussing the disappearance of hundreds of their neighbours with their father. Her daughter's calm demeanour suggested they had not. Doubtless, her husband Abraham had similar thoughts when he and their son had walked this same route some hours earlier.

The Nazi-led police squad had stormed into the tiny ghetto earlier in the day and emptied it, street by street, of all the community's men – aged 14 and above. The armed men, made up largely of Lithuanian collaborators, then marched off groups of a few hundred at a time in the same direction as the two women were now heading.

When the Aktion finally took place, it was no shock really. The only surprise was that her lawyer husband was not taken days earlier along with other formerly well-to-do and prominent members of the community.

She looked down at the road for a moment, praying her brother Meyer and his family was safe in Shavl. They should have headed

47

there when they had the freedom to make such a decision, she thought for the hundredth time. Weeks earlier, when the barbed wire was erected around the ghetto they had convinced themselves that as Abraham was a respected lawyer so surely nothing would happen to them.

❧

THIS DAY WAS the culmination of two months of hell for the Jews of Ponevezh. The German army had entered the town on June 26, the same day as it had taken Shavl. The almost 10,000 strong Jewish community, the third largest in the country, was subjected to a series of horrific pogroms, carried out by fascists in their midst. They were horrified to discover that numbered among the ringleaders were people holding the most prominent and respected positions in the town. One was the high school principal, another was the school inspector, the deputy provincial prosecutor, and the secretary to the provincial court, to mention just a few.

As in the rest of the country, the homegrown fascists did not wait for the German army to arrive before attacking the Jews – they got a two-day start. Jews were marched around town and beaten on the way. Townsfolk stood around in huge numbers. Some watched and remained silent while others hurled stones at their Jewish neighbours.

In the early days, farmers co-opted young and able-bodied Jews as slave labour. Many never returned from their day's unpaid work and so the whittling away of the community began, one by one, a dozen here, a dozen there.

Many of the Jews' persecutors would consider themselves good and faithful Christians. In many parts of central and east Europe, particularly in rural areas medieval myths and prejudices still dominated religious teachings. Jews were Christ's killers. They were the physical incarnation of evil on earth.

At the beginning of July, the local authorities forced the Schatz family out of their comfortable, two-storey home. The authorities herded the family, along with the rest of the Jewish community, into a ghetto, adjacent to the town abattoir. At 6 p.m. promptly on July 11, the area was fenced off and some of the police that lined the road this day took turns to stand guard, 24 hours a day.

Those that had previously inhabited the ghetto streets may have lost their homes but soon found themselves enjoying the homes vacated by the Jewish community. It was a pattern of events repeated throughout Lithuania.

The authorities closed the ghetto and took 70 dignitaries hostage to discourage escape attempts. Subsequently the leaders were spirited away to the forest where they were shot and buried.

Armed men frequently entered the ghetto at nightfall. Once there they would force their way into houses, terrorize their Jewish victims and help themselves to whatever they pleased.

One particular story shook Abraham and Tzilia to the core, as it did every other person who heard it. It concerned a farmer who was not satisfied with the day's slave work of his captives. At his behest, some of his sadistic cohorts took the Jews to a nearby cement factory. Inside there were vats full of concentrated lime, to which the Jews were ordered to add water. When the lime began to froth and bubble, the leaders ordered them to jump and swim around in the water. They pushed in the Jews who refused to jump and they savagely beat those who subsequently tried to climb out with rifle butts.

Eventually they released their victims from the pits but they never returned home for they were living – barely – proof of the savagery. The story leaked out anyway, spilled by one of the participants over a beer in a local hostelry.

As July wore on and the heat of August arrived, the numbers taken out of the ghetto grew to be many dozens at a time. Finally, it was the turn of the Schatz family.

TZILIA'S THOUGHTS RETURNED to the present. She eyed the hundreds of police and local residents that lined the roadside ditches, many recruited for the day to make sure no captive escaped.

The silence of the marchers was broken first by sobbing and then more hysterical cries as one by one the unwilling marchers realized what was to become of them. The greatest outburst coincided with their entrance to a clearing in the woods. Agitated minders struck out at the crying women.

At that point, there was no official order to make Lithuania *Judenfrei* – free of all Jews. However, the *Schutzstaffel*, better known simply as the SS, had generous guidelines in choosing the victims they deemed would most likely hinder the progress of their advance.

Efficient killing squads, known as *Einsatzkommando*, led by SS officers, using Lithuanian auxiliary units to do the dirty work, got a head start on what would be termed the *Final Solution to the Jewish Question* in January 1942.

At the site, the executioners that greeted the arriving Jews were flush-faced not because of their strenuous efforts but because of their breakfast rations of vodka. The SS knew that some of those tasked with the final duties would show a weakness of spirit without a belly full of liquid courage. The mainly young riflemen dutifully ordered their victims to take off their clothes and pile them in the clearing. They would later be collected and doled out to the 'poor' in Ponevezh.

The naked Tzilia shivered. The air may have been warm but the sight of the recently dug 60-yard long trenches sent a chill down her spine. As she got closer she could see the trench nearest to her was already half full. The stench was unbearable. Faeces mixed with urine everywhere. Bodies lay contorted, frozen during their owners' death throes. The faces of some were missing. Some fainted around her. She squeezed the hand of her daughter, who remained quiet. Their group filed down the earth ramp at the end of the trench.

The latest batch for victims lay flat on the corpses as ordered. Some stared down into people they had known all of their lives, while others were cheek-to-cheek with the grotesquely contorted faces of complete strangers.

Armed with rifles, the 80-plus guards fired a hail of bullets into the prostrate Jews from both sides of the four-foot deep pit. Those that showed signs of life after the shooting had stopped received a 'merciful' single shot to the head from a Walther P38 pistol fired by an obliging SS officer.

As the day wore on, group after group followed each other to the killing fields until no Jew remained standing. The last group included patients from the Jewish hospital and all the medical staff. The doctors and the nurses were still wearing their medical whites when they arrived at the pits. Witnesses later reported that surgeon Dr. Theodore Gutman was among them. He addressed his team, encouraging them to accept their death with dignity. Rather too confidently, he assured them that future generations would avenge their deaths.

After the final shots of the day had felled the doctor and his fellow medics, the Russian prisoners of war charged with filling in the graves began their grisly task. A few of the supposed dead were not. The Russians surreptitiously pulled the wounded Jews from the pit and helped them to the safety of the bushes.

However, these roving killer squads were sharp-eyed and had come to expect such heroics from their misguided gravediggers. They beat the Russians and finished off those wretched souls they had attempted to save. Among those rescued was a child but he was executed summarily despite pleas from some of the killers with weaker stomachs. The commander insisted, "The child cannot be permitted to get away. Better to kill him and so ensure that there is no one left to avenge the blood of the Jews." He then aimed his pistol at the child, shot him through the head and walked away.

Such a day's work often ended with the host community feting the killers in a local hall, sometimes even a church building, and today would conclude in the same way. Even men of the cloth were actively involved with some of the squads. Dozens of priests recruited executioners and some even pulled the trigger. They doubtless believed they had the blessing of Archbishop Skvireckas, who recorded his approval of Hitler's anti-Semitic beliefs in his personal diary. Most would later flee to Germany to escape prosecution by the succeeding Soviet regime.

Among the drunken revellers in those church halls, there was much boastful talk. One grisly tale told of separating babies from their mothers, tossing them into the air and then shooting them like game fowl as they dropped into the pit. Not likely possible with only long guns at their disposal. However, its unashamed repetition many would suggest speaks to the bestiality of the executioners.

They could have told stories of mass rape but they may have considered them too offensive, or perhaps the perpetrators feared their wives or girlfriends might take exception to such sport.

BACK IN THE ghetto, another group formed from the local citizenry took one more run through the empty ghetto to make sure they had plundered everything of value that had belonged to their now deceased neighbours.

The day's murderous activities marked the final stage of the German-directed extermination of the Ponevezh Jews. By the end of the day, the Nazi bookkeepers were gleefully recording the elimination of 7,523 Jews (1,312 men, 4,602 women, 1,609 children) on that day alone, bringing the final death toll to 8,745.

They had missed only one young Jew. His Catholic girlfriend hid him for the next four years.

It was now time for the squad to turn its attention to the next community on the hit list. That unofficial hit list was considerably shorter than when they began their work in early July.

Shavl – Early July 1941

A MONTH EARLIER, it appeared no such similar fate lay in store for the Jews of Shavl, 40 miles west of Ponevezh as the crow flies. In fact, after the Germans had clamped down on the local fascists for their pogroms, some Jews dared to think that life under the Reich might be tolerable.

They even took solace from the striking of a Jewish committee – known as the *Judenrat* – to represent the community. Gita's cousin and former Lithuanian army officer, Mendel Leibovich, headed the group, which included Ber Kartun, a neighbour of the Krons and a business partner of her father. Another notable was schoolteacher Eliezer Yerushalmi, who performed the duties as scribe. His words would live beyond the ghetto and his accounts of ghetto life would convict some of those responsible for the atrocities.

Meyer was less optimistic than many, having witnessed firsthand what had happened to Jews in Germany. Nevertheless, he was relieved there would now be a unified body to deal with their new masters. As he told Gita one evening, "They are undertaking a very responsible and dangerous job as go-between. Though I'm sure at times they will feel as though they are caught between a hammer and an anvil, appreciated by neither."

Future events would prove his prediction an accurate forecast. The Nazis decided to place a buffer between themselves and the local population in general by appointing existing civic leaders to do their bidding. Petras Linkevicius, the former director of the Dairy Trust, began his duties as Mayor on July 10. One of the Mayor's earliest decrees signalled what was to come: it forbade Jews from displaying Lithuanian national flags in their homes. There really was no fear of such a rule being broken. Some Jews found the flag rule almost amusing but further restrictions imposed in the coming weeks would be no laughing matter.

෴

GITA'S COUSIN WULF was the physician of choice among a number of the town's Gentile elite. He was flattered but knew that gradually his list would shrink now the Germans were here.

Some of those who previously revered him would shun him. Some were already breaking appointments, mainly those who considered they had much more to gain by staying in the good books of the Nazis.

One morning while looking at his appointments, his eye fell on the name of a woman married to the town's chief judge. Ah yes, she would not likely show up, he thought. He was wrong, on this occasion.

The handsome physician greeted her with his warmest smile, one he reserved for attractive young women. A brief examination revealed there was nothing wrong with her. Nevertheless, he said the right things to please her and suggested how she might take a break from her schedule and rest a little more. An uneasy silence followed his final words of advice. Perhaps she was there for a different reason other than to consult the good doctor about an imagined ailment. He could see she wanted to get something more off her chest. She looked towards the window as she spoke, avoiding eye contact.

"Doctor, in the smaller towns there is an epidemic raging of a type that hits only the Jews.

"It really is quite incurable," she said, turning to face him and look directly into the steely blue eyes that had caused many female hearts to flutter.

Wulf needed no more elaboration.

"Thank you, I will make some further discreet inquiries as we wouldn't want to cause a panic, would we?"

"Of course, Doctor, but I can assure you I have obtained this information on good authority," she continued rather more forcefully, a little hurt that he was not ready to take her at her word.

"Goodness, I didn't doubt the veracity of the information for one moment. It's just it would be helpful to know just how severe the epidemic is and whether it is likely to come our way."

She nodded, placated by his response. "Quite so, doctor. I will, of course, keep you posted on that."

❧

WULF HAD HEARD the rumours from his Gentile colleagues about executions in the woods by hit squads recruited by the Germans. He shared his intelligence with the newly struck Judenrat, most of whom had heard the same tales of terror.

A few days later, Wulf led a small party to visit another of his high-profile patients – the newly minted Mayor Linkevicius. The official treated his visitors graciously, urging them to sit before proceeding with any discussion. He could see they were anxious about something and his show of courtesy put them at ease . . . temporarily.

It made them feel like equals, which, of course, they were not. Linkevicius hoped the matter would be something he could resolve without recourse to the invaders. He listened without comment at first. He then dropped the pretence when he heard their plea for him to use his influence to secure the safety of the town's Jews. He responded coldly.

"Gentlemen, there is absolutely nothing I can do as the 'Jewish problem' is now exclusively handled by Captain Stankus and beyond my sphere of influence."

Antanas Stankus, a captain in the Lithuanian reserve corps, was notorious for publicly expressing his anti-Jewish sentiments. If he had his way, the Jews would be 'cleansed' from the whole region. Soon he would seek an opportunity to fulfill that wish. The Nazi administration had chosen well. He could be trusted to carry out all of their orders with zeal.

Wulf wondered if the reference by Linkevicius to the 'Jewish problem' was merely a case of quoting his new masters verbatim or perhaps he was describing what he truly believed to be a problem in need of a solution by whatever measures deemed expedient.

An uneasy few seconds passed before another member of the delegation attempted to re-engage the mayor. Linkevicius merely repeated his previous remarks, word for word, nodding his head as he did apparently for emphasis. It was clear there was to be no further discussion.

With that realization, the small group rose as one and headed towards the door. They were determined to leave by choice rather than suffer the indignity of a dismissal, thus shattering what remained of the illusion that they enjoyed equal standing in this meeting. Wulf decided to hang back, hoping to make a quiet personal plea. He opened his mouth to speak but the Mayor raised his hand in a gesture that indicated he would be wasting his breath. After feeling the Mayor's chill, Wulf was surprised when the man warmly put his arm around his shoulders. He almost jumped.

"Of course, doctor, given our long relationship, I'm sure it would be possible to be helpful should you wish to pursue your career elsewhere."

Wulf looked sheepish and thanked the Mayor but avoided accepting the offer.

"Well, get back to me if you wish, doctor," said the Mayor as he closed his heavy office door behind him.

It was an offer of personal help repeated many times in the coming weeks by other notables. One person even offered to arrange transportation to a Baltic port where he would join a ship bound for Sweden.

"Thank you but I still have too much work to do here to even consider taking such a vacation," he said with a smile, on that occasion. How such a flight could happen when the Nazis had firm control of the Baltic coast, an area populated with ethnic Germans, was beyond him anyway.

The Jews at large became very jittery as they read the poisonous outpourings of the LAF newspapers and newsletters. The publications circulated widely and fell into the hands of local Jewry. The edition of Tevyne – The Fatherland - published July 13 raised Meyer's eyebrows.

"Listen to this, Gita," he said before reading the offending piece aloud.

"About 600 Jews used to work in Siauliai's (Shavl) leather industry. Presently, most of the Jews have been dismissed with only five per cent, or 30 people, remaining."

Meyer looked up for a moment, commenting that his numbers did not tally with those in the Tevyne story. Those left were only those required to keep the machines going.

The next statement was the cause for alarm.

"Even with these remaining Jews, Lithuanians are working and will take over the machines in one or two months. In a short time, we will not have a single Jew in the leather industry. We shall prove that conversations about irreplaceable Jewish specialists are mere fairy tales."

Meyer put down the paper, wiping the ink from his hands and looking at Gita, hoping she would dismiss the contents as merely the ramblings of malcontents. He was disappointed.

"Mara, this means our usefulness to the Germans will be for just a short time and then what?"

Meyer was quick to answer, "And then nothing."

She gasped, fearing he meant death would follow, but this time Meyer was the optimist.

To her relief, he explained his response: "No, those are big brave words, nothing else. The Lithuanians do not have the skills to perform these tasks."

On a less confident note, he added, "Besides, forcing us to work for them will be cheaper and easier." He forced a smile.

He returned to reading his paper. Gita left the room. The lines blurred and he just stared at the text. Meyer prayed that his business case for Jewish survival mirrored that of the Germans. The alternative did not bear thinking about. In his quiet conversations with Wulf, he had learned of the stories circulating about the wholesale killing of Jews in other small communities.

Meyer worried about the wellbeing of his sister Tzilia in Ponevezh and his brother Yaakov, in Riga, and their respective families. He thought about how much his brother – then years his senior – and his wife Eva had already endured tragedy with the loss of their eldest son. Matya died following a burst appendix that he suffered shortly after Tamara was born. Only younger son Zali remained.

Meyer recalled how he had sneaked off on business. It was merely a cover so he could secretly attend the funeral in Riga. He feared that if he broke the news to Gita, who was sick following Tamara's birth, and to his ailing mother, he would have had more to worry about at home.

Some days later after his return, the ruse was exposed. While Gita and his mother expressed worry as to why Yaakov had neither visited nor written, the tragic news broke from an unexpected source.

"Well, because Matya is dead," said young Ruta. "Papa went to his funeral, didn't you know?"

Gita was stunned and the shock was too much for Shana, who sunk into decline from that moment.

Gita jolted Meyer back to the present.

"What are you thinking about, Mara?"

"Oh, nothing," he lied, determined not to let her relive that episode in their life together. He turned to the next page as though he had just finished reading a story and was moving to the next.

She could read him like a book but decided to forgo reading him anymore that night.

⌒

TWO DAYS LATER, a poster appeared all over town requiring all Jews to hand in their radio sets, under threat of some unspecified legal action. Now that did worry Meyer.

"This is our lifeline to the rest of the world."

Gita knew what he was thinking.

"You have to do as they say, Mara. You know what the Nazi idea of legal action is. We will find other ways of learning about what is happening."

He half smiled: "Yes, Wulf is never short of news. He will be our lifeline."

Three days later, on July 18, there came exactly what the Krons had expected, a list of restrictions similar to those imposed first on German Jews before the outbreak of war.

The Mayor had posted a Skelbimas, an announcement detailing in point form what was proscribed for Jews. The first of eight points pronounced that Jews who had fled Shavl would not be allowed to return. Those that did would be arrested, as would anybody aiding them. All Jews were ordered to wear a yellow Star of David and obey a strict curfew.

However, the most disconcerting content was at the end of the published declaration: all Jewish property was to be registered and real estate sold so that the Jewish community might be moved to a designated area of town – in other words, a ghetto.

The Mayor and Stankus called a meeting of the Jewish committee to delineate more clearly the geographical area of the ghetto, as ordered by the German command.

The Kaukazas area of town between the Jewish cemetery and Vilna Street, opposite Frenkel's, was to become their new home. There were about 100 rundown homes in this area, occupied by 400 of the poorest people in town. It would come to pass that they, like their brethren in Ponevezh, would profit from this arrangement by moving into the homes vacated by the Jews. Naturally, the Germans and some of the newly elevated city bureaucracy would have first pick of the very finest Jewish residences: the Krons' home being one of them.

However, before that selection was to take place, the Krons would first suffer the indignity of having their valuables taken by members of Stankus's brigade of legal looters. A persistent loud banging on the door with a heavy object heralded their arrival. Without waiting for a response four men burst in with rifles, shouting orders in Lithuanian to the Krons to hand over their rings and other valuables.

The couple had a bag ready to hand over, though their most valuable possessions were already long gone. The official announcement of intent had forewarned and forearmed the community. Many, like the Krons, had found places to secrete their belongings for collection "when all of this nonsense is over." Some had buried their treasures while others had lodged their valuables with neighbours and Gentile friends. The Krons more realistically saw their stash as a means of bartering in the future, for whatever they may need to get them through the inevitable hard times ahead.

Giving a little something would appease the robbers, the Krons had thought in preparation for the expected visitation. However, the men were not satisfied and began what would be a fruitless search for more booty to boost the Reich's treasury and enrich their own earthly wealth. These men were motivated more by their own personal greed than a commitment to the new order.

Gita looked down at her hands, hoping to avoid looking at these marauders as though the absence of eye contact would somehow keep her safe. She feared gold and silver might not be the only things of interest to them. They were animals and she had heard horrid stories about such men raping women in front of their loved ones.

Meyer was across the room with Ruta, while a terrified Tamara was hiding behind her skirts. Surely, she thought, if they have one ounce of humanity these thugs will take the money and run, so to speak. They must know Meyer was a man of some influence in the town: was being the operative word.

As Gita bowed her head, her eyes alighted on her wedding ring. She sought refuge in her happy memories of May 3, 1934. The scene playing out in her imagination was the vivid recollection of her wedding in the garden of her parents' city home just a short walk away on Basanaviciaus Street. It might as well have been a world away.

One of the Stankus mob discarded a wine decanter and it crashed into tiny pieces as it hit the hard floor of the kitchen. Gita did not move a muscle for its shattering had coincided with her recollection of the sound of the wine glass breaking beneath the groom's foot as their covenant was sealed. It was an audible replay of those past cries of "Mazeltov!" that greeted Meyer and his young bride Gita when they emerged smiling from beneath the chuppah. It also shut out the present day crash of furniture upended by the search team.

Their future then looked bright. It was a great match of which any yentl – matchmaker – would have been proud. As far as the twosome was concerned, no third party involvement was necessary. However, Gita's older sisters, Bluma and Iudite, might argue that point.

Meyer and Gita first dated in 1933 while Iudite was home for a visit from Rome where she lived with her husband Luigi. She had run into her old school friend Meyer on the street and agreed to accompany him to a concert. However, she conspired with Bluma. She would fake sickness and then when Meyer arrived Bluma would suggest he take their younger sister instead. It was the start of something big!

At the time, Meyer was the shoe factory's handsome chief engineer and Gita a pretty, blonde young woman who had temporarily sacrificed her career ambition to become a lawyer in exchange for becoming Mrs. Kron. The adoring way she looked at her man on their wedding day would have persuaded any guest that her choice was really no sacrifice at all.

Gita was jolted back to the present. One of the looters began yelling at Meyer, clearly frustrated by his lack of success in securing anything of great value. She looked again at the gold ring engraved with the date of their wedding and quickly slipped it off. Ruta watched her mother put it into her mouth. She wondered why mama had done that but knew better than to ask. Tamara was still crying between sniffles. Ruta remained rooted to the spot and quiet.

The men left abruptly to ransack more of the Jewish homes. The Krons looked at each other in silence. Meyer never took his eyes off his bride as he gently stroked Ruta's hair reassuringly. Gita held his gaze and likewise comforted Tamara.

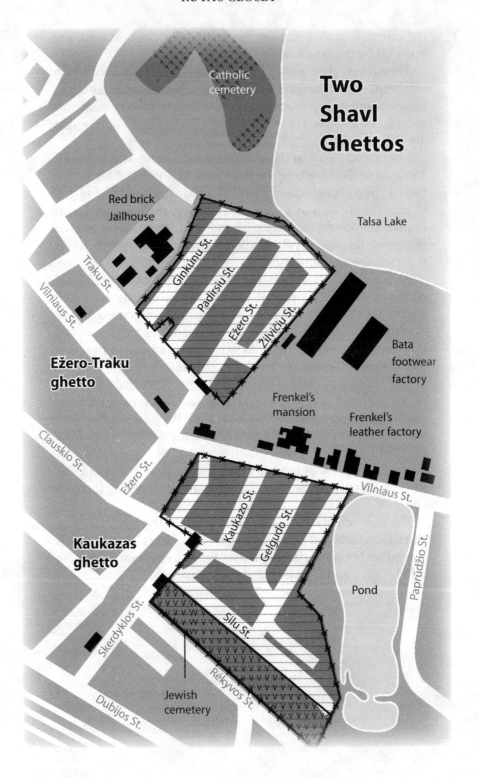

Catholic cemetery

Two Shavl Ghettos

Talsa Lake

Red brick Jailhouse

Traku St.

Vilniaus St.

Ginkūnu St.

Padirsiu St.

Ežero St.

Žilvičiu St.

Bata footwear factory

Ežero-Traku ghetto

Frenkel's mansion

Frenkel's leather factory

Clauskio St.

Ežero St.

Vilniaus St.

Kaukazo St.

Gelgudo St.

Kaukazas ghetto

Paprūdžio St.

Pond

Skerdyklos St.

Silu St.

Dubijos St.

Jewish cemetery

Rėkyvos St.

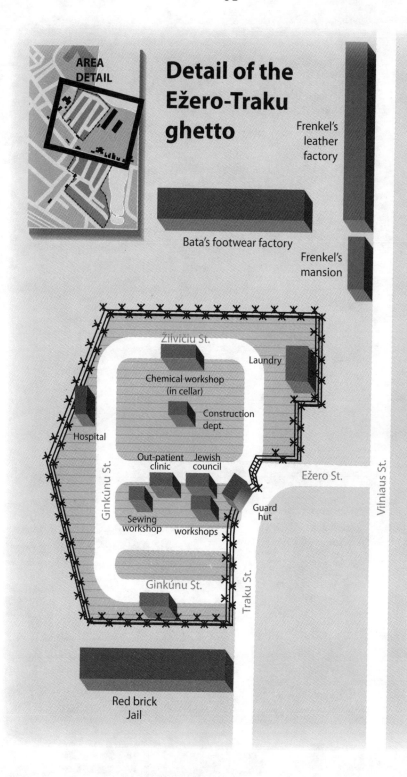

AREA DETAIL

Detail of the Eẑero-Traku ghetto

Frenkel's leather factory

Bata's footwear factory

Frenkel's mansion

Ẑilviciu St.

Laundry

Chemical workshop (in cellar)

Construction dept.

Hospital

Ginkúnu St.

Out-patient clinic

Jewish council

Eẑero St.

Vilniaus St.

Sewing workshop

workshops

Guard hut

Ginkúnu St.

Traku St.

Red brick Jail

CHAPTER FIVE

In the ghetto

Ezero-Traku Ghetto – Tuesday July 22, 1941.

THE KRONS MOVED INTO a tiny, single-level hovel with two rooms and a kitchen, on Ginkunu Street.

The Krons, Wulf, Moshe Shifman and a young girl, unknown to them, shared one room. Meyer's mother was in the second room along with a family of four – a tailor, his wife and their two teenage children.

It was going to be especially tough on Grandma Kron, who had fallen sick some weeks earlier and was bedridden. Wulf diagnosed it as nothing more than a cold. However, when he was through examining her, he called Meyer out of the room and revealed she had cancer of the liver. This cancer growth was only the size of a pea but Wulf had found it.

Ruta looked around in shock at her new abode. There was not much to look at. To call it humble would be wildly flattering. The paint on the wall – if that is what it was, more likely distemper – was peeling. The windows were small and filthy, likely unwashed in a decade.

The family that vacated the green-coloured house undoubtedly got the better end of the real estate deal, re-housed across town in what had once been a Jewish household. It would not be as grand as the Kron family home, for senior members of the Nazi administration snapped up such desirable residences.

Ruta longed to be back already in their spacious two-storey home on Vilna Street. It was set back in a courtyard, reached through an arch at the end of a semi-circular driveway. The Krons lived upstairs in a tastefully furnished apartment, across the hall from Ruta's grandparents. That is where they held Shabbat dinner and all family gatherings. Now it would be a place for the Nazi hierarchy to gorge on the best of food and drink and play with their newfound female friends, far away from their wives and girlfriends.

Ruta would run around there and play where there were no space restrictions. When she interrupted whatever game she was playing and opened her mouth to speak, grandma would pop some food in. Filling up Ruta seemed to be a major priority for the adults in the family. The skinny youngster was always on the go and seemed unable to sit still long enough to consume and digest a meal. Finding the food to feed her now and the rest of the family would become an all-consuming challenge. Running carefree and receiving food treats would not be happening here, Ruta thought.

She turned to look at the area described as the kitchen. The kitchen in town had all the latest appliances and was large enough for the whole family to gather. Now they were all on top of each other. Mama never cooked there but she would here, standing on a dirt floor.

When Ruta looked out of the window of her old home, she could see the girls' school next door and the street, where parades passed on special occasions. Ruta skipped over to see what her new view of the outside world offered. She smiled when she saw a little garden, which reminded her of the one at home. A child's imagination is ever optimistic. Papa would soon have it planted with cabbages, tomatoes, cucumbers and radishes. That was not so fanciful a thought as Meyer would soon secure seeds from his many contacts beyond the fence.

At least the Krons had somewhere. The ghetto area was originally to be located exclusively in Kaukazas area, opposite the factory. The Jewish representatives protested the space allocated for the ghetto was not sufficient to house the large community. City leaders ignored their repeated requests to expand the ghetto. In desperation, they visited the Wehrmacht Kommandant, who to their pleasant surprise agreed and ordered Linkevicius to create a second adjacent area. Thus, the Ezero-Traku ghetto was created, between high-walled red brick jail, as it was known, and Ezero Street.

MOST OF THE ghetto inhabitants worked outside of the ghetto in a variety of places largely dedicated to supporting the German war effort. These forced labourers would go to the ghetto gates each morning and from there, groups accompanied by guards would fan out to different work places. They walked to and from work in columns, not on the sidewalks but down the middle of the street. This publicly showed the ghetto residents' inferiority.

In the town, the Venclauskas family opened factories and workshops to employ Jews, often creating fictitious sales and profits just to ensure they could keep their Jewish workers alive. It was a remarkable act of defiance from a well-to-do family, who need not have taken any risks to survive the war.

Meyer often opined that his place of work was the very best place to work. The old tannery was a producer of vital equipment for the warring soldiers on the Eastern Front and thus a place where there would be work until the end, whatever the end might be.

REINERT AND KAISER replaced the first German director of the factory, Müller, while a man called Siegel became technical director. Meyer did much of the work, but Siegel took the credit. In peacetime that would have riled Meyer but he was just happy to be alive and pleased to make Siegel look good.

There were more Jewish workers on the factory floor than were truly needed but the Germans did not seem to notice. The Jews were, naturally, not interested in producing too much and sometimes that defiance brought painful consequences. Siegel would wander around laying a beating on slackers. Many escaped a battering because Meyer would phone ahead to each department to let the workers know in which direction Siegel was heading.

BY AUGUST 31, the German administration had closed the two ghetto areas to further admissions. Meyer noted in his written recollections later that people "were piled in like herring." The Krons were among 3,000 housed in Ezero-Traku and another 2,950 in Kaukazas. That left at least a couple of thousand more without a home. They would be taken to Zhager, where they would be more comfortable, said the administration. However, the Jewish leaders feared holders of a ticket to Zhager would meet the same gory end as the Schatz family of Ponevezh.

The leadership lobbied for a third ghetto. Anxious to calm down the Jews, Linkevicius and Stankus acceded to their wishes. Well, at least they said they would when they announced a third ghetto in the Kalniukas neighbourhood.

It would take some preparation so the displaced Jews agreed to take up temporary residence in the Village Traders' Synagogue, the Jewish Home for the elderly and the Central Choral Synagogue. The truth was they were merely collection stations. A few hundred at a time were shepherded into the buildings over the course of the next month. They were taken then to the Luponiai Forest near Kuzh, where they were shot and buried in pits dug before their arrival.

The ghetto areas were fenced, placed under guard and only workers with passes could leave or enter. The Mayor and Stankus ordered the listing of all residents who were sick or unable to work. In the next few days, more than 400 of those on the list were executed in the nearby Gubernija Forest.

Those early days were extremely unsettled; the residents were never sure whether they would see another dawn. There were lightning raids on homes by Lithuanian police doing the bidding of the German command, or at least that was the assumption. Few of their captives returned.

Young Nathan Katz, a neighbour of Wulf Peisachowitz, lost his mother to such a visitation. It was a case of mistaken identity for she was just 41 and very capable of work. The alert mother spotted the truck turn on to the street and knew its arrival heralded trouble for somebody. She shooed the teenager out of the back door ordering him to hide in the woodshed. The men that knocked on their door asked for 'Tatz' but the overly helpful neighbours said there was only a 'Katz' there. That was close enough for them. They marched the proud Rachel Katz to the truck.

Most who suffered the same loss never saw conclusive proof of what happened to their loved ones. The Katz family was fortunate, or unfortunate, depending on your viewpoint, as to the value of closure over the precious hope offered by not knowing what happened. Nathan's father was working in the city on the road when he saw his wife pass aboard the truck. They waved their last goodbye – discreetly.

Days later, the young Katz saw the proof of her undeserved end. He worked in the German administration offices and one of his duties was sorting through the clothing brought back from the killing sites. He looked down to find the dress in his hands was the one his mother had worn when taken. He began to cry uncontrollably. His fellow workers, realizing what had happened, sought to calm him down. Continuing to draw attention to himself in such a way would likely earn him a final ride on that truck, once it was unloaded and the Germans had extracted everything of value.

He braced himself and got back to the soul-destroying work. However, he could not shut out of his mind what had happened to his mother. The distraught young man believed the responsibility for the vicious murder of his mother lay squarely on the narrow shoulders of an insignificant looking little man. A man he had seen in the flesh.

On March 23, 1939, in his hometown of Memel, as a curious 18-year-old he had joined the thousands anxiously waiting for the arrival of Adolf Hitler. It was the day after the frightened Lithuanian government had handed back Memelland to the Reich, which it had occupied since 1920.

At 1:30 p.m., Hitler left his vessel the Deutschland anchored off shore and landed in the town at 2 p.m. aboard the torpedo boat Leopard. After reviewing the new military masters installed at this strategically placed Baltic port, he journeyed by car to the central square to speak to the waiting masses.

Katz was attracted to Theatre Square like a moth to a flame, curious about the cause of the excitement around him. It never occurred to him that his presence there was fraught with danger. On the other hand, no self-respecting Nazi would suspect a cowardly Jew would dare to enter his domain.

A roar of the magnitude normally heard in a soccer stadium from the victorious team's fanatical followers greeted Hitler's appearance on the balcony of the theatre. This too was a triumph for his supporters, who jumped up and down around Katz, waving flags and banners.

Katz could see the whites of the orator's eyes, only a stone's throw away from his position in the square. If the enthusiastic greeting of the crowd surprised Katz, the reaction to the speaker's words proved still more disturbing. The Führer's opening remarks electrified the thousands in attendance.

"I greet you today in the name of the entire German people. I am happy to receive you into our Greater German Empire."

He talked of the new Germany that "shall not entrust its destiny to foreigners; it stands ready and willing to master its own destiny, to fashion it, whether or not this suits an outside world."

Each confident assertion of entitlement whipped up the crowd. By the time he delivered his trademark *"Sieg Heil!"* at the close, it was in a state of delirium. Before the clock struck four, the strutting little man was gone and on the way back to his seat of awesome power in Berlin.

The bemused young man had never seen so many people in one place and he had never seen people react so hysterically to a speech, screaming *"Heil Hitler!"* at the top of their voices.

After what had happened to his mother, Katz was now more determined to do whatever he could to make life difficult for the Nazis and that little man. His work position outside of the ghetto within the German administration headquarters would give him many opportunities. Something Dr. Peisachowitz would be happy to exploit for the good of the ghetto in the months to come.

UNBEKNOWNST TO MOST residents, the Shavl ghetto's days were nearly over before they had barely begun. By early September the Einsatzgruppen were running out of Jews to kill. Its commanders were therefore delighted with an invitation from Stankus and his cohorts to visit Shavl to solve the resident Jewish problem.

News of this evil intent reached Wulf's ears. It came from a Venclauskas family member with whom he had regular contact at the hospital. A girlfriend of hers was dating a local lad, who had volunteered for the murderous troop. Wulf immediately informed the Judenrat of this intelligence and took it upon himself to talk to Gebietskommissar Hans Gewecke, the head of the German civil administration.

Getting an audience with Gewecke was not just a matter of picking up the phone, even with the supposed weight of the Judenrat behind the request. As the occupation continued, Wulf would find himself before the Nazi hierarchy on a number of occasions, sometimes by design but other times under less desirable circumstances. However, on this occasion, he used subterfuge to get before the man in command. He deliberately broke curfew and a German street patrol obligingly stopped him as he had hoped. Wulf told them he had to get to the hospital to treat an important patient. Not without permission, they told him.

Minutes later, he was standing before Gewecke asking for written authority to make such trips. While waiting he bravely struck up a conversation with the German.

"Sir, in my travels I hear rumours and one I heard the other day, I believe would not serve you well," said Wulf.

He had Gewecke's attention and repeated the essence of the rumour, though talking about "resettlement' rather than execution.

"This would lead to bad consequences for the German soldiers on the Eastern Front, where it is extremely cold. Where else are they going to get the clothing they need to fight during the cold winter they face?"

The man of few words unexpectedly thanked Wulf for the information and dismissed him while passing him a valuable piece of paper giving him permission to leave the ghetto after dark.

The wisdom of Peisachowitz's words was clear to Gewecke. Berlin would judge him by the productivity of the enterprises under his control. However, these mad murderers were obsessed with killing Jews and not the need to feed the war machine.

When the mobile killing squad commander arrived along with his 150-strong Lithuanian volunteer executioners, as predicted, Gewecke lit into the arrogant SS chief. Gewecke wasted no time in involving higher authorities and the killer commando left with his tail between his legs. The Jews of Shavl were spared.

By the end of the month, there would be only one such killer squadron active in Lithuania. Its successor in the task of making Europe free of Jews was taking shape in Poland, where the first experimental use of gas chambers began at a little known Nazi concentration camp, shrouded in secrecy, called Auschwitz.

Amaliai Schoolhouse, Sunday, September 6, 1941.

ONA KUPAITIS ALWAYS greeted people with a smile, especially family members. However, she was frowning when she told her daughter Ona Ragauskas and son-in-law Antanas about what she had just witnessed on her way over to their home. What she had witnessed deeply troubled her.

"It was very odd," she began. "The truck was full of school children all in their uniforms as though they were going to perform somewhere or go on a picnic."

Antanas impatiently interrupted to ask the obvious question of the confused and anxious woman before them.

"Where, mother? – Was it near here or closer to the farm?" he asked somewhat impatiently.

A little irritated, she answered, "Near our house. It was parked in the lane that leads to the woods. There were no Germans around that I could see, just one man with a long gun, who was guarding them."

"Did he say anything?" her daughter asked, trying to encourage her mother to tell the whole story. The older woman frowned in thought for a few moments, as it was a challenge to recall.

"No, he just waved me on," she finally responded, also waving to demonstrate how he dismissed her.

By then all in the room feared the worst had happened to the youngsters. It was a relief when the subject was dropped abruptly in favour of a more mundane topic.

If Ona Kupaitis had left home half an hour earlier, she might have seen two or three trucks in the same spot also loaded with smartly dressed schoolchildren. The collaborator Romualdas Koloksa, a former lawyer from Uzventis, had raided the Jewish orphanage with his men earlier in the day. They had forced the 47 children with two teachers onto waiting trucks.

The truck Ona's mother saw was the last one, waiting to take its turn transporting its young passengers to a clearing in the woods at the end of the pretty lane. The execution squad would bury them in freshly dug trenches. Lithuania was becoming a nation of killing fields. Though the sins of Koloksa were later uncovered, he escaped punishment.

LAF MEMBERS APPEARED in the ghetto on September 15 along with dozens of police. Residents feared the rumours they had heard about mass executions might now be proven fact rather than gossip. They were thankfully mistaken.

Earlier, the ghetto residents capable of work received blue *Arbeitsscheine*. In addition, those whose work took them outside of the ghetto got pink passes – *Passierscheine*. Those that qualified for neither soon found themselves herded into a nearby synagogue before transportation to the site of their execution.

The unexpected visit by LAF men was to ascertain who would get new yellow passes. Those denied would again contribute to reducing the ghetto population. The Nazis would take them away and kill them. The Judenrat realized that the innocuous looking yellow permits could be lifesavers. They must get as many as possible into the hands of their people.

These sober souls smartly developed a plan that would take advantage of one of their persecutor's reputation for insobriety. Halfway through the selection, Stankus arrived and the Jewish leaders proceeded to ply him with drink. As he lapsed into a stupor, they removed 500 yellow forms from his bag and whisked them away. Those deemed expendable by the Stankus brigade would receive most of them. They would hide the rest for other Jews who might find their way to the comparative safety of the Shavl ghetto.

FEAR STALKED THE GHETTO, 24 hours a day. On whose door would the occupiers or their agents knock next? They needed little excuse to rid the ghetto of a few more persons.

Parents feared the Nazis might cull their children, left to roam the ghetto during the day, at any moment. Thus, they told their offspring to stay away from anybody in a uniform. They never fully explained the actual nature of the threat. It was not necessary, for the parents clearly transmitted their fear in their body language.

That said, the children of the ghetto got on with being children and that meant playing outside at every opportunity. A makeshift school brought some order to the younger generation, as the transplanted community got used to its new life.

Ruta and Tamara were too young for school. They continued to run wild from the moment their parents left for the factory to the moment they saw them return home at the end of a hard day. The first sight of mama and papa meant food was on its way. Once she was within earshot, mama was greeted with questions as to what that sustenance might be. It must have appeared that children cared only about having a full belly, not that any appetites could be satiated on the rations available. The children's inner thoughts remained unspoken: "Mama and papa are home safe again."

One night in the fall of that first year in the ghetto, Gita walked smiling towards Ruta. For a moment, it reminded the little girl of happier past times when she was the only one. That smile was the one Ruta saw when she and mama dressed in their best and went out together for tea or hot chocolate and richly frosted cake at Milstein's Café. Gita sometimes rewarded Ruta with chocolate eggs, which melted and coated her lips on the way home.

"Call me Gita, when we are out," her mother said repeatedly. Ruta did not know why that was so important but the chocolates were bribe enough to secure her cooperation. Besides, it suited Ruta anyway. On these occasions, Gita was her special friend, big sister, whereas her nanny was more of the traditional mother.

Then along came Tamara on March 3, 1939, and the fun was all over. In fact, Tamara nearly took Ruta's 'big sister' away from her permanently.

Two weeks after the birth, Gita became very ill with a blood infection. Her temperature was dangerously high and there were shooting pains in her legs. Cousin Wulf was unable to help so he summoned a gynaecologist. While under examination, a blood clot in Gita's legs broke away and travelled to her lungs. Any more movement and it might travel to her brain and kill her instantly.

The visiting doctor's advice was to stop eating solid food and he prescribed a diet of cognac: a bottle a day, no less. What kind of quack prescription was this? Naturally, Gita became very drunk, very quickly, and the pain worsened.

A second specialist merely ordered complete rest and said she should not move at all for between eight and ten weeks. It would not be an easy regimen to follow. Slowly she improved, but not before undergoing all kinds of remedies, some dangerous, some sickening, including leeches. The little beasts that sucked the blood from her mother's legs and dropped to the ground, fattened to bursting, horrified Ruta.

Ruta felt ignored and for the duration, Tamara got all the attention, limited though it was. She was upset and jealous of this newcomer.

She once bit Tamara out of sheer frustration and anger at having her position as mama's favourite usurped. That was the first and last time her father had ever taken off his belt and given her backside a few whacks.

The rivalry continued in the ghetto but then it was more a case of Tamara getting in the way of Ruta having fun with her peers. She resented having to look after her sister. When they played hide and seek, Ruta would hide and hope this obstacle to her freedom and enjoyment would not find her!

Gita's arrival interrupted Ruta's flashback. The grubby faced kid . looked up to her mother's smiling face and asked the expected.

"Oh, we have enough soup to get us through tonight, I think."

"Soup again, mama?"

There was no point waiting for an answer; it was always the same one about food being scarce and they must make do with what was available. She and Tamara would eat together and then while they got ready for bed their parents would have their supper.

Bedtime was when Ruta got some special attention from her father. He would read poems by Aleksandr Pushkin to her, which she adored. Ruta treasured those quiet times because she still believed Tamara got special treatment in the ghetto. One day, papa brought home an orange – goodness knows where he got that from – and fed it piece by piece only to Tamara. It was an exercise repeated periodically over a period of weeks until her scurvy had cleared up. The significance of the fruit as a form of medication was lost on Ruta.

At least they did get to share the *Gogol mogol*, a Russian dessert made from egg yolks and sugar, made only very occasionally. Ruta noted it usually happened shortly after papa had slipped out at night and returned with meat and vegetables. The source of the bounty was unknown to her. Not that she cared.

Whatever they ate, Ruta was full of beans the next day. No sooner had her parents turned the corner towards the ghetto gate than Ruta was tearing out of the house with Tamara, who was desperately trying to keep up with her big sister.

Soon a gang of children would gather at the corner of one street or another. It was not hard to find the chosen location of the day as the ghetto was only a few blocks square. As the weather worsened, it did not deter them from chasing through the mud-filled, unpaved streets.

Under grey skies, they ran and screamed, sheltering only when hail or snow slowed them down. There were not many adults around; occasionally they would hear the sharp edge of the tongue of a night worker, desperately trying to get some sleep before heading back to the factory.

There was also Hannah the *Meshugganah*, as some adults unkindly referred to her. The kids parroted that name but they did not really understand the meaning of the word. They just knew she was a crazy woman, who acted strangely and talked about hearing voices in her head. They would tease her, chase her, and jump out from behind buildings to scare her. She would bellow at them and chase them too. Then one day she was not there anymore.

CHAPTER SIX

Putting bread on the table

Ezero Street, Shavl – Thursday, January 8, 1942.

THE COLUMN OF WORKERS halted just a few steps out of the ghetto at the corner of Ezero and Vilna Streets to wait for military vehicles to pass along the main road.

It was a bitterly cold day and the wait seemed interminable. The sorry-looking crew, dressed in the most threadbare of clothing, shivered and rubbed their hands together in a desperate attempt to keep the circulation going.

Meyer soon tired of counting the trucks and Wehrmacht staff cars and began to look around the street for something else to occupy his mind. He sensed a presence at his left shoulder. Dare he look? If it were a guard, he might find himself cuffed across the face or worse for having the nerve to stare at a superior – in all senses of the word.

Curiosity got the better of him. He turned to face the man standing on the sidewalk. It was Jonas Jocius; a man he feared would one day be his nemesis. Now he was shaking for reasons other than the cold.

Meyer first encountered him one day back in 1934, when unusually he responded to a loud knock on the front door. Meyer did not know his visitor and was a little intimidated by the man, who filled the doorframe.

He introduced himself as Jonas Jocius, the last time Meyer ever heard or used the man's given name. The man's plea shattered Meyer's initial impression: "My mother is sick and I need a job desperately . . . I've been a political prisoner for the past four years because I was accused of being a communist sympathizer."

It was a poor political choice in anti-communist Lithuania. At the close of the First World War, the country had declared its independence from the two giants – Germany and the Russia – that took turns in controlling it for their own strategic and economic good.

Such political intrigues did not concern Meyer. The compassionate chief of tanning was touched by the story told by the bearded man with unruly long blond hair and hired him on the spot. Jocius trained to operate the lacquer kitchen, which produced the concoction that hardened the leather and gave it that unmistakable gleam. The painstaking work called for a high level of skill and great care.

Back then, the process of making patent required mixing volatile chemicals with linseed oil before boiling in a process that could take up to 25 hours. Once the mixture reached a certain critical temperature, it had to be quickly but carefully moved or else there was a risk of a flash fire.

Jocius soon validated Meyer's decision: he was a fast learner and a good worker. Yes, there was the occasional flare-up but the skilled Jocius soon extinguished it without setting back the hectic production schedule – at least for the first six years, until the kitchen burned down while Jocius was attending a clandestine communist meeting. Meyer had to fire him.

HERE WAS JOCIUS, by Meyer's side again. Meyer looked at him as nervously as he did the day they first met.

Jocius broke the ice: "How are you doing?"

Meyer stuttered a little, taken aback. He had to say something. He decided that blunt honesty was the best policy. What had he to lose?

"I am not doing very well at all. There's nothing to eat and we are all very cold."

The Nazis' idea of sustenance was a weekly ration of 700 grams of black bread, 113 grams of flour, 100 grams of beans and 125 grams of horsemeat. The Judenrat distributed the food along with the measly pay the Germans assigned for the work performed by the Jews. Families lived on nothing more than the watered down soup that Ruta detested so much, most of the time.

Barely were the words out of his mouth before the march started up again. As Meyer moved on, he heard Jocius say in a loud whisper that he hoped would not be audible to anybody else:

"Don't worry my friend I will help you."

"Friend," thought Meyer. "The best way you can help me is to forget about me."

A short time later, Meyer received a message from Jocius through an intermediary at the factory, telling him to wait for him at a location near the ghetto fence that night at 8 p.m. A preposterous proposition, thought Meyer, but he would discuss it with Gita when he got home.

They wondered whether it was a trick so that Jocius could finally get his revenge. Their debate was inconclusive. Meyer was too desperate not to take a chance. Food was very scarce. They were cold and hungry. He pulled on his threadbare coat, wrapped a scarf around his neck and then headed out.

ON THE CHOSEN night, the recently fallen snow almost made the outside world beyond the fence look pretty. Meyer waited, shivering in hiding behind a building wall. He could not afford the luxury of pacing back and forth to keep warm. Even if he were not seen, his footprints in the snow would be a giveaway and prompt a search.

When the sentries were some distance away, Jocius suddenly appeared with a sleigh. He had been nearby for some time, out of sight but close enough to observe the movements of the guards. They did not loiter long in any one spot. At the gates, a hot stove beckoned with the promise of a mug of steaming tea – or at least what passed for tea.

Jocius began throwing things over the wire. Meyer watched in disbelief as the contraband dropped with a dull thud in the snow. There was meat, butter and food the family had not seen for months. He was hesitant to pick it up, as he was worried that a guard would appear from nowhere and arrest him or just shoot him in his freshly made tracks. Then how would his family survive?

He swallowed hard and stepped out of the shadows to pick up the food and scramble away. Jocius just nodded and smiled. There was no time for an exchange of verbal pleasantries. Besides, fear had caused Meyer to forget his good manners.

He must have looked over his shoulder a hundred times during the five-minute run home. He asked himself the same number of times why Jocius would do this. No answer sprang to mind but Meyer would get a surprising answer in the near future, directly from the horse's mouth.

The unexpected hamper kept the Krons alive and in good spirits for weeks. It enabled them to stockpile their meagre official rations and enjoy the fresh food, which by the time the last morsel was consumed it was perhaps past its best. There were no complaints.

Meyer again received a timely message to make his way to the fence under cover of darkness, soon after the family consumed the last of the bounty. Every few weeks, the process repeated. Jocius would bring more food, in spite of the fact that this was equally dangerous for both the donor and the grateful recipient.

Many months after their first uneasy encounter, Meyer ran into Jocius again while out in the town on tannery business. At first, it was a stilted conversation. Meyer's head swivelled around in an unnaturally jerky motion, his eyes constantly checking to see if they were under observation.

"Relax, no one is watching," Jocius reassured Meyer, and beckoned him to step into the narrow covered alley between two stores.

Jocius tried first to engage his Jewish 'friend' in a civil conversation. It appeared to calm Meyer, who, after a few innocuous pleasantries, let loose. He told Jocius how he feared him because he had fired him.

There was a twinkle in the big man's eyes as he leaned into Meyer: "You had a good reason to be afraid."

Meyer recoiled a little.

"But I never forgot what you did for me by hiring me when I was in need of help. You put food on my family's table and now it is my turn to put food on yours."

Meyer was stunned. The man's words moved him for a second time, the first being their first meeting at the doorstep when Meyer had given Jocius a job at the factory.

Jocius then got down to business and established a less haphazard way of making future contact. They settled on one of the few Lithuanian workers at the factory. The man worked there under the communist regime but in spite of that association, the Germans retained him.

Jocius got his walking papers the moment the Germans took over and truly, he was lucky to be alive. A troublemaker was a troublemaker no matter who was in power, in the Nazis' book. Giving a second chance was not part of their 'employment practices'. Jocius's previous factory floor antics and known political affiliation certainly qualified him as a troublemaker.

Those earlier publicly professed leftward leanings of Jocius did not convince Meyer either. He thought the man was somewhat fickle, willing to swear allegiance to the party that would best serve the needs of his family. Whatever it takes to survive, thought Meyer. It was a thought that would occur to him many times more in relation to the continued survival of his own dear family.

Jocius's latest occupation was more capitalistic than communist. He was committed to the propagation of a flourishing black market. He would go out into the country to procure meat and other fresh produce to sell at good prices – for him – in the city. It was a dicey pastime but very rewarding financially. Nevertheless, there was a still more risky side to his entrepreneurial ventures.

Jocius had ploughed his profits back into farmland where he kept cows, pigs and chickens. He dutifully registered his livestock with the Nazis though his counts were somewhat inaccurate. The ghost livestock produced a stream of ghost income.

There was another twist in his dealings, designed to ease concealment and boost his profits. Jocius sold some of the milk from his cows for Russian Roubles rather than the special Reichsmark currency introduced by the German authorities in the conquered eastern territories. He was sure Germans would lose the war and thus the new currency would become worthless. It was a gamble he knew that could cost him his life or make him wealthy; a game of Russian roulette.

Jocius was an enigma. Some described him as an opportunistic, risk-taking, money-grubbing, capitalist but he was also a generous benefactor. He was ready to sacrifice his own life to ensure the Krons received adequate nutrition. There would come a time that he would play a vital role in saving all of their lives.

EVEN THE LIFE giving provisions generously donated by Jocius could not keep Meyer's mother alive. Shana finally succumbed to liver cancer on April 2, 1942, the Saturday before Passover. The family had not revealed the extent of her sickness to outsiders, fearing it would seal her death warrant. The Krons managed to arrange a funeral through outside contacts, in much the same way as they had done when Gita's mother had died shortly after the German takeover. They buried Shana next to her husband Leibe.

After her burial, Meyer and Gita took their minds off their personal loss, talking about Passover traditions. They recalled the times of plenty when Passover meant feasting. Feasting was no longer an option. It was not the first time Meyer had faced starvation. The conversation turned to a dreadful period in the latter stages of the First World War.

Gita settled down to listen to her husband; it was therapeutic for Meyer in this time of mourning to talk of the past, the good, and the bad. It also reminded her how Meyer had become such a resourceful man. So what if she had heard the tales before? He began with a favourite fun story about his time in post-revolution Moscow that perhaps, in the telling, helped him deal with the darker side of the tale.

"One evening I was desperate. All my attempts to sneak into the Bolshoi among a crowd had failed," said the lifelong lover of opera and ballet.

"I went to the end of the horseshoe-like corridor, which surrounded the great performance hall and where I noticed a camouflaged door. I tried to open it and it gave way. I entered a dark place with a winding staircase leading upward. It took me to the top floor and directly into a box with a beautiful view of the stage. After that I had no problems getting into the theatre."

For a few moments, he smiled as he privately relived the experience. Gita would have let him prolong that moment forever if she had the power, for he now had little to make him smile.

The purpose of such visits to Moscow was not one of which fond memories were easily made, everlasting, yes, but not necessarily pleasant. Food shortages drove Meyer to make the train journeys to the Russian capital – the very problem he faced again. The Great War was raging and many of Shavl's Jews had fled to the safety of Russia. The Krons were living in Bogorodsk, about 35 miles outside of Moscow, where Frenkel's tannery had also moved its operations. At that time, Meyer's father handled the books for the firm.

Meyer stopped briefly. Gita knew the rest of the account would not be a fun story but she wanted to hear it again. It would remind her how her Mara was made of stern stuff, something for which she would be eternally grateful.

"The only way of getting food was through the black market," he explained, as though his bright bride was hearing that for the first time.

"There were some very large textile factories around Bogorodsk, called Morozoff Manufacturing, which produced mostly silk. The people at the factory used to steal it to sell on the black market.

"I used to get bolts of silk from neighbours, unravel the material then twist it around my body. Then I would get dressed and smuggle the silk into Moscow by train.

"It was very dangerous and was made more so by the fact that the silk could be noisy when you moved. I would go to the train very early – at 5 a.m. – board it and lie down on the top luggage shelf."

Meyer smiled as he pondered his next line. Gita knew which part of the story was about to be told.

"There I would lie until we arrived in Moscow, which sometimes took up to four hours and did not always go smoothly. Sometimes there were complaints from the people who were "downstairs" from me.

"They wondered where the 'rain' was coming from. I was a young boy and could not always contain myself. They couldn't do much about it, however, because the train was so jammed that they could not move to call the police."

The police at Kurski station checked almost everybody but always ignored the young boy Kron. Speculators bought the material from him, providing the young wheeler-dealer with funds for food. Meyer would arrive at number 9 Krivokolenny Lane in Moscow, the home of his older sisters Mary and Chaytze, wilting under the weight of a sack filled with potatoes, carrots and bread. The rest he would take back to Bogorodsk. His black market activities of yesteryear would serve him well in the coming months.

Meyer's face clouded again as he recalled one trip that almost cost him his life. Gita was tempted to interrupt to ease the tension, which was palpable. She let him continue.

"It was a very cold night and I had to walk for about an hour from the station to the city," he recalled, his voice now devoid of the child-like excitement evident when he told of his mischief in the Bolshoi.

"When I came to my sisters' door it was locked and, as I might have expected, the bell was not working. I tried and tried again but there was no response to my banging.

"Eventually I decided to lie down and, using my sack as a pillow, fell asleep in front of the door. Luckily, one of the tenants of the ten-storey building came home in time and found me before I froze. I was half-dead and at that temperature could not have survived for more than ten or fifteen minutes longer."

Fortunately, both of his sisters arrived just in time and, being doctors, took over the work of the Good Samaritan reviving their brother, warming him gradually and enabling him to evade the clutches of hypothermia.

"I was lucky that time." He turned around to look straight at her: "Have I told you about that before?"

"No, not that bit, Mara," she answered, lying for the best possible reasons.

She feigned partial ignorance again later when he talked about the end of the First World War when papa Kron was very sick with colitis. The Bar Mitzvah marks ceremonial passage of a Jewish boy to manhood at age 13, but in Meyer's case, there was nothing symbolic about this occasion. Meyer had proudly accepted his ailing father's mantle of responsibility for the family. Elder brother Jacob by this time was long gone, living elsewhere in Russia.

"I had to procure fuel for the ovens so I used to bring wood from the forest by sleigh and chop it up in a shed near our home. While I was chopping wood I heard a kind of hollow sound come from beneath the floor."

Meyer made motions with his hands as though he were lifting up the floor: "I found a space under the floor where, to my surprise, I found a huge box full of table salt packed into neat packages of one pound each. I have no idea who put them there.

"At that time money had little value but salt was scarce so we used it to barter for other kinds of food. It kept the whole family alive for a long time."

As times became harder, even Meyer's special currency was unable to buy food because there was simply none to buy.

"Then I heard that more food was available in the south of Russia, around the Volga, and many people went down there in search of it."

Meyer sat up in the rickety chair and stroked his hair purposefully, pausing for a few seconds to make sure his audience was paying attention.

"Naturally, this was a job for grown-up men but, not having anyone else in our family who would be able to do something about the situation, I joined some neighbours who were going south. I took some packages of salt and, somehow, I had managed to obtain a pair of shoes to trade for food and I also took Jacob's coat!"

The trains were very crowded, he recalled. People travelled on the steps of the wagons and even outside on the tops of the carriage. However, Meyer's group somehow managed to get on the train. They disembarked in a field at a station called Myl'naya, near the Volga. The closest village was nearly ten miles away so they had no choice but to walk it.

"It was an extremely trying journey in very hot weather. I scarcely had the strength to drive myself forward.

"However, I got there and we separated to mount our individual searches for food. I knocked at the door of a house and, as it turned out, it was the doctor's house. He and his family put me in the kitchen together with a maid, gave me food and promised to help me barter for food supplies to take home.

"At the end of a day or two I was a rich man," he said, laughing aloud. "I had accumulated about 800 pounds of grain, butter, meal, meat, watermelons and many other kinds of foodstuffs."

The doctor got a ride for Meyer back to the railway station where he reunited with his group.

"Then the difficulties began. Tens of thousands of people were sitting on the fields with their sacks of goods. There were people as far as you could see in all directions, but no trains came."

This area was a critically strategic location for the combatants in the civil war that was tearing apart the countryside. It was close to the only bridge over the Volga and the counter revolutionary army was approaching from the other side. The bridge blew up while they waited. That was the end for northbound trains.

In typical Soviet communist fashion, a committee was formed to remedy the situation. The only thing they could do was send telegrams to Lenin and to Trotsky asking for trains.

"At first we hoped to get a train in a day or two. Later on, week passed after week. Only after five weeks of waiting did the first set of wagons arrive. You can imagine what kind of a fight broke out as to who should be the first to get on the train.

"I was lucky again. Because of this and because I was the youngest of all of them I was the first to be put on the train with my goods."

It was not a passenger carriage but a cattle wagon. Meyer did not care. He was going home.

"It took another two weeks before I arrived home. The secret police stopped us at several stations along the way to search our goods. Then somebody in authority decided not to let anyone take more than forty pounds of food home. However, through all kinds of tricks, we managed to secure about three-quarters of our bounty. We had to give the rest away to the authorities."

The inside of the train was unbearably hot and dirty. All kinds of insects, including lice, covered everyone.

"The trains used to stand for hours at a station waiting for a locomotive and that's when we would swim in the nearest river, wash our clothes in a pool, or get hot water for a cup of tea.

"The rest of the waiting was boring. The men used to sit under the wagons to keep in the shade and play cards. Money had no value so they gambled for grain."

"One day I heard a shot. A fellow in our group had lost all his goods playing cards. Most likely, he had had a good shot of vodka as well. In any case, he couldn't stand the loss and shot himself."

The final sentence tumbled out of Meyer's mouth and he swallowed, ridding himself of the awful taste the words left behind. Back home he would have reached for a glass of vodka but there was no such comfort in the ghetto – not yet, anyway.

There was a sharp intake of breath from Gita. She had not heard that bit of the story before.

"It was a miracle that I finally got home. I did not go into the house until I had thrown away my clothes and burned them so as not to bring any lice in. I do not think mama would have cared because she was just so relieved to see me alive.

"My journey was supposed to have lasted three or four days, but it took many, many weeks. I was not scared but I can imagine how my mother suffered, not knowing of my whereabouts when hearing of the destruction of the Syzran Bridge.

"I was told later that mama never went to bed all this time. As a result of this trip and the goods I brought home, the situation in our family improved greatly."

Mama never mentioned the pain she suffered then or the pain that wracked her frail body in her last days.

JOCIUS'S FOOD DELIVERIES CONTRIBUTED greatly to maintaining the health of the Krons but alone they were not enough to sustain them. Meyer and Gita knew that remaining healthy and fit to work was the key to survival. The Nazis would undoubtedly dispose of anybody who could no longer contribute to their war machine.

The Jewish police played a vital role in smuggling food themselves, as they had permission to leave the ghetto at any time. Most of their bounty went to feed the mouths of their own. Nevertheless, they often facilitated clandestine deliveries to the gates by the likes of farmers and bakers sympathetic to the plight of those within. Clearly, this was not a dependable way of securing food. If families wanted additional food, then securing a supply would be a constant test of their ingenuity and bravery.

It was time for the Krons to retrieve some of the valuables they had left for safekeeping beyond the ghetto fence. Gita would take on that dangerous responsibility for the good of her family. Her husband's pre-war bravery and resourcefulness in keeping his family's stomachs full inspired her. Of course, such independent acts of daring went against Meyer's protective instincts. However, he rationalized the risk had to be taken. He knew better than to challenge his wife when it came to maintaining her family's well-being.

The Jewish police at the gate took on the role of alerting their fellow inmates when it was safe to leave the ghetto without fear of detection by German officers or the local police guards.

Periodically, the blonde, almost Gentile-looking Gita would take advantage of those safe times. Once outside she would strip off her yellow star and walk the sidewalks as a non-Jew would. She visited former neighbours and friends to retrieve goods for barter, sometimes hiding eggs in the fur trim of her long coat.

It was not always a successful exercise. Some so-called friends offered little in return for the more valuable jewellery Gita presented. Then there were those who wanted nothing more to do with their Jewish neighbour. They threatened to call in the Gestapo – the occupational police force – if she did not get out of their sight. It was the same story many of her ghetto neighbours could tell.

Though her blonde mane made her less noticeable, she still had some close encounters almost running into off-duty guards, who would have happily betrayed her to the Nazis.

The sound of laughter was never heard in the ghetto, some would claim in later years. However, inside the hovels they called home, Jewish families did sometimes find humour in their plight. One such occasion occurred after one of Gita's more successful summer outings. Gita found butter for the family. Her providers cut up the two kilos into thin slabs, strapping them to her lower back beneath her dress.

It was beginning to melt by the time she returned home. Rachel Peisachowitz, recently married to cousin Chaim, whisked her away from male eyes and deftly removed the dress. Then, as Gita giggled uncontrollably, she scraped the butter from her tuchas where it had slipped. The knife doubtless tickled but it was hard to tell whether the tears that accompanied the mirth were a product of the absurdity of the situation or relief to be back in her family's care.

Meyer did his fair share of smuggling too. His position at Frenkel's enabled him to make business trips out of the factory and at those times, he invariably found ways of procuring food.

The next challenge was establishing how safe it was to return home at the end of the day with groceries. From one of the factory windows he could see his attic window in the ghetto. When it was time for him to leave, Gita, who was generally home by then, would appear in that window wearing a white kerchief to let him know if it were safe and there was a sympathetic guard on duty at the gate. If there was danger, she wore a red kerchief.

Some of the guards turned a blind eye simply because they wanted to help their fellow Shavl citizens. Others were delighted to cash in on their position as gatekeepers and accept bribes. No matter what their motive, they too had to be most cautious because many of their other colleagues were Jew haters by conviction.

On more than one occasion, would-be food smugglers had to dump food or toss it over the wire when they returned to find one of the 'wrong' guards on shift. The guards arrested those caught with food and inflicted the severest of physical punishment on them. Some of those arrested never returned from the red brick jail.

WULF WAS MORE concerned with the scarcity of medicine than food and seized upon every opportunity to smuggle it back into the ghetto from the Shavl hospital. He brought in the medications needed to treat such diseases as typhoid and diphtheria. He was supposed to report such outbreaks to the Nazis but he knew that providing such information would result in a death sentence for the sufferers so he kept quiet. He also enlisted the help of Nathan Katz as a drug runner. Wulf could count on the young man to obtain medications by whatever means necessary from the general pharmacy in town, which sometimes included the occasional break-in.

When Joseph Leibovich, the brother of the Judenrat chairman, was diagnosed with tuberculosis, Wulf determined the only way to cure him was to get him out of the ghetto. He being a member of the Jewish police force made that somewhat easier.

Leibovich was whisked away to the city hospital and into a quiet room away from the general patient population. Once there, Wulf set about performing a procedure to clear the sick man's lungs. However, just as Wulf plunged the syringe needle into the chest of his patient, two members of the Gestapo burst in. They dragged Leibovich from the operating table, snapping the needle in two as they did so. One of the nursing staff had betrayed Wulf.

Both men were frog marched to the police headquarters, on Ausros Street, just a few doors away from Gebietskommissariat. They led Leibovich unceremoniously to the cellars. Wulf could hear his patient's screams, as he was tortured. He survived and later overcame TB with further treatment – in secret.

Then it was Wulf's turn. To his great surprise, his torturer merely sat him down and issued a succession of threatening orders, hitting everything but Wulf with various instruments of torture. The Nazi's wife was Wulf's patient.

WULF'S NEXT BRUSH WITH the law came one night in February 1942 when two policemen appeared in the ghetto. Their chief, Albinas Grebliunas, was seriously ill, supposedly with typhoid. It was a misdiagnosis and Wulf quickly established he was suffering from blood poisoning. Wulf looked like a miracle worker a few days later when Grebliunas rose from his bed. In reality, it was just a case of carrying out a thorough examination and prescribing the right drug.

Grebliunas called him in a few days later and asked what he wanted in return for his 'miracle' treatment. He asked for a private meeting between the officer, himself, and some of the Judenrat members. The Jewish leaders told the chief how the Nazis had seriously cut back food rations to the ghetto.

Days later, a police squad, charged with supervising the ghetto, moved into a house by the ghetto entrance. Their unofficial orders were to look the other way when food was smuggled into the ghetto, a gift from Grebliunas.

However, the cozy arrangement did not continue for too many months. In late August 1942, the Nazis showed just how serious they were about punishing smugglers. Unexpectedly, dozens of soldiers, supported by police, arrived at the ghetto gates as their slave labourers were marching wearily home. Instantly, contraband food littered the street.

This time they outwitted their searchers but the worst was yet to come. The Nazis knew the Jews had made fools of them. They later issued a shocking ultimatum to the Judenrat to turn over 50 Schwarzhändler – food smugglers – on September 2, who would then face a firing squad.

The Judenrat members wrestled once again with the task of doing the Nazis' dirty work, knowing that if they did not draw up the execution list the Germans would just select 50 Jews at random. They would not stand for it this time. On September 2, the members of the Judenrat turned themselves in to Gewecke. The furious Gewecke's high-pitched voice climbed an octave and might have shattered glass. He ranted and raved but as he did so, a plan was forming to save face. After a painfully long few moments of silence for the listeners, he delivered a new ultimatum. He would call off the execution for a payment of 20,000 Reichsmark – a sum that the Judenrat managed to collect with great difficulty from the ghetto's Jews. The cash would not likely see the inside of Hitler's treasury.

THE SCARE REDUCED THE level of smuggling but only temporarily because dire needs among the population left no option but to come up with new and different ways to keep families fed. When the Krons' resources outside dried up, Meyer and Gita began discussing other ways of financing their forays for food.

Meyer hatched a plan that would have guaranteed his permanent demise if caught – and likely the rest of his family. His new source of income would be booze. He convinced the factory's German directors that he needed five litres of pure alcohol a month for analytic purposes.

He used not one drop for analysis. Meyer and his pharmacist colleague Israel Shapiro merely invented the results that would please Director Siegel. Instead, the twosome used the alcohol to produce a passable imitation of vodka, lapped up by Meyer's non-Jewish colleagues. The factory's non-Jews would bring in meat, bread and butter to work to trade for Meyer's marvellous concoctions. The liquid rotgut was marvellous for the men, starved of their favourite tipple.

Meyer's bootlegging partner provided the recipes for the liqueurs they also ambitiously created. Both men were not averse to sampling their own products, sometimes to excess. They lived on a knife-edge, neither knowing what tomorrow would bring.

Aside from the liquor manufacturing enterprise, Meyer had a secondary source of income. He built up excess supplies of a dye compound called Methylene Blue. A manufacturer in town needed the dye badly and Meyer was able to supply it through an unidentified third party.

The vodka was the most stable source of income and it seemed as if the Kron-Shapiro distillery would continue undetected. Then one day, a worried Shapiro showed up in Meyer's cubbyhole, which passed for an office. By the time the conversation was over, Meyer was white-faced.

Twenty-two people had died of poisoning and several more became blind after drinking from a drum delivered to Frenkel's, which they thought was vodka. It may have smelled like vodka, but it was methyl alcohol mistakenly sent in place of the sulphuric acid ordered by Meyer for the tanning process. This brand of 'vodka' was smuggled out in pails and sold on the Black Market. The fatalities came fast and furiously.

The anxious Meyer wrung his hands and repeated almost continuously: "I wrote the order. They will blame me. I'm finished."

Shapiro tried to calm his colleague but Meyer never heard the reassurances. He just repeated his fear, lost in thought as to how he would get out of this mess.

Miraculously, the tragedy passed without any further recriminations, or at least any directed towards Meyer. The Gestapo traced the error to the supply centre and meted out an appropriate punishment, or at least what the Nazis deemed appropriate. Not for the last time, fate smiled upon Meyer Kron.

CHAPTER SEVEN

The last pregnancy

Police Headquarters, Thursday, March 5, 1942.

THE PEOPLE OF THE ghetto awakened every day wondering what cruelty their merciless captors would subject them to that day. The men, especially, had hardened themselves to the verbal attacks and smacks around the head by a gloved hand or, more painfully, by the butt of a rifle. Despite all of the terrible ordeals each and every family had suffered during the first nine months of the occupation, no one could have predicted the monstrous Diktat the Germans were about to issue to the Judenrat.

However, when Dr. Peisachowitz, Judenrat chairman Mendel Leibovich and Ber Kartun were summoned to the Nazi administration offices, they each surmised what they were about to hear would spell more despair for their fellow Jews.

They emerged stony-faced and stunned after a short meeting with *SS Oberscharführer* Hermann Schlöf. He was straight to the point as though issuing no more than a minor order to clean up the streets. He had a dirty job for them to perform. He told them coldly that they must ensure that no more Jews were born in the ghetto after August 5, 1942. Simply put, he warned, if any child was born after that arbitrary date the whole family would be 'removed' – a ghastly euphemism for execution by firing squad.

Peisachowitz broke the news to his fellow ghetto doctors, which prompted gynaecologist Dr. Joseph Luntz to seek a private audience with Schlöf. The SS officer had a grudging respect for the doctor, who hailed from a well-respected Jewish family so he agreed to see Luntz. However, once there, Luntz soon learned that the depth of the Nazi's respect for him was somewhat shallow. Schlöf spared the niceties and quickly spelled out his position, so there would be no misunderstanding:

91

"The order is approved at the highest level and it will be obeyed," he said, before passing a few uncomfortable moments looking down at the papers on his desk, clearly a signal that the meeting was over before it had really started.

Schlöf would offer no reason for what he called a 'ban on births'. The Nazi's position was that he did not need to explain and, besides, the doctor's persistence was irritating him. This meeting would end shortly before it became nasty. Schlöf was astute enough to know that while he had the power to fling this Jew out there might be a time when he would have need of him, though not of his professional services, of course.

Such a ban would mean fewer mouths to feed and ultimately there would be fewer Jews to kill later. Yes, all in the ghetto knew their time left on this earth was limited and at the whim of the men in black. Hitler had made it very clear that he would not rest until Europe's Jewry was no more.

News of similar bans in other ghettos had quickly reached the ears of the Jewish leadership. Of course, Luntz knew before he arrived that his attempts to dissuade Schlöf would be futile. Nevertheless, he had to make an effort to prick the conscience of the man before him.

He knew that there would be no exceptions for Shavl but perhaps he could buy some time. To that end, he sought an assurance they would seize no child born before that date. In the doctor's fertile imagination, an ambitious plan was already being conceived, one that required such a guarantee. He must try to save as many of the unborn as possible within the time left.

Luntz bit his lip as he waited for a response to the plea for time. Schlöf looked up. He had heard something he could respond to positively. A more civil conversation ensued and after some bargaining, Schlöf finally agreed to make that guarantee public, well, at least to Luntz and the Judenrat. The Nazis extended the date by ten days some months later, not much of a break but every extra day could mean the birth of more healthy Jewish babies. Luntz had nothing to offer in exchange for such concessions. Not then, but the payback would come later.

No time to waste thought Luntz as he returned to the ghetto. He consulted his dear friend and colleague Peisachowitz and together they hatched a fully-fledged plan based on an idea that had swirled in Luntz's head just a few short hours earlier in the German's office. With whatever means at their disposal, they would induce births in cases of the women whose termination dates were on or about the date of the ban.

To make sure there was good chance of the newborns surviving the team would have to wait until closer to the August deadline. In the meantime, there was no choice but to abort fetuses in the first trimester of development.

For the inductions, Luntz devised a surgical method that made use of the limited medical instruments at their disposal – largely equipment smuggled out of the city hospital by Peisachowitz – and drugs obtained illicitly and ferried back into the ghetto by young Nathan Katz. Caesarean sections were out of the question so Luntz had to draw upon all of his skill and experience to ensure there were no tragic mishaps. They kept no personal records of how many children were born. There was no point in giving the Nazis ammunition to aid them in their future actions.

Privately, a couple of evenings later, Peisachowitz proudly told Meyer and Gita that the doctors enjoyed a 100 percent success rate, not one mother or child fell ill even though some infants were born quite prematurely. Then he fell quiet.

"On the other side of the ledger," he admitted, "we also terminated a lot of Jewish children before they had a chance to breathe."

Gita stared at her favourite cousin for a moment and snapped him out of his momentary trance.

"Wulf, it's tragic but by extinguishing some lives, you have saved many others."

Meyer reinforced his wife's point: "The Judenrat has had to make similar decisions for the greater good many times."

Peisachowitz remained silent, which was most unusual for this loquacious man.

"Clearly, the women also arrived at the same conclusion or else they would not have presented themselves willingly to you and Joseph."

Meyer made one final attempt to reassure their distressed relative.

"You can't torture yourself with this."

The doctor would continue to torture himself for the rest of his life but for that moment, he set aside the guilt. He smiled unconvincingly and changed the subject.

WULF AND LUNTZ's sickening termination work was complete for the time being. However, the news from the front would have a greater influence on how long they could keep their termination tools locked up than they could ever imagine.

The German attack on Stalingrad began on August 19, 1942. It would be a propagandist's dream to take the city named for Josef Stalin and it would enable the aggressors to take control of the Caucasus oil fields.

The Red Army fighters defended their city from within, forcing its enemy to enter and fight on the streets, a perilous way for troops entering unknown territory.

Three months later, on November 19, as winter began to bite the Germans, three Russian armies surrounded the city and launched a huge counter attack from outside, joined a day later by two more. The Germans were defeated. After two months more of fighting in frigid conditions, they were 300,000 fewer in strength. The repelling Soviet force had lost 500,000 but its sheer weight of numbers available to fight had guaranteed their victory.

The first clues the Shavl Jews received as to just how badly things were going for the Germans came early in the fighting. Dozens of frost bitten and severely wounded young combatants arrived daily for treatment at the hospital housed in Frenkel's mansion. Word spread quickly.

In January 1943, radios secreted around the ghetto carried the big news on the BBC broadcast from London. Wulf heard the latest development in a basement room at the public hospital where one of the staff hid a radio.

"Germans surrender at Stalingrad," said the cultured English voice in Russian, delivering the headline that would get everybody's attention.

The newsreader continued: "The Soviet Government has announced the final defeat of the German 6th Army at the port of Stalingrad, in southern Russia.

"A statement late this evening said: 'Our forces have now completed the liquidation of the German Fascist troops encircled in the area of Stalingrad. The last centre of enemy resistance in the Stalingrad area has thus been crushed.'

"The declaration brings to an end five months of heavy fighting for the city. The battle has been described as among the most terrible of the war so far."

At that point, Wulf heard somebody walking towards the darkened room so he switched off the radio. It could have been a sympathetic colleague approaching but it could also have been somebody who would have taken delight in reporting his act of surreptitious radio listening. He switched on the light so the intruder would think Wulf had just arrived there himself. It was a maintenance man who just walked right on by the room.

Wulf did not bother turning the radio back on, but packed up his belongings and prepared to return to the ghetto to spread the news to his family. The end of the bulletin revealed that the Red Army had taken 45,000 German soldiers prisoner, doubling the total in custody at a single stroke. The Russians kept their prisoners in appalling conditions in temperatures of -30° Celsius, a fact that would elicit little sympathy from ghetto listeners.

THERE WERE NOW more pregnancies in the ghetto. Such positive news out of Russia had reached the ears of ghetto residents in dribs and drabs for the past five months. It had encouraged these women not to acquiesce to their captors' demands to submit to abortions. They kept assuring themselves and their families that a German defeat was only just around the corner and their babies would be born healthy and free.

As January went by and February turned into March, some of the expectant women became despondent and voluntarily submitted to the life destroying procedure but not all. Others were pondering what to do; perhaps half hoping that somebody else would make the decision for them. If that were their wish, they would not be disappointed.

On March 24, 1943, the Judenrat held an emergency meeting to plan how they might deal with the new pregnancies that threatened the lives of many healthy adults. Leibovich and the rest of the respected gathering present that day had hoped they would not have to revisit this painful and divisive issue again. This time it would be more difficult to remedy the situation because these women and their husbands had consciously ignored the orders.

Leibovich brought the meeting to order, looked down, and introduced the only item on the agenda: How should they prevent births in the ghetto? – Eliezer Yerushalmi took notes but his report of the meeting would never be available for perusal by the Nazis.

❧

"THE BAN ON giving birth to children, which has been imposed on the Jews, is being applied with the utmost severity in all of the ghettos," Leibovich announced, following up with a sordid example of what they had heard occurred in another ghetto.

"There was a birth recently in Kaunas and all members of the family were shot and killed."

The frustrated elder continued: "But it seems no attention is being paid to this threat here and people are behaving most irresponsibly. There are already several cases of pregnancy in the ghetto but, fortunately, so far no measures have been taken against them."

Dr. Kalman Blecher responded by asking rhetorically if the council could really force the women to submit to abortions. No comment, though everybody had an answer. No member really wanted to tackle the thorny issue that threatened to turn families against the leadership and divide the council.

After a few moments, Luntz broke the uneasy silence: "We have had three births since August 15 of last year. I don't know how or where exactly they took place because I did not treat the cases prior to birth."

All three births took place after the Nazi-imposed ban on births deadline. Then he volunteered the numbers they really did not want to hear.

"I can tell you that at the present time there are about 20 pregnant women in the ghetto, most of them in the first few months of pregnancy but some are already in the fourth or fifth month and one even in the eighth month."

There were loud sighs around the table, as the extent of the problem hit home.

Luntz continued: "Only two of the pregnant women approached so far refuse to have an abortion; for one of them this would be the third abortion and she is threatened by the danger of subsequent childlessness and another is the one who has reached the eighth month."

Peisachowitz joined in the discussion, tapping the table to make his point firmly: "They must be persuaded to agree to have an abortion. They must be told about what happened in Kaunas. If necessary one must make use of a white lie in this emergency and tell them that the security police are already looking for these cases."

Attitudes began to harden in the room.

Dr. Moshe Burstein suggested the council forbid the medical team, including the midwives, from attending births. Blecher, in support, went a step further proposing that they should register all pregnancies. It was a step too far, for Leibovich, if the doctor meant the council should name and shame the women into compliance.

The normally calm Leibovich certainly took it that way and reacted angrily, not asking for a clarification:

"We must not make propaganda against births in public! – The matter could reach ears that should not hear it. We must discuss the matter only with those concerned."

Leibovich said the Judenrat should summon all pregnant women to the ghetto hospital. Once there, they would warn them, in the presence of the doctor, of the danger that awaited them if they went through with the pregnancy.

The tension within the room increased when Luntz called the attention of the meeting to the delicate ethical matter of operating on a woman in the latter stages of pregnancy. It was one thing to induce birth at eight months as they had blessedly, and successfully, done prior to the ban but a late termination was another matter entirely.

"How can one perform an abortion on a woman who has already reached the eighth month of her pregnancy?" he asked, silencing the gathering. He allowed what he was saying to sink in before continuing.

"Surely we must understand the feelings of the mother. It will surely be impossible to convince her. What will happen to the infant if we cause a premature birth?

"We cannot carry out an operation like that in a private home and it is forbidden to leave the child at the ghetto hospital. What will happen if despite everything we do the child is born alive? Shall we kill it?"

There, he had said it. He concluded: "I cannot accept such a responsibility."

Blecher's chilling response caused some listeners to shiver and others to flinch:

"No doctor will take upon himself the responsibility of killing a live child, for that would be murder."

Peisachowitz suggested allowing the child to be born and then smuggling it out of the ghetto to a Christian family. That was a welcome straw for them all to clutch. However, it slipped from their collective grasp, as the exasperated Leibovich nixed that notion:

"We cannot allow the child to be born because we are required to report every case of a birth," he said, wringing his hands as he spoke. "We have been asked three times so far whether there have been any births recently and each time we have answered in the negative. We will be found out and then others will be sacrificed." His pained delivery of the statement revealed his inner turmoil for all to recognize.

Ber Kartun said what was at the forefront of everybody's mind.

"If the only threat was to the family of the infant, we could leave the matter to its members. However, it endangers the whole ghetto and the consequences are liable to be most terrible."

Council secretary Aaron Katz sensed the mood of the room was beginning to shift towards taking action.

"The doctors should negotiate with the pregnant women. If nothing results from their discussions, they should hand over the case to a member of the Judenrat and he should apply sanctions against the family. He should take away their ration cards, move the family members to the worst working places and deny them medical treatment, firewood and other things."

There were some gasps from the gathering but he was not finished yet.

"In the event of those sanctions failing the pregnant woman should then be presented with the following ultimatum: accept an abortion or the Judenrat will let the security police know."

He rapped the table hard to emphasize the importance of each step. He still was not finished. He looked around the table, trying to get a sense of how his colleagues were taking this before uttering his final dreadful sentence. He could learn nothing from the sour expressions that greeted him. He carried on regardless.

"In the case of the woman in her eighth month the child should not be born alive because if it is it will serve as an example to others."

Silence descended and in it, troubled minds began to change.

Dr. Girsas Dyrektorovich was the first to speak. He would go along with the hard line approach and offered an ethical compromise to appease those troubled by the killing of a newborn.

"It would be like sacrificing a child when there is a danger to the mother's life." Heads nodded.

Luntz, who had devoted his professional life to bringing children into the world, found such expedient rationale unacceptable.

"I cannot do this!" said the distraught Luntz.

Even the gynaecologist's dear friend Peisachowitz was now more accepting of the need to take drastic measures. It would not be the last time that his Hippocratic Oath to preserve life would be challenged.

Quietly, he suggested a deception, which he rationalized was in the interests of the greater good of the community: "It may be possible to cause an early birth in the hospital and have another doctor deliver the child. Then the killing of the child might be achieved by a nurse simply administering a lethal injection elsewhere, without her knowing, of course, just what she was doing."

Luntz said no more. This course of action would haunt the members of the Judenrat for the rest of their lives. It was a deal with the devil, in the shape of the Third Reich.

Katz summed up in a chilling, detached manner:

"One should bring about an early birth immediately in the case of the woman who is eight months pregnant. In every other case of pregnancy one should take all measures to convince the woman to abort before introducing sanctions and ultimately threatening them with exposure to the authorities."

The meeting closed. Yerushalmi the scribe took away his notes and hid them in the usual place, a metal box he buried in the ground away from the Judenrat office. There his accounts of life in the ghetto would remain until the Nazis left this land.

∾

THERE COULD BE no further delays; the doctors began the task of taking lives rather than saving them. The terminations had to occur without the Nazis learning of them for fear that they may decide to execute the women and punish the Judenrat for sitting on the information.

Rachel Peisachowitz was a midwife by profession and therefore the obvious choice of assistant for her brother-in-law. She could be relied upon to be efficient and above all, discreet.

In the days that followed, a procession of women dropped by the ghetto hospital to end their dreams of motherhood. Some sobbed quietly, others bawled loudly but most just climbed on the table unaided and submitted to the act of destruction with barely a word spoken. The lack of emotion shown by the latter was perhaps the most worrying to observe. How would they deal with this trauma the day after and all of their days after, especially if they were now destined never to experience the joys of giving birth?

THE FINAL DAY of surgical terminations was long and exhausting, both physically and emotionally, for those with fresh blood on their hands. The Peisachowitzs looked at each other, as the last woman left with her husband

"That's it, Rachel, isn't it?"

"Yes, well at least for today," she responded, guessing there may be half a dozen more in another month or so.

"Yes, indeed, I fear you may be right, my dear."

They remained quiet while Rachel slowly cleaned herself up, fastidiously scrubbing the blood from her hands. It was unlike Rachel to do anything slowly. He followed her slow lead. He wanted to say something but was not sure what would provide comfort to his beloved Rachel. It was unusual for him to be lost for words.

Instead, Rachel picked up the thread of what she had said a few quiet moments ago.

"Who knows how many more will discover that they are pregnant and must … and must …."

The rest of the sentence stuck in her throat.

Peisachowitz could have said "yes, indeed" again but he did not. He wanted to pick his next words carefully but toiled over the content. His sister-in-law saved him.

"Oh, well, I guess it's time," she said.

Without saying anything more, she climbed on the table for now it was her turn to abort the child she and her husband Chaim had prayed for and tried to create for so long. Their joy had been short lived and she would never experience the pleasures and rewards of motherhood.

It was a similar story in all the ghettos that remained. It is unknown how many abortions there were. The numbers were not included in the estimated six million Jews murdered by the Nazis.

THERE WAS ONE more pregnancy in the ghetto. Riva Gotz conceived the baby in womb less than a month after the ban on births came into force.

Her husband Zava was against her having the child as was her mother Bella and the rest of the family. He repeated the threat the pregnancy posed. His position as the second-in-command of the Kaukazas ghetto police ensured he had a high profile. Therefore, he feared their secret would not remain so for long and that would mean the execution of the newborn, both of its parents and most likely the rest of the family.

However, the 30-year-old woman was not prepared to submit to an abortion and she made that clear when she discovered she was more than four months pregnant in January of 1943. She had already suffered a miscarriage and feared this might be her last chance at motherhood.

Prior to a visit to the doctor, prompted by what turned out to be a bout of pneumonia, she and her husband had no suspicions about her condition. Many of the women in the ghetto suffered from an erratic menstrual cycle caused by the appalling living conditions and poor nutrition.

Moments after breaking the happy news, that should have warmed the room that winter day; there was a distinct chill in the air. The room, barely 5 feet by 10, was home to Riva, her husband Zava, her mother Bella, brother Yankl Ton, his partner Esther Ziv and her daughter Haviva, and two complete strangers, who, fortunately, were absent that day. Their conversation likely followed the same lines as many others had elsewhere in the ghetto during the last year.

"We waited a long time until we had a nice apartment to have a child . . . and then I lost the baby," the dark-haired beauty told her husband. Zava did not need reminding of the miscarriage they endured a little more than three years earlier during the Russian occupation. The quiet, reserved man let her continue.

"Now we are here in the ghetto. I am 30 and I want this baby. I may not get another chance," she said somewhat pessimistically, he thought.

Zava idly looked up at the peeling ceiling as though searching for inspiration from above. What a state of disrepair this place had fallen into, something his father would never have allowed to happen when he lived there. Yes, the Gotz family members were likely the only ghetto residents living in surroundings so familiar to them. It was formerly a splendid house and store on Vilna St., opposite Frenkel's factory, big enough to house a family of nine comfortably, including seven children. Now almost 50 people were crammed into the building.

The tall, slender man unfolded himself from the worn seat that once resembled an armchair, his head barely missing the low ceiling as he stood.

"Now of all times it has to happen," he said after a few moments contemplation of their dreadful situation.

He became lost in his thoughts again as she repeated her commitment to going through with the pregnancy. He was in shock.

Then he uncharacteristically raised his voice to his wife.

"I work in the ghetto administration, this makes it impossible," reasoned the man, who would be made head of the Kaukazas ghetto police by mid-summer.

"I have to help persuade other women to undergo abortions, yet my own wife refuses. This cannot be."

She spat out a reply: "This is not about your job. It is about our future, our family."

Her mother had listened quietly, but she snapped, coming to the defence of her son-in-law:

"We may not have a future if you insist on having this child. There will be other opportunities for you to have a child."

The determined Riva would not move from her rigid position.

"Quieten down both of you. We are not alone," cautioned Zava, wary of the dozens of pairs of ears that may overhear them.

It was not how many people might learn their secret, but whom. Among those around them was Girsas Rabinovich, who worked within the office of the Gebietskommissar. His daughter, Dora, like Zava, worked for the ghetto administration. Another resident's duties attached him to the main Nazi administration, one other worked in the police headquarters in town and two more worked directly for the SS. The risks of betrayal were huge.

"We don't know these people and to save themselves they may betray us," reasoned Zava.

"Then we will not tell anybody," said Riva, staring them both down with her bright blue eyes.

The risks her family talked about could not break down her stubborn opposition to a termination. There was to be no more discussion that day but the topic was one they would return to almost daily in an attempt to wear her down.

During a later heated discussion, Riva repeated an optimistic sentiment shared and often voiced by most of the women in her delicate state.

"Look the war is not going well for the Germans. Hitler will be dead before I give birth."

Riva grew more determined with each snippet of news about a Red Army victory. However, some of the others in her condition were not so optimistic and so she was the last pregnant woman in the ghetto. The woman who was near term at the time of the Judenrat meeting had given up her child. It was born alive but found dead the next day, apparently smothered. There was no need for Peisachowitz to say more and no Judenrat member pressed for a more detailed explanation. Of course, such deaths can happen naturally in beings so fragile.

The pressure became unbearable for Zava. The Jewish administration leaders called on him two or three times a week to deliver his wife to the hospital for an abortion. He resigned his position.

Riva felt badly for her husband but she had come this far and she must not give in to the monsters from another land. There soon came a time when she could no longer conceal her child no matter how billowing her dress. The labour board stopped assigning her as a seamstress, fixing uniforms, for the German officers. Seamstresses were in great supply so her absence went unnoticed.

Riva would lie down on her bunk bed under the window and look out at the clouds sailing by. Standing up was dangerous because it would advertise her presence there during the working day. Besides, the street view below would not allow her an escape, mentally or physically, from this prison of her own making.

She passed the time visualizing how her baby might look. It would be long in body like her beloved Zava. It may have her blue eyes. It would certainly be the most beautiful baby in the world. In the clouds, she would see her baby's head and features and hair, curly hair, she decided.

In her dark moments, and there were many, she felt like a prisoner. Her situation and the danger she was posing to others was a heavy weight on her conscience. At times, she felt guilty, even ashamed.

The lonely weeks passed by. Then news filtered through the barbed wire fence that lifted her spirits. The Wehrmacht had surrendered at Stalingrad. Perhaps they really would be defeated before her baby was born. Falling bombs nearby convinced her that release was imminent.

The birth was also imminent.

Zava and Yankl prepared a place for her. It was a large closet in the kitchen across from their room, where food and firewood was stored.

They scrubbed the windowless enclosed area until it was spotless. They collected paper and made a paste by adding water and even some flour – a rare commodity. They papered the walls, hoping this would muffle the inevitable screams and cries that would accompany a birth.

Zava smuggled in a kerosene lamp so they could work by night. He found a cot, a table, and a bench within the ghetto and brought them home under cover of darkness. He piled wood against the closet door to discourage entry by any other resident.

The family collected soap and constructed a kerosene stove out of parts gathered from around the ghetto to heat water. A washbasin materialized from somewhere. Zava, through his contacts in the administration, obtained a rubber sheet along with sterile cotton and gauze from the ghetto hospital.

Zava thought his pilfering and wheeler dealing was going unnoticed but the likes of Peisachowitz and Luntz knew exactly what was going on. However, they decided to obey the letter of the law but not the spirit. They would not be there at the birth but they would be available to help after the fact, if necessary.

On May 31, with a little more than a week to go, all hell broke loose outside and inside the ghetto. The Nazis carried out a search at the ghetto gate and found two Jews with food hidden beneath their work clothes. After the previous situation, in which Gewecke was embarrassed, this time there would be vengeance.

One of those arrested was a baker named Sol Mazovetsky, one of a family of ten housed in the same building as the Gotz family. The S.S. burst in, looking for other evidence that would garner them many more victims than the two they had already under lock and key. Where better to start than the home of the smuggler? Riva cowered in her secret room. The guards never came near her haven, concentrating almost exclusively on the Mazovetsky quarters.

On the night of June 3, Riva was extremely restless. At 4:30 a.m. the following morning her water broke. She calmly got up and walked a couple of unsteady strides to where her mother lay.

"Be calm and go back to bed," her drowsy mother told her. "We have plenty of time. Be patient."

Riva could not settle down. She paced the floor in the darkness, fearing to turn on the single electric light. On a whim, she went into the kitchen and lit the kerosene lamp there so she could see her way to boiling some water. As it bubbled, she eyed the closet door where she would soon enter, leaving only when she had a babe in her arms. She then poured the water into the sink and washed her hair. Goodness knows why; but it relaxed her.

At around 7 a.m., her family and others in the house left for work. Zava remained behind. Immediately her pains became regular and ten minutes apart. She and Bella went into the closet and closed the door. Zava piled the wood against the door and left.

They were now in their own private world. Just the two of them, soon to be three, Riva thought. Bella ordered her to lie down on the cot. Riva was relaxed at first. Then the pains came more frequently. She began crawling around, hoping to relieve the excruciating pain.

"You can't do that," her mother almost screamed. "Lie down. Bite on this.' She said, passing her a clean rag. The day passed and the family returned from work. Zava opened the closet.

"Go away," she yelled. He did.

When the child was born some hours later, the exhausted mother collapsed. She remembered nothing until she awoke sometime around midnight to the soothing words of Dr. Luntz.

"Be calm my dear, you have lost a lot of blood but you are going to be fine if you rest and remain where you are."

When he had entered the makeshift birthing room, Luntz's stomach turned. He was risking his own life. If she should die and his complicity was discovered it meant certain death. He felt guilty about even having such thoughts.

"When I saw the handsome, healthy baby born in the terrible conditions of our ghetto life, I experienced a moment of inward joy," he excitedly told his wife hours later in the safety of his own home – such that it was. "I saw in him the symbol of the salvation of Israel."

It was also a comfort to him. He grieved for the dozens of healthy embryos he had aborted with his friend Peisachowitz. There was blood on his hands but somehow this infant's birth cleansed them.

Riva clung to her baby boy. She named him after her father, Ben Tzion – son of Zion. The infant seemed healthy enough. The new grandmother estimated he weighed in at about nine and a half pounds.

The closet became a nursery. Riva and her son rarely strayed from its protective walls. The baby was never more than an arm's length away. The moment he woke, she nursed him at her breast so that he would not cry out.

Neighbours even dropped by to look at the miracle born under their noses. They were no longer alone. Those that worked for the Nazis stayed away and the family was glad of that.

Three months passed and mother and child remained undetected. The war was going poorly for the Nazis and the Russians were getting closer. The mood in the ghetto swung between extremes as its inmates pondered what this meant for them. Some feared it would signal their end while fewer thought liberation might be near.

There were rumours from other ghettos about the Nazis mounting surprise raids to round up and permanently remove all the children – a *Kinderaktion*. There were also reports of some ghettos closing and the former inmates being marched to secret locations.

Initially, Riva would not hear of parting with her child. After what she had been through, no one was going to take her little Benya, as the family affectionately referred to this special child. Eventually, she gave into the suggestions of her husband and brother. Her child's best hope was on the other side of the fence in the care of a Christian family. Yankl worked in the machine shop of a vehicle repair garage in town so his daily work brought him to regular contact with non-Jews. He already had a family in mind. They did not need any persuading to take the youngster. They agreed to raise him as their own, until happier and peaceful times returned to Lithuania and his natural parents were able to take over his rearing.

A day later, Yankl slipped away from his work and secretly approached a Catholic priest called Father Justinus Lapis. He had heard rumours that the priest was a friend of the Jews. He arranged for the forging of many baptismal certificates for Jewish children and provided one bearing the name Benediktas Martinaitis for Yankl's nephew.

Now the next challenge was how to smuggle out the baby. Arye Krupnik was the official driver appointed to serve the Judenrat and had surreptitiously removed other children to safety. In the early days of the ghetto, Arye had even smuggled in, rather than out, a severely disabled young man. The man's parents feared the Germans would immediately remove and kill their son if he entered the conventional way. That particular act would one day soon enable the saving of a man set to face a Nazi firing squad. If the Nazis uncovered Arye's human smuggling activities, the cost to the whole community would be great. Fortunately, they never did.

There was also the 'latrine man'. He would arrive on a cart with a huge barrel on the back. He would often exit not with the ghetto waste but children bound for safety in the care of rescuers.

It was too risky. Ben Gotz was not capable of holding on once inside the barrel.

One trick tried by others was to distract the guards while somebody smuggled a child out beneath an adult's coat. The anxious parents feared that would not work either because the baby might cry.

It was time for Peisachowitz to play a role he had played at other times. At the appointed time, one rainy night, he showed up at the Gotz home, with a small bottle in his coat pocket. With a little cotton wool, he dabbed baby Benya with a drop or two of ether, just as he had done before for one of his own young cousins, Aviva Leibovich.

Zava placed his soundly sleeping infant in a battered suitcase with a few holes punched in it to allow air to tickle the nostrils of the baby within. Riva, comforted by her mother, sobbed as her husband walked swiftly through the darkness of the early evening towards the fence. It was all clear. The guards were not straying far from the shelter of the gate on this miserable night.

Zava kissed the case and tossed it towards his brother-in-law on the other side of the wire, who caught it cleanly and turned on his heel. Uncle Yankl then headed down the back streets to the repair garage where he would hand over little Benya. He then returned home, after making the delivery, via the main gate. The guards knew he often worked late on SS staff cars so did not question him as he went by. Besides, they would have got wet.

For the next week, Riva expressed her milk daily into a small bottle and Yankl took it to work. There he passed it to his nephew's rescuer. It kept her connected with her child. The vital maternal link that kept Riva going was broken when Ben's new parents weaned him off his mother's milk. Now she began to feel guilty, believing she had abandoned the child rather than save him. It was an interpretation of events shared by nobody else.

She dreamed about sneaking out of the ghetto to see him, so much so that she later convinced herself she had done so. Her family would not contradict her when she shared such stories. Her fantasy had become her reality and it helped her cope with her loss.

CHAPTER EIGHT

Matters of life and death

Ezero Street - May 31, 1943.

As Shavl's slave labourers returned home in the evening, people on the sidewalks warned them in loud whispers that the Nazis were searching everybody before they reached the ghetto gate.

Those were the good neighbours but bad neighbours outnumbered them. The latter stalked the columns of workers waiting to pounce on contraband food discarded surreptitiously by frightened Jews. They too were hungry and not averse to profiting from the misfortune of their neighbours.

Meyer and Gita returned empty handed this day as they were still 'feasting' on that supplied by their generous provider, Jocius. They looked at each other, relieved that they did not have to waste good food discarding for the human jackals to scoop up.

Others in the line were less inclined to let go of what they had secured with their dwindling resources. They held tight to their food until they made their final turn into the street leading to the fenced compound they called home.

Meyer almost tripped over a stale loaf dropped by a man in front of them; gnarly potatoes rolled unevenly on the cobbles, kicked aside by people marching behind. As they shot from beneath the column across the street, urchins leapt out from the sidewalk to grab them and take them home for the family pot.

Gita spied a couple of broken eggs in the gutter, almost certainly dropped by somebody nearer the front of the line. She doubted one of the residents of the ramshackle houses on either side of her would so carelessly have dropped them.

She took her mind off the danger ahead, imagining what she could have made with those two eggs. Ruta's favourite treat was

Gogol Mogol. She did not have any sugar in her secret food stash but she would find some way of sweetening the gooey, eggnog like mixture.

Reality returned with a thud as a fellow marcher dropped what looked like a hunk of beef wrapped loosely in a newspaper. It was big enough to feed a family of four in peacetime, 12 in the ghetto. He or she must have stolen it, thought Gita, because no one was going to give up such a rare treat willingly. Some Jews worked as domestic servants for the high-ranking Nazis so one of them likely removed it from the larder of a German officer.

They were taking a considerable risk because even the occupiers were not so laden with life's riches that they would not notice the disappearance of their weekend dinner. That was more the case now than ever as the war was going so badly for the invaders and supplies were becoming more difficult to obtain for these unwelcome guests.

The Germans were agitated by what was happening on the battlefront and thus quick to take out their frustrations on the ghetto residents. A gradual retreat on all fronts followed the humiliating military defeat in January at Stalingrad, where the once-mighty Sixth Army surrendered. It angered those among the higher echelons, who shared Hitler's vision for the German people. It also worried their underlings, who feared a transfer from their cozy assignment in Shavl to the Russian front. There they would become cannon fodder for the Red Army, serving with demoralized comrades, who had suffered the ravages of a Russian winter. Already the less fortunate were back in Shavl in the hospital housed in Frenkel's mansion – known as The Palace locally – next door to the factory.

The ghetto gate was now only a short distance away and there was no longer any discarded food to avoid while taking those final few steps. Meyer raised his eyebrows and nudged Gita:

"What have we done to deserve such a warm welcome from Gebietskommissar Gewecke?" he asked sarcastically, bravado concealing his anxiety.

Meyer noted Gewecke's second-in-command, Ewald Bub, was also present, a man he had found most unpleasant in his dealings with the German bureaucracy. Alongside were administration official Schwant and some German police he did not recognize. Of course, the regular guards carried out the search. They were 'only obeying orders', thought Meyer, sarcastically.

The city's Deputy Police Chief Albinas Grebliunas was also wandering around barking orders and hitting any Jew within his reach with a stick. A crowd of Jews was cowering, kneeling down, and preparing to feel the pain of his blows.

The guards found nothing on those who entered Ezero-Traku that day but it was a different story at the entrance to the Kaukazas ghetto, across Vilna Street a couple of blocks away.

Not everybody had heeded the warnings. Lena Bayer, a music teacher in times when there was reason to sing with joy, was found with some bread beneath her clothes. On Sol Mazovetsky, the searchers found a veritable grocery list of supplies, relative to the lean times at least. The baker was carrying a pound of meat, some bread and a few cigarettes – just enough smokes to calm him in the evening quiet of the ghetto. It was as though they had found the whole contents of the nearby Army storeroom on him.

The young woman was bundled into the rear seat of a Volkswagen. The tall Mazovetsky was folded over and pushed into the trunk of the so-called People's Car. Fortunately, it was a short ride of no more than a block or two to the jail.

In the hours that followed the line often repeated was, "For a few cigarettes they will only beat him up and let him go." It did not take long for a guard friendly with some of the Jewish police to confirm the first part of the common wisdom. Sadistic SS men set about him with a kippel – a long rubber hose with a piece of metal affixed to one end. The inside man was visibly shaken by the beating he had witnessed, saying at its cessation Mazovetsky's "whole body was a bleeding wound." Despite his injuries, he refused to reveal who had supplied him with the contraband food.

A couple of days later, friendly sources at the German labour assignment office quietly told members of the Judenrat that there was a drunken party the day before at the German administration offices. During the event, Gewecke had promised to make an example of the unlucky pair by hanging them. Bub immediately invited his staff and friends to attend what would be a public execution. At least those invited could decline such an offer but on June 3, the Nazis officially informed the Judenrat of the punishment and advised them that every resident of the ghetto must attend, without exception.

Gewecke also demanded that the body recruit two Jews to build the gallows for a fee of 2,000 Ostmarks – the currency of the occupied territories. It was a further humiliation; for the mischievous Gebietskommissar knew for all the outward signs of solidarity among the community, some would sell their souls for this 'honour'.

A 35-year-old cobbler named Chaim Kerbel, thought by the Judenrat to be an informant for the police, took the job of constructing the gallows in a small garden in the Kaukazas ghetto. His partner was 33 year-old Ben Davidovich, a storekeeper at the army food centre, also described as a professional thief.

In the ghetto later that night, a heated meeting pitted the elders against youthful underground leaders. Members of the Massadeh group argued passionately for armed resistance, using the handguns hidden around the ghetto.

Aaron Katz reasoned: "We have already lost many of our people. Once we are outside of the gates, we can offer no resistance to the German army with just a few handguns. If we do this, it will end up in mass murder. Are you prepared to take responsibility for almost 5,000 people?"

A dozen people tried to talk at once. Finally, in exasperation Katz asked:

"And where is everybody going to go once they are through the gates?"

There was no reasonable answer to that. There was only one option, plead for mercy.

The next day as the hammers swung and the nails secured the temporary gallows, Leibovich met with Bub in an attempt to persuade the officer to back down and release the two prisoners.

The Judenrat head reasoned that it would be bad for morale and production would decline at a time when the war effort needed more support than ever before. The elders had used the morale argument successfully before in getting others out of difficult situations. Reminding Bub that the war was not going well was a risky tack but one Leibovich thought worth taking if it saved two young lives. It would be difficult to back down on this, even if Bub had a mind to, because it would be a sign of weakness and the Nazis were all about strength.

Leibovich could see his powers of persuasion were failing as he later engaged Bub. In a final appeal to reason, the Jewish leader asked Bub why a local crook recently caught with a large amount of flour, which he was planning to sell on the black market, only received a sentence of three months in jail.

Bub, losing patience, prodded Leibovich's chest striking at the middle of the older man's yellow Star of David, saying as he did.

"Do not forget that these two are Jews."

If all reason fails, try bribery, thought Leibovich. He thought it might come to this and had such an offer in his back pocket. There was gold, jewellery to offer and, thanks to his cousin's husband, Meyer Kron, even a pair of men's leather boots.

Meyer knew of the vanity shared by the senior administration staff such as Bub and other Nazi officers for well-made boots. Bub was not likely to benefit personally from the gold and jewellery for it would go into Hitler's treasury. Ah, but those boots would look good on him and Bub would figure he deserved them for his dedication to the Führer. Bub reached a compromise with which he was sure Gewecke could live. Mazovetsky's sentence of death was irreversible but the trinkets and those fine leather boots would save the woman.

Nathan Katz, who was frequently in the presence of Bub during his work at the Komissariat, made one final foolhardy attempt to intercede on the part of his friend Mazovetsky. Bub heard him out then threw his head back in laughter. What did this whippersnapper have to offer him? Katz was trying to appeal to the man's finer feelings but Bub's response left him in no doubt that they did not exist.

"What do you Jews do after a hanging ceremony? Do you sing or do you dance?"

He roared with laughter again before waiting for an answer.

"From us you will see tears and sorrow," Katz responded, wondering whether he had pushed the German too far as the word sorrow left his mouth.

Bub removed a piece of chocolate from his desk and threw it at his German Shepherd dog, who rose suddenly snapping it in his jaws before it was able to fall to the carpet.

"Enjoy it, Rolf. This Katz does not need to eat chocolate. We will hang him too, sooner or later."

The Judenrat knew how events would unfold but not surprisingly did not reveal the nature of the deal with Bub. Many in the ghetto were still convinced that at the last minute there would be a reprieve. That notion gained popularity when ghetto work coordinator Chernovsky spread the story that he figured there would be no lynching. He was supposedly in tune with the inner machinations of the Nazi administration, or at least that is what many of his listeners figured.

Kaukazas ghetto – June 6, 1943.

MEYER AND GITA readied Tamara and Ruta for a family outing that Sunday in much the same way as they had done before the war. The difference was this time there was no enthusiasm among them for a morning walk around the neighbourhood.

It was a family scene repeated around both ghettos for they would all be unwilling witnesses to the public execution of Lena Bayer and Sol Mazovetsky.

By 9 a.m., all were present at the makeshift execution site in an orchard. No spectator was pushing for a better vantage point. The wait began. It seemed like hours. The first clue that the worst was about to unfold came with the arrival of several men from the Gebietskommissariat, who took up prime viewing positions.

Beyond the fence, curious townsfolk perched in trees and on house roofs. They looked like black crows, observer Levi Salit would later write in his secret diary.

After a few minutes, the sound of marching boots on cobbles filled the air. Heavy ankle chains shackled the two prisoners and rope tied their hands behind their backs. The woman bowed her head. It was difficult to see whether she bore the scars of a beating. It was easy to see that Mazovetsky had suffered greatly at the hands of his captors; his face was swollen, black, and blue.

Belkstys, the thug in a police uniform, prodded the doomed pair, ordering them to pick up the pace in the direction of the scaffold. A machine gun swung from his right shoulder, banging his side as he pushed them more vigorously in response to their unsurprising reluctance to obey. Chernovsky whispered reassuringly to Mazovetsky as he passed: "They will not hang you; they will commute the sentence."

The escort of four police officers looked around furtively, trying to spot potential troublemakers and perhaps fearing for their own safety. Maybe an informant had told them about the fiery Judenrat meeting where there was a call to arms.

Bub stepped up. There was silence, not a peep even from the youngsters among the crowd. He was succinct in his address. There was no point in spoiling his whole day with this unpleasantness.

"All who attempt to bring contraband into the ghetto will meet this same fate," he warned, surveying the crowd before him as he spoke, occasionally locking on to the eyes of the unfortunate individuals with 'ringside' seats.

It looked to all as though Chernovsky's optimism was misplaced. The Germans were going to carry out the sentence, after all. Even the Judenrat members were beginning to wonder if all their efforts were in vain and their bribe wasted.

Bub savoured the palpable fear in the crowd for a few moments before ordering Lena Bayer be freed. There was a collective and audible sigh of relief from the crowd. Some may have been tempted to applaud but they restrained themselves. Her leg irons removed, she fled into the crowd. She would not wait to see if Bub would change his mind. She hoped others would hear him repeat the reprieve for Mazovetsky.

That was not to be. Bub pronounced the death sentence on the young father. Kerbel and Davidovich checked to make sure they had knotted the rope correctly. Mazovetsky was very calm for a man facing death. He asked almost politely for his hands to be untied. The instant refusal did not change his expression. Beneath bruises, a smile was breaking out. He even had smiles for his executioners and the Germans lined up below him.

Ghetto police chief Ephraim Gens interceded, asking if Mazovetsky could say goodbye to his wife Chaitza, young daughter and mother.

"Nein," snapped Bub, impatient for a speedy end to this interruption on his day off.

There was a murmur in the crowd but his wife drowned it out with a hysterical wail that chilled all who heard it. She broke away from her family and flung herself to the ground before the Germans, kissing their feet and begging for a last minute pardon. They kicked out at her and Bub ordered the guards to take her away.

Mazovetsky did not react to his wife's final futile attempts to save him. He suddenly stepped forward and put his own head into the noose, pausing only to speak his last words.

"Forgive me for the trouble I have caused you," he begged, addressing the ghetto at large though his voice barely reached beyond the first few rows of onlookers. It mattered not, for those that did hear would repeat his final declarations for those out of earshot.

"My coat is borrowed; please return it to its owner. Comfort my wife and child and take of care of my mother."

Turning to the hangman, he said, "Do not be afraid. Continue with your work."

Mazovetsky spared the appointed executioners further anguish and jumped before they were able to remove the platform beneath his feet – a kitchen table.

His surprise move also caught out the mothers in the crowd who had hoped to cover the innocent eyes of their children before Mazovetsky hanged. Gita's hands fell like a camera shutter over Ruta's eyes, but not before the shocking image of Mazovetsky, dangling from the rope, etched itself forever in Ruta's memory bank, the stuff of a thousand nightmares. Fortunately, little Tamara had looked away by chance at the critical moment. Gita placed herself between the youngster and the ugly scene.

The shouting from the reluctant spectators grew into a roar. It took the Germans and their Lithuanian collaborators by surprise. It unsettled them. The fear was now in their eyes. Maybe the Jews would revolt. Yes, many of them would die in a spray of machine gun fire but some would succeed in overpowering and killing their captors. The uniformed minority were doubtless relieved to see the Jews disperse quickly, heading back to their homes to take in what they had seen and console each other that they weren't the ones swinging from a rope in the spring breeze.

Maybe this execution would cow them or maybe it would spur them on to take action in the future, foolhardy though it might be. After all, what did they have to lose? They were already in hell.

That may have been the way the aggressors thought but then they had the benefit of knowing what was in store for these Jews. The Jews had a different mindset. They figured that as long as they drew breath there was hope. Besides, soon maybe Stalin's armies would deliver them from this hell.

Ghetto doctor David Druyan declared Mazovetsky dead but Bub ordered he swing until noon. A reminder to all of what they could expect if they tried to bring in nourishment for their loved ones.

Gita and Meyer shooed both of their children in the opposite direction from the gallows. They would take their place early in the march back to the Ezero-Traku ghetto. They need not look back.

WHEN NATHAN KATZ WENT to work the next day, the sadistic Bub could not resist toying with him.

"Did you enjoy the ceremony, Katz?"

Katz was grateful the man did not wait for a reply for he may have been tempted to say something unwise in the heat of the moment.

"From now on there will be stricter checks for smuggled food," he warned. "The gallows will remain functioning for those who are caught."

Bub continued on to his office, leaving the young man to ponder his chilling words.

CHAPTER NINE

The doctor and
the Kommando

Ghetto Administration Headquarters – mid-summer 1943

WHEN SS HAUPTSTURMFÜHRER Heinrich Forster first showed up in the Shavl ghetto in the summer 1943, he was a very sick man.

The 45-year-old Bavarian had previously served as a member of the Einsatzkommando 3, a unit of the roaming killing squads responsible for the murder of more than 130,000 Lithuanian Jews since 1941. In fact, the SS chiefs praised his particular squad for being the most productive. The efficient shooting and disposal of hundreds, sometimes thousands, in a single day earned Forster and his comrades-in-arms this dubious recognition. At the time, no Judenrat member was aware of the enormity of the death toll. However, they all knew he was a man to fear simply by his association.

This was no time for the captain to be ill for he would need all of his strength and guile to take on the new assignment that would reach its deadly conclusion in a few short months. Nevertheless, he could cover up his medical problems no longer, so he headed for a 12-day stay in the Frenkel mansion hospital.

Most of the patients there were seriously injured foot soldiers returned from the front. There were times during his stay when Forster would have traded the young soldiers' battle wounds for his severe abdominal pain; at least they knew what ailed them. The finest doctors in the Reich had examined him before his transfer.

For reasons he could not comprehend, none was able to diagnose his excruciating painful condition.

The bed rest did him no good. When he returned to work, Forster could not hide the searing pain from his colleague. He bent double frequently, even when dosed up on painkillers. A couple of his colleagues showed up at his office to suggest he try his luck with a Jewish doctor in the ghetto. The thought of a Jew manhandling him did not appeal to the vehement anti-Semite, even though at home he and his family visited a doctor of the same faith. There had not been much choice, in truth. As each wave of pain rolled across his stomach, the idea of a visit to this Peisachowitz fellow became more appealing.

THE JUDENRAT INFORMED Wulf that he must report to the Nazi administration to consult with a German officer who required medical attention. The appointment was finalized a couple of days later. Wulf was terrified in the intervening period. It was an extremely unusual request and that meant it was serious. The thought of it all going horribly wrong and him paying for it with his life tormented him. However, there was no question of him refusing to treat the man. It was not something for which he could seek a second opinion from Meyer or Gita. For them to know about this would only put their lives at risk.

Shortly after 7:30 a.m. on the appointed day, two police guards knocked on his door and escorted him to the ghetto gate where two SS men were waiting. He walked in the gutter, as Jews were required to do while his escorts strolled along the sidewalks, other pedestrians scattering as the uniformed men approached. Some recognized the Jewish doctor; some may even have owed their lives to him. They wondered why he was getting such close attention from the SS.

The two men quickened the pace and barked at the limping Wulf to keep up. He had injured his leg as a boy, while on the way to school. Wulf had tripped, dropping the bottle of milk he had brought along to wash down his lunch. It shattered on the ground and Wulf cut his knee deeply as he landed on a shard of glass. It healed but he was never able again to flex his knee, not that he ever let it slow him down. Today it ached like never before.

He began to wonder if it was all a ruse to get him away from the ghetto without causing any fuss. Maybe they had found out about his pharmaceutical smuggling activities. He was sure his Gentile colleagues at the Shavl hospital ignored his appropriation of medications for use in the ghetto hospital. He still worked there as a so-called medical assistant though he actually continued to function as a doctor and had full access to drugs. He could not think of anybody that had it in for him.

Wulf was sweating with fear rather than exertion by the time he had completed the 15-minute walk across town to SS headquarters, which was based in a fine house once owned by a family now residing, like him, in the ghetto.

Wulf was a frequent visitor to the offices of the various German departments because of his role as chief of health for the ghetto. Therefore, he was not given a second look by staff when he walked in. If he had been, those more familiar with him might have noticed a look of anxiety had replaced Wulf's normal air of confidence and importance.

A young soldier showed him to the second floor where he was offered a chair. Such niceties were not normally extended to Jews; not that many came in through the front entrance. Most would arrive bloodied and bruised through the back entrance floors below. Guards would then push them into an interrogation room for a beating.

They left Wulf alone with his worst thoughts for an hour. People came and went, passing papers to the corporal at the desk by the door. The door to the office of the bigwig never opened once in that time. The phone rang occasionally and the young gatekeeper occasionally put them through to his boss, having established the call was important enough for him to disturb the great one.

Periodically, the blond soldier behind the desk cast furtive glances in the doctor's direction. He was new and was one of the few who did not know Wulf. He wondered what business this Jew had with his superior. Wulf's same query would be answered soon, though the corporal would never be any the wiser and that was probably just as well.

Wulf was daydreaming about happier times in this house. He had attended a number of parties when the wine flowed and he had feasted on his favourite foods. A single shrill ring from the phone brought him abruptly back to occupied Lithuania. The young officer replaced the receiver in less than ten seconds and told Wulf the captain would see him in another ten minutes.

He still did not know the identity of his prospective patient. He could not make out the nameplate on the office door from where he sat. At least he now had a rank to work with; it was only a middle-rank in the SS but still one to fear. Really, Jews had reason to fear the holders of any SS rank.

Exactly ten minutes later, the desk officer rose and ushered Wulf through the door. Standing before him was Hauptsturmführer Forster, the three silver pips and two silver stripes on the black collar patch of the uniform confirmed his rank. Wulf had become quite knowledgeable about SS plumage; it was good to know one's enemy.

Wulf had glimpsed the nameplate as he had passed through the doorjamb and gulped as he recognized the name. This man's ruthless reputation preceded him; there was much talk among the Judenrat of the man's arrival.

Only months earlier Wulf was instrumental in helping avert the mass killing of all of Shavl's Jews at the hands of one of Forster's superiors, SS-Standartenführer Karl Jäger, a key player in the drive to exterminate Baltic Jewry. There was no doubt in his mind that Jewish blood stained Forster's hands. Maybe soon he would finish the job Jäger wanted to do.

Forster wore the *SS-Ehrenring*, unofficially known as the Totenkopfring or death's head ring. It was originally an SS honour personally bestowed by Heinrich Himmler for valour and leadership skill in battle. After 1939, it lost much of its shine as any officer with three years' service could wear the bauble. Wulf had no doubt that the man had earned it the hard way.

Forster motioned Wulf to sit down.

"Thank you . . . how should I address you?" asked Wulf, good-naturedly.

"That is not important," the man responded rudely but quietly. "The only important thing is that you should have medical knowledge and be able to allay my pains."

His voice was now barely audible to Wulf, who leaned forward and cocked an ear in the officer's direction. If he was struggling to hear, then it was certainly out of the range of hearing of the corporal beyond the closed door.

This man, who once would gladly have placed his hands around Wulf's throat and squeezed the life out of him, now needed his expertise. That notion almost brought a smile to Wulf's face.

Forster described his symptoms and explained that his ailment remained undiagnosed, even after consulting the best in Berlin. It was time for Wulf to perspire a little.

Forster abruptly rose and walked gingerly to the door, wincing with each step. He opened it and Wulf heard him tell the corporal that no one should disturb him until further notice. As if to emphasize that command, he clumsily turned the key creating a clatter that the young soldier at the other side of the door must have heard.

Wulf asked the man to remove his jacket and shirt, quite timidly. Forster obeyed Wulf's orders without question and presented himself for examination. Wulf focused his attention on the man's abdominal area where his patient complained the pain was the most acute. It was a cursory examination at best, though he was quickly able to find the tender spots. How he would have loved to squeeze until the man collapsed. Wulf told him he would need to give him a thorough examination and place him under observation. He suggested that the officer visit the town hospital. That did not sit well with Forster for he had hoped all of this business could occur within the privacy of his office.

He stared out of the window for a few minutes; a slight grimace distorted his face as he looked away from Wulf. Then he turned back to face the doctor and it was his turn to lean forward.

"I will come to the hospital after normal hours," the Nazi stated.

"You have a pass that enables you to leave the ghetto at any time of day?" Forster asked but continued without waiting for answer.

"I will not be in uniform. You will make sure that you are alone."

Wulf interrupted: "But I will need a nurse . . ."

"No, you will be alone," he repeated, allowing his voice to increase in volume.

Then he seemed to realize that if he was to regain his health he really had to deal with this annoying man on his terms. He would not be staying overnight for observation, as the doctor put it. After the further examination, he would be returning to his apartment in the rear of the SS headquarters. He agreed to Wulf's request for a nurse to assist.

"But it must be somebody who is trustworthy."

Wulf had just the nurse to fit that requirement: Berta Luntz, wife of his dear friend Joseph Luntz, the ghetto gynaecologist.

Forster nodded his head in reluctant agreement; he knew of Luntz, though not his spouse. He motioned to the door. He was finished.

Wulf rose, turned on his heel, and made for the door. The whole meeting had taken barely 20 minutes. As he unlocked the door, less dramatically than the German, Forster spat out one more order.

"Herr Doktor, you will tell no one about our consultation now or ever."

The command hung ominously in the air. There was no need to explain further the consequences of disobeying his demand. This was not just a restatement of every patient's right to privacy. Wulf nodded courteously without saying a word and left the office.

Well, he had his answer but he was not sure whether to feel relieved or petrified. The corporal looked at Wulf questioningly as he left. Now there were still more questions buzzing around his head about the possible consequences of him failing to find what ailed this vile man or still worse, causing him harm with the treatment he might prescribe. Maybe Forster just wanted a diagnosis to pass on to a German doctor.

THROUGHOUT THE EXAMINATION some days later, Forster remained quiet. He looked worried. He was a human being, after all. His future actions would cause Wulf to reconsider that charitable assessment. Berta Luntz did the blood tests and prepared him for the X-rays that followed. Then she left the two men alone. As the Nazi had made it clear he was not going to stay for a few days for further observation, Wulf would get one shot at this diagnosis.

"Well, what is it?" asked Forster, with a sneer that showed he was not convinced that Wulf was capable of supplying a satisfactory answer.

Wulf looked up from his notes and told him, in non-technical language, that he was suffering from an ulcer that was leaking acid into his pancreas. The patient exploded into a rage, his whole face turning the ruddiest shade Wulf had ever seen. Wulf did not think it would be smart to reveal this condition could ultimately kill him if untreated.

The irate officer banged his fists on the flimsy desktop, which Wulf thought would break up before his eyes if the Nazi's bombardment continued. The furious German repeated that the brightest medical minds in the Reich were unable to diagnose his problem.

Wulf puzzled over the point of this assertion. Was the officer mad at the Berlin doctors? Was he angry that this lowly Jew had diagnosed what they had failed to spot? Did he just not believe the ghetto physician? Wulf decided not to seek clarification.

Forster stormed out. Wulf collected his papers together and placed them in a folder he would hold away from the prying eyes of others. He then returned to the ghetto, bracing himself for the worst. This was one very unhappy patient. An hour or two later Forster sought out Wulf in the Judenrat office where he had adjourned for the evening to catch up on some paperwork.

"This is it. This is the end," Wulf thought when he again encountered the man he felt sure would be his nemesis. The office emptied rather quickly, leaving the two men alone.

"Write down your diagnosis and your reasons for arriving at the conclusions and what treatment you recommend for it," ordered Forster.

Yes, thought Wulf, he was going to send the report to Berlin and that would get him off the hook. What a relief. Wulf could barely contain himself.

"Of course, I'll do it right away and send it over to you in the morning," said Wulf agreeably, already reaching for the file in his private drawer.

"No, you will deliver it to me, doctor. This must not be placed in anybody else's hands."

With that final command, he left without saying goodbye. Why lie? He would most likely rather have wished this conceited Jew a permanent farewell.

Just two days later at 6 a.m., a Jewish police officer knocked on Wulf's front door. It was an order summoning him to Forster's office at 8 a.m. He waited for an hour before his audience with the demanding patient. Forster handed an official-looking letter to Wulf. It was from a specialist in Berlin, who confirmed the diagnosis was correct.

"Well, of course, it is," thought Wulf, who had a streak of arrogance. That trait made him so capable in his chosen profession. He had easily diagnosed what had confounded the Nazi doctors. Then came the 'but'.

"But they disagree with your treatment recommendation," said Forster. "They say it is too dangerous. They are not prepared to do it."

Wulf guessed the injections he had recommended to relieve the pain was causing his Berlin counterparts considerable consternation. (It pained him to think of them as counterparts.) The rest of the treatment was not contentious or risky but just a matter of sticking to a strict regimen of medication. Still, there was no point in saying anything in response to the report from Berlin. Wulf knew what was coming next.

"So, you will do it?"

Wulf waffled: "I don't have the necessary . . . ."

Forster anticipated the final words of the sentence.

"You will tell me what drugs you need and I will see to it that your requisition is filled promptly."

Wulf thought it remarkable that this man could be so calm in delivering these orders. He was talking about his own wellbeing, damn it, his very survival. Despite Berlin confirming the gravity of the situation, Forster was beginning to talk dismissively about his complaint as though it were some minor ailment. To admit more would make him even more indebted to Wulf for his medical intervention. That would never do for an SS officer, soon to be called upon to execute a most terrible order.

True to his word, the drugs arrived and Wulf prescribed a short two-week course of the medication. Meanwhile, Wulf would deal with the pain that would undoubtedly continue for some time. Forster had found himself in a backwater with a doctor who had a skill shared by only a handful of doctors. Wulf trained in Prague to perform sympathetic ganglion injections. It was a procedure he believed would cure his patient's debilitating bouts of pain. A couple of injections into the spinal area may have sounded simple to the SS officer but it was far from being so. Wulf had to administer them with great precision in exactly the right spot or else . . . . well, that did not bear thinking about. The two injections took place in the Nazi's office a week apart, with no fuss.

"You will get progressively better now," he told his patient, confident the medications would do their healing work and the injections remove the pain. What else was he going to say? If it all went wrong then the gallows left standing following the hanging of Mazovetsky might be back in action soon. Wulf fingered his neck and throat as he thought about the possible consequences of what he had just done. If that was self-doubt, it lasted only seconds.

"Yes, you will be fine. I have every confidence."

Did he detect a moistening of the eyes in the Nazi? No, that is not possible, thought Wulf. It was merely a trick of the bright light catching the eye of the ruthless and cold-hearted man.

"Thank you, doctor."

That was a first, thought Wulf.

"You will tell no one, not even your family . . . ," said Forster, repeating his earlier order.

This time Wulf sought to reassure his patient though it was more for his own peace of mind than that of Forster.

"I wouldn't dream . . ."

Forster cut him off.

"Actually such a dream would be your last nightmare. I can promise you that."

Just in case there was any misunderstanding, he spelled out the consequences

"If you do, you will not live to repeat your story and neither will your family members."

Now that was more like what Wulf expected from the man before him. He delivered his final remarks in a softer tone, which sounded strange coming from a man who had just threatened Wulf's life.

"You will find me better friend than foe, Doctor Peisachowitz," he said, enunciating the syllables of Wulf's surname.

"I will remember what you have done and one day maybe I will be able to be of assistance to you."

His parting words were still more surprising, maybe an afterthought that he should not have verbalized.

"In our family the Jewish doctor always had the last word."

Except in this case the Jew didn't have the final say, because after placing a note in Wulf's hand, the hospital door closed quietly and the Nazi was gone.

Before reading the note, Wulf wondered whether the promise of future help was sincere. He grinned. So, this was not the first time this rabid Jew hater or his family had benefited from the medical skills of a Jewish doctor. Wulf chuckled.

Then he opened up the note. In recognition of the doctor's contribution to the continued health of the SS officer, he would permit Wulf to use the facilities of the municipal hospital for ghetto patients. In light of that concession, Wulf pondered if there was an ounce of good in this man. He would get the chance to find out in the near future.

CHAPTER TEN

Messengers of fate

Shavl railway station – September 26, 1943

T HE SHAVL JEWS DOING track maintenance at the station watched despairingly as each freight train passed through loaded with weaponry and vital supplies heading for the Eastern Front.

Nevertheless, in the early autumn, they began to notice that some of the locomotives were pulling cattle cars loaded with human cargo, of the Jewish kind. Their despair deepened.

Some trains were bound for Estonia while others were travelling in the opposite direction to destinations unknown. They would soon come to know and fear what lay in store at the end of the line. The rumours were already flying about mass deportations to work camps near Tallinn, in Estonia, and to concentration camps in Nazi occupied Poland and beyond.

Late on Sunday, September 26, a long line of cattle cars slowed to a gradual halt in Shavl. It may even have been the early hours of Monday; eyewitnesses without watches do not make the best witnesses. However, there is no mistake about what then happened. Within a short time of its arrival, showers of small pieces of paper began falling from the barred slits at the top of the cars. The paper flurries caught the eyes of nearby workers, assigned to work on the extension to the rail line. When the bemused workers did not immediately break off their work to investigate, it seems the hidden messengers became anxious. Arms and hands suddenly appeared from within, gyrating awkwardly, constricted in their motion by the narrowness of the open gap. It was a remarkable sight but the purpose of the gestures was clear.

The workers moved cautiously across the tracks trying not to alert their supervisors, who seemed oblivious to the snowfall of paper. They moved closer to the wagons driven by their curiosity, waiting for the opportunity to grab one or more of the messages. Once they were sure they were unobserved by the guards, those nearest to the notes stepped quickly forward to retrieve what they could reach, looking over their shoulders as they made their grab.

Some of the messages were concerned with the needs of the moment: they asked for bread and water. The workers quickly handed over their own food and water. Some of the bodiless hands became more frenzied in their jerky arm motions as they realized some of their fellow travellers were getting sustenance and they were not.

They wanted to call out for help but could not for fear that the flow of food and refreshment would cease if the guards became aware of what was happening. The frantic waving was the only way of making their needs known.

The mission of mercy came to an abrupt end when one of the guards noticed workers getting a little close to the train. A shouted order caused the Jews to scurry away. They hid the crumpled messages, within their tattered clothes and discreetly delivered them to the Judenrat office later.

Most of the notes simply explained that their writers were from the Vilna ghetto. One chilling note had only two words crudely scratched upon it: "Kittel Destruction." The subject of the note was Bruno Kittel, head of the Gestapo section responsible for the so-called Jewish problem in Vilna. Kittel is also the name of the white robe worn by Jews on such special occasions as a wedding – the white symbolizing purity. It was an irony often commented upon by those threatened by his existence.

The liquidation of the Vilna ghetto got underway in early August. Around 2,500 ended up in work camps in Estonia and another 5,200 left in early September. The ghetto's 8,000 remaining Jews left in the days just before this train's arrival. The correspondents were the last remaining Vilna Jews heading to an unknown destination.

It could only be a matter of time before the Shavl ghetto faced a similar dissolution. There was no immediate danger because the Nazis still needed their labour. Kittel liquidated Vilna prematurely because he feared an armed resistance was in the offing, something he did not intend to waste good bullets putting down. That said the defiant reaction from the crowd after the Mazovetsky hanging must have given the Nazis in Shavl cause for thought.

THE HASTILY WRITTEN notes were not the only testimony to what happened to the Vilna Jews. That evening, the rail workers also returned to the ghetto with a young woman, who had miraculously escaped the train. They found her wandering around the rail yards, soaked to the skin and shivering after the train had left.

The 20-year-old, whose name was Parazeita, later explained to the Judenrat that all the way from Vilna she sawed away at a bar with a knife she had hidden beneath her clothes. Eventually it gave way just as the train approached Shavl.

Helped up by other car occupants, she pulled her head through the gap and then gripped the roof outside to enable her to haul the rest of her emaciated body out of the carriage. She had a soft landing in the swamp on the edge of town. She roamed through the forest, following the rail line up to the service yards, where luckily she encountered the Jewish workers.

She was now safe – temporarily – the Judenrat would find a way of keeping her in the ghetto, likely under an assumed name of somebody who had recently died or, less likely, had escaped. Parazeita would not be the last welcome stranger to wander into the care of the resourceful and merciful Judenrat of the Shavl ghetto. However, the next visitor of note would not just wander in.

Shavl Ghetto – September 1943

THE CRUEL WINTER weather would soon batter the Shavl ghetto, chilling its residents to the bone and killing the weaker among them in the process.

However, what some heard in late September chilled their souls. The civil administrator Gewecke was no longer in charge of the ghetto and his successor would not head any popularity list. It was Schlöf, the SS man with a reputation for ruthlessness.

The Warsaw Ghetto Uprising, an event now known to all the ghetto residents, convinced Berlin that the SS were better equipped to deal with unruly Jews. Ghettos that served no purpose in the war effort were closed. Reichsführer-SS Heinrich Himmler ordered that all remaining ghettos were to become Konzentrationlager - concentration camps controlled by his men.

The transition in Shavl began in September and by October 1 Schlöf had control of the former ghetto. His ascension heralded a violent period after what had been an extended period of relative calm.

Schlöf removed the Lithuanian police guards and replaced them with men he believed he could trust not to accept bribes from the inmates. The new guard troop consisted of 30 SS men from Romania.

Within a very short time, he moved 1,550 Jews to work camps such as the Wehrmacht's airfield at Zoniai, which became permanent residential camps. The Kaukazas ghetto closed in mid-October and the remaining residents crammed into the Ezero-Traku ghetto. It may have been designated a concentration camp but it was still referred to in conversation as a ghetto, by jailor and prisoner alike. The autumn days were getting darker.

MEYER'S GRAPEVINE FOREWARNED him about the change in management and on the evening of the official takeover, he decided it was time to talk to Gita and her father about an escape plan.

Once the girls were asleep, he beckoned both to a corner of the room. They had to whisper, as both children were only a raised voice away from awakening in the family's shared room.

Moshe Shifman sat with his back to the children while Meyer and Gita squatted barely a yard away in front of him. After each sentence Meyer looked over his father-in-law's shoulder to make sure neither girl was stirring.

"Kaiser took me into his office today ostensibly to talk about improving production but he spent more time talking about his concerns about the SS controlling the fate of his workforce," said Meyer.

"Oh, if that were the only thing we had to worry about, Mara," responded Gita, shaking her head. Her father remained quiet, anxious to hear the rest of the story.

"Well, to be fair he does have to answer personally for any decline in quality or fall off in production. Nice though he is, he can't possibly put himself in our shoes."

Moshe chipped in: "A nice German. That's hard to imagine."

Meyer let the remark go for this was not the time to defend the German director, who stuck his neck out many times to make sure his staff escaped the cruelty of his military contemporaries.

"He confirmed the rumours we've all heard. Back in April the Nazis attempted to liquidate the Warsaw ghetto only to meet stiff, armed opposition," Meyer explained. "They apparently held out for a month but were then crushed by overwhelming firepower."

Kaiser would not go into more detail about what happened to the tens of thousands of Jews shipped out of Warsaw. He certainly knew they were going to large concentration camps in Poland and Germany but possibly did not know what the SS had in store for them on arrival.

"He said nothing that would discourage me from thinking that we will likely face just the same treatment when the Russians break through. The children and you, papa, may be at risk sooner. Gita and I will be fine as long as there is war work. They have no use for people who cannot work for them. We have to get your father and the children out."

Moshe frowned. Gita was about to speak but could see her father was about to so she held back.

"I'm an old man, where am I going to go? Remember what your cousin Mendel told us about the underground wanting to foment an uprising here. So you shoot a few Germans and break out but where do we go then that's safe?"

"No, papa, that's not what Meyer is suggesting," his daughter explained.

"He's not suggesting a revolt. We know how that worked out in Warsaw. No, we have to find places for all of you to hide until the Russians arrive."

"Precisely," confirmed Meyer. "We still know people beyond the gate and we have land we can promise in exchange for a hiding place.

"We have to move quickly because my guess is we don't have much longer and in the meantime half the families in the ghetto will be thinking along the same lines as we are: those that keep their ears to the ground, at least."

Meyer and Gita both looked over at the children during the lull in conversation. Particularly worrying for them were the stories of so-called Kinderaktions, in which the soldiers surround the ghettos and emptied them of children.

Moshe picked up the thread: "If you find somewhere for me and the children what's going to happen to you?"

Meyer had a quick and confident answer. Well, it was quick. As to whether he was confident is a different matter but at least it might reassure his older relative and perhaps Gita. No, Gita would not be taken in for a moment and he knew that but thinking she might eased his burden.

"We can't all go at once because they would come looking for us, me especially because of my position at the tannery. They will not miss either you or the girls.

"I believe we will get warnings when the ghetto is to be liquidated. We know enough people in the know on this side of the fence and more importantly on the other side of the gate.

"I'm sure it will become evident when something is afoot. Kaiser may even warn me. Gita and I will devise our own escape plan and we will stand much more chance of survival if it is just the two of us on the run."

His wife echoed his sentiments: "Yes, papa, we stand much more chance of surviving if we split up. What about Barbora Jakubaitis and her brother, Pranas?"

They were farming neighbours of the Shifmans, who got on well with the Jewish family in the past. Gita knew the woman but not her brother.

"Yes, she offered to help before we came to this place," said Moshe, spitting out the final two words. "We'd have to offer them something in exchange for my safety."

"The farm," said Gita.

"You are not serious; it has been in our family . . ."

Gita knew what was coming but she cut him short.

"Your life is more important than a bit of land. It is settled. I will find a way of visiting them shortly."

Moshe was tempted to tell his daughter that was too dangerous but he knew that was a wasted remark. How his youngest child impressed him with her bravery and ingenuity. Her mother would have been extremely proud.

Meyer stared at the love of his life for a few moments. His thoughts were doubtless similar to those passing through the mind of Papa Shifman. Gita glanced away from the two men in her life, to make sure the girls remained asleep. Before Meyer could restart the conversation, Gita was speaking to the next item on their agenda.

"We must also look for a home for the girls. There are families who will take in Jewish children. Though I can't think of any I would trust given our recent experiences trying to get our valuables back from the safekeeping of our so-called Gentile friends."

Meyer was oblivious to her sarcasm as he was too deep in thought. Then he responded to her suggestion: "It is terribly risky.

If we find somebody and they are then caught they will pay for their humanity with their lives."

There was a momentary silence. Ruta was a quiet girl and mainly obedient but Tamara was nervous and excitable and woke up in the night, often screaming. It would be a tall order for one family to take both children and yet if they separated whoever took Tamara was in for a hard time.

Meyer continued: "Jocius."

"Oh, no Mara, he has already risked enough for us," countered Gita.

"He will take one of them. I'm sure," said Meyer, not giving up on his idea.

Gita softened her position: "Maybe, but Jocius is not exactly the most anonymous member of the Lithuanian community. He is well-known and I'm sure he's under suspicion by the Nazis for any number of what they consider transgressions."

Meyer was not so sure about the latter. "If the Nazis had even the slightest suspicion he would have been arrested before today. Point taken though, he is known and doubtless has enemies who might betray him if they can gain some advantage. As times get tougher it will take less and less for people to turn in their friends and neighbours."

Meyer was starting to talk himself out of asking Jocius for assistance. Gita suggested as a compromise they at least tell him they were looking for somewhere for Ruta and Tamara.

"Yes, with his contacts maybe he can locate somebody to help," said Meyer. "We could be assured that he would vet any possible candidates very carefully."

Moshe chipped in: "But if something happens before we smuggle them out?"

His son-in-law was quick to respond: "We have to have a backup plan to hide them temporarily in the ghetto if they come for the children while we are at work."

Silence reigned again as they racked their brains for somewhere safe to hide the children. Parents throughout the ghetto were having similar thoughts and conversations. All would likely conclude there was no safe place but there were spots where their offspring would have a fighting chance of evading capture.

Meyer had an idea: "I figure that the only place we could use would be our woodshed. Tomorrow evening, when it is quiet and we are alone, I will move the chopped wood away from the wall and leave a space behind that could just accommodate the girls.

"Wulf would surely get us some sleeping pills to calm them, particularly Tamara."

Gita nodded but she was not convinced the woodshed would provide more than a temporary hiding place. Anybody determined to take the children would easily find it but all she said was: "Yes, Wulf may be able to help us."

She had a better hiding place in mind for the girls but she would keep that thought private until she had talked it over with her cousin.

All three were now almost hoarse. An hour of talking in an unnatural, guttural whisper in order that each of them could hear and understand without waking the sleeping children had taken its toll. The impromptu meeting closed with the resolve to find hiding places for papa and the children beyond the fence.

On Wednesday, October 27, 1943, Ona Ragauskas walked by the ghetto gate and past a work party waiting to leave. As she walked by the back of the column, somebody tapped her on the shoulder. Contact between ghetto inmates and the general population was forbidden so she hesitated to respond. However, curiosity got the better of her.

"Ona we need your help," said the man quietly, ducking behind his wife so as not to be seen talking.

It was Joseph and Felya Zilberman, who had fixed some of Ona's broken pans in the early days of the ghetto when the Jews could talk to and trade a little with non-Jews.

"Hello, yes, I remember you well," responded Ona. "What can I do for you – is it food you need?"

She was taken aback by what she heard or thought she heard. The man lowered his voice to a whisper and looked about him before speaking. It was not the volume that caused her to ask him to repeat himself.

"We would like you to take our daughter," he repeated. The second time around there was no hesitation in finding the right words.

"There are rumours that the ghetto will soon be liquidated and we hear stories of children and old people being removed from other ghettos."

A staccato delivery of the reasons why Ona should not worry about taking their daughter into her care followed. After each sentence, the couple peered along the line to make sure the guards were not looking:

"Janina is almost three. She will be no trouble. She is blonde and has blue eyes so she will fit in. She is a good little girl and she will do as you say. Please take her . . . ."

She only heard his first words. It was enough to confirm she had it right the first time. It was just so unexpected. She did not need any further explanation because she had heard the same rumours.

As Joseph continued, Ona's thoughts drowned him out. She had promised herself she would rescue a child if she could. Here was that opportunity to keep her word.

This would be her initiative to take the child because she had not really talked to Antanas about it. Well, not in direct terms, though she had alluded to helping somehow. However, in doing so she ascertained to her own satisfaction that he would not object if she showed up with a child. His mother Zophia was a different story. She would go along with her son though. Besides, she was a guest in the house, she thought, immediately feeling guilty about thinking of her mother-in-law as a mere guest.

The torrent of thoughts stopped as she heard Joseph say: "Please take her." This family had more than its fair share of loss. Rabbi Aaron Baksht, shot within days of the German takeover, was Felya's father.

Ona stared at the two pleading parents for a moment or two longer. Felya mistook the pause as a signal that a refusal was imminent.

"Please take her," Felya said, her voice wavering as she repeated her husband's last words.

Ona was thinking about her own tragic loss. Her three-year-old son Rimantas had died in February of diphtheria. She knew the pain Felya was suffering and she would make her wait no longer for an answer. An inner voice told her 'try to do something that was not done for you'. For Ona it was a command from God.

"You are right; I remember the little girl and her looks will not give her away. I will come back on Friday at this time. Can you smuggle her out beneath your skirts?" she asked Felya. She did not wait for an answer.

"It will be busy and she can just walk off with me."

That was easier said than done. They all knew that but the Zilbermans nodded in agreement. They wanted to hug her tightly as they would hold their daughter when they handed her over to this godly woman. It would not have been a welcome sign of affection for it would have drawn attention to them. Ona felt their warmth and knew what was going through their minds. She walked away before they gave in to their instincts.

As Ona walked away she never looked back, instead she cast her eyes at the guards standing by the gate smoking and warming their hands on tin cups full with a steaming beverage. If the 'wrong' guards were there on duty Friday she would simply come back another time, she thought dismissively. Schlöf may have thought the ghetto gates were inviolate with his trusted guards but he would be wrong. Some of these war weary men were as susceptible to a bribe as were their Lithuanian predecessors.

Ona never did get around to discussing her plan with Antanas. She would just turn up with the child and the moment he caught sight of her blonde hair he would be reassured. Janina would be a wonderful playmate for her daughter Grazina, who was less than a year old. They would grow up together as sisters if the war continued for many more years or something unfortunate should happen to her parents. She pushed such thoughts out of her mind.

Two days later, Ona made her way into town to do her shopping, not that there was much to buy at the end of the long queues. She abandoned her wait at the bakery after half an hour. She could wait no longer. She was full of this strange mix of excitement and trepidation at what she was about to do. She strolled over to the ghetto, spotting the Zilbermans in the work line up before they saw her.

Where was the little girl? Could they not smuggle her out with the work party? Were the wrong guards on duty? Had they changed their minds? A feeling of helplessness swirled inside. She so wanted to help them. She wanted to have a young child in the house again.

As she approached, Joseph saw her. His smile suggested nothing untoward had happened and there was no change of heart on their part. Anticipating the question he quickly explained: "We would like to keep her one more week. Tonight we will celebrate Shabbat together for the last time."

Ona sought to reassure the Zilbermans, taking his words too literally.

"There will be other times . . . you will be together again," she said hurriedly, hoping they might change their minds. She sensed a danger in such a delay but she did not attempt to express that fear in words.

"Yes, yes, I'm sure we will," said Felya, recognizing a fellow mother's concern.

"But we must prepare ourselves for the possibility that we may not do so for a long time until this war is over. It is important that we share this Shabbat as a family.

"And Friday is a good day for an exchange because it is busy in town."

Spirituality was an important part of Ona's life so this desire to break bread together was certainly not lost on her. She said no more on the subject.

After agreeing to meet at the same spot on the following Friday, Felya handed Ona a hessian bag containing some of her daughter's clothes.

"Less to carry next time," she said.

Ona pulled the bag close to her chest, allowing the straps to dangle loosely. Then, with her shopping bag strap slung over her right shoulder, she began her trek home.

∽

ANYONE WITNESSING the afternoon stroll through the ghetto taken by *SS Hauptsturmführer* Forster on Thursday, November 4, might have suggested that parents such as the Zilbermans were being overly pessimistic.

The officer smiled as four-year old Aviva Luntz approached him to stroke his German Shepherd dog. Somewhere beneath that black uniform beat a heart. He always allowed her to stroke the dog's coat and he always greeted her as his favourite though not in a language the pretty child knew. She would sing songs to Forster as she played with the dog and in turn, he would pat her head appreciatively. In a moment of weakness he had revealed she "melted his heart with her songs," within earshot of the Judenrat scribe Yerushalmi.

Forster fed chocolate to all of his favourites among the ghetto children that day. This wickedly cynical man knew then what the next day would bring for these innocent children.

Ruth (Ruta) and Ona reunite in Shavl in the summer of 2000.

Iudite, Gita and Aunt Hanna

Iudite and Gita

Moshe Shifman, Gita's father, pictured by his mother's grave.

Gita and Meyer Kron on their wedding day, May 3, 1934.

Meyer and Ruth on the beach at Palanga, on the Baltic, before the war

Gita, Meyer and Ruth vacationing in Palanga.

Gita and Ruth - location and year unknown.

Ruth ready for an afternoon with mama at Milstein's Cafe in Shavl.

Meyer, Gita and Ruth in Riga, Latvia, July 1938.

Picture courtesy of Siauliai Jewish Museum

Only three of this Jewish Kindergarten class survived the German occupation. We do know the third little girl from the left, two rows from the back with the big bow in her hair, did, for she is Ruth.

Dr. Wulf Peisachowitz, Gita's cousin and ghetto director of health.

Jonas Jocius: perceived nemesis-turned-family-saviour.

Picture courtesy of Siauliai Museum

Picture courtesy of Siauliai Museum

Father Adolfas Kleiba, rescuer of Jews.

Dr. Domas Jasaitis came to the aid of the Krons and many other Jews.

Picture courtesy of Ragauskas Family
Antanas Ragauskas, Ruth's rescuer.

Picture courtesy of Ragauskas Family

Ona Ragauskas, who rescued Ruth along with husband Antanas.

Picture courtesy of Ragauskas Family

A young Ona Ragauskas with her son Rimantas, who died of diphtheria in February 1943, aged three years.

Ruth standing by the memorial to the former Jewish residents at the entrance to the Shavl ghetto.

Ruth points to the red brick jail where guards spotted her and sister, Tamara, emerging from their hiding place, during the Kinderaktion.

Ruth in the farmyard at the rear of what was her schoolhouse sanctuary.

Ruth outside a typical ghetto home. In 2000, people were still living there.

Ruth in the farmyard at the rear of what was her schoolhouse sanctuary.

Manya and the late Bill (Wulf) Levin at their home in
New York. Bill, who died recently, was a member of
the Jewish Police in the Shavl ghetto

Simcha Brudno, now deceased, was a Kron family
friend.

Saul (Zava), Ben, Amos, Regina (Riva) Gotz in 1957, three months after Ben, the last child born in the Shavl ghetto, was reunited with his parents in the U.S.

Frenkel's mansion also known as the 'Palace'. It became a hospital for injured German soldiers from the Eastern Front.

The walled section between the fences was once a gate and the spot where Meyer and Gita Kron escaped the ghetto.

Ruth in front of the house where Jonas Jocius lived.

Violka - the rural farm owned by the Shifmans, Gita's parents. Her mother Lina was shot here during the early hours of the German invasion.

Behind this window, Meyer and Gita Kron hid and lived in constant fear of detection after fleeing the ghetto.

The Krons slept here, while waiting for liberation by
the Soviets

CHAPTER ELEVEN

Taking of the innocents

Shavl Ghetto – Early morning, Friday, November 5, 1943.

THE UNWILLING WORKERS GATHERED in the early morning half-light by the ghetto gates as usual, forming into rows of five. Soon they would march across the wet cobbles to the factories and workshops where they would endure another long day of forced travail in support of the Nazi war machine.

Some stared at the sky, straining their eyes to look for a hint of what kind of weather was in store for this day. In that grey light that signals a winter dawn, those with younger eyes would likely make out the shapes of darker clouds that heralded a chilly change from rain to snow. Before Shabbat ushered in the returning night at the end of their shifts that November day, keeping their families warm would be their least concern.

There was not much conversation between those in the line but then there never was. What was there to talk about? Why attract the attention of their sadistic keepers unnecessarily? There were, however, some whispered questions about the delay in opening the gate. There were no authoritative answers. The previous day they had left the ghetto in total darkness but today the first signs of dawn were lighting their miserable surroundings.

The unusual wait was not the only change from the norm. With the spreading light, the ghetto inmates noticed there was a lot of unusual activity around the gate area. There were more SS men standing around and it was possible to make out the shapes of uniformed figures beyond the fence. The lighter it got the clearer their presence became to the naked eye and that provoked more conversation. Some read it as a sign of what was rumoured for months and a wave of panic flooded the ghetto.

159

There were more stories that originated from other ghettos about actions in which the Nazis and their collaborators removed the children, the sick, and the elderly and transported them to mystery destinations. Was it now the turn of Shavl's Jews? Maybe they would empty the whole ghetto as was threatened in the past when the Einsatzkommando leaders lobbied hard to liquidate the entire population. On that occasion, Gewecke, for selfish reasons, had proved to be the Jews' saviour. Now the SS was firmly in charge and it would be a different story.

Many of the workers who had not yet joined the line but noticed the unusual activity hastily pushed their offspring into hiding places, ordering them not to come out until their return. The Lurie family, who worked with the Krons and were neighbours, hid six-year-old son Arie in a cellar among rotting potatoes where he would remain safely hidden all day along with six other children.

Meyer and Gita were among those already at the gate and thus unable to return home without attracting the ire of the guards. They glanced around, growing ever more fearful as the senior SS men gathered at the gate and still more uniformed soldiers appeared on the other side of the fence.

The couple said little but the worried glances they exchanged spoke loudly of their shared fear. Each comforted themselves with the knowledge that they had left their two children in the care of their Papa Shifman, who knew exactly what to do if there was danger. They were so sure of the inevitability of the threat that they had even practiced for such an event. Nevertheless, they also realized the senior family member would be a target for arrest. Their initial confidence began to give way to darker thoughts as they tortured themselves with the question: what if papa does not notice anything unusual until it is too late.

Gita had left the ghetto a number of times in recent weeks looking for places to hide Ruta, without success. She had left with work parties, only to duck down an alley, remove her star and venture back onto the open street, where she would walk purposefully towards the address of a possible saviour. Many others had also walked that well-trodden path in search of a safe haven. Some were successful but just like Gita most were not.

When the gate opened a half hour later than normal, some desperate parents smuggled out their youngsters beneath their coats or skirts. They would worry about where to take their children once they were out of this godforsaken place. Maybe it would be safe to bring them back to hide them within the ghetto after the trouble had passed.

Shortly after 7 a.m., a guard at the gate announced that his orders were to let nobody else through. The gate closed. Word soon spread among those left behind, those being the older members of the community, the sick, workers from the hospital and administration office and, of course, the children.

Judenrat member Abraham Katz ran to the gate gesticulating wildly and ordering the Jewish police to permit all to pass. Not wishing to wait for a negative response, a dozen or so of the able bodied moved toward the gate. With one gesture from the SS officer, the accompanying guard troop raised their weapons clearly indicating that nobody would pass and live to tell of their disobedience.

Half an hour later, just before the barely visible sun rose for the last time before Shabbat, Forster entered the ghetto flanked by other SS men. At last, the ghetto would learn what his important assignment was.

Once he was satisfied that the gate was secure, Forster strutted a few short paces to the Judenrat office where Katz joined him, ready to take his protest to the German. The respected Judenrat member had not relished confronting the SS-man, based on his previous dealings with the short-tempered senior officer.

Katz held his tongue. The perceptive elder detected a smirk dancing around the lips of the cold face before him. Forster purposefully stepped towards the table and laid a copy of his orders before the gathered members of the council.

He tipped his head as though to read his printed order. He need not have bothered for he knew every word contained in the document off by heart. Officiously he told the Judenrat: "I hereby inform you that I have received the order to take out of the ghetto all the children up to the age of 13 and all the old people and those who were unfit for work."

There was a stunned silence. Each member weighed the intruder's words and awaited his next revelation. They knew there would be more; there always was when this wretched man so theatrically paused for effect, as he had done before when delivering an ultimatum or demand. Forster let his dramatic opening statement linger in the air for a few moments before continuing. He looked into each of their eyes, watching for any signs of dissent among his audience. Once he was certain that the initial message had sunk in, he delivered his lines without further reference to his script.

"They will be taken to a children's home in Kaunas, and the old people will look after them. All the Jewish children from the camps will be gathered in that place."

He glanced around the room, savouring the pain his words inflicted upon his listeners. Their expressions clearly showed that his scattergun delivery had scored direct hits.

The anxiety so evident in their faces told Forster they were not buying the fairy tale ending to his monologue. Perhaps he was enjoying this too much.

He reassured them that nothing ill would become of their scattered flock. The last thing he needed was an open revolt. Under any other circumstances, he would not care about spilling the blood of Jews but the Reich had need of their skills to support the war on the Eastern Front.

"Two members of the Judenrat, Ber Kartun and Abraham Katz, can travel with them. After settling in the children, the members of the Judenrat will return and give a farewell greeting from the children."

He rattled off the last words impatiently as though what he was saying was nothing to worry or concern them. Once it was obvious Forster had no more to say, the sullen faced gathering of Jewish elders collectively pleaded: "How is it possible to separate small children from their parents?"

Forster's limited patience now had worn thin and he would brook no further opposition.

"Enough. Your police have the duty to carry out the order and if they do not my troops will enter the ghetto to execute the order."

Before his grand entrance, the Judenrat members had seen the armed guards with their dogs, spaced 35 feet apart, on the other side of the fence. Overheard snippets of conversation suggested most were Ukrainians but other witnesses would later identify some as White Russians from what is modern day Belarus.

Moreover, they could be sure that the lurking presence of the complete SS guard from Kaunas, Forster's last posting, would make short work of anybody not following their orders to the letter. That group had been standing out of sight in the shadows of the neighbouring streets since 4 a.m.

In addition, 300 armed men stood by in Riga St. in order to cut off the road to the Russian cemetery and to the rest of the town, in case of escape attempts by the Jews or some unexpected opposition from the locals.

The Nazis figured the latter was far from likely, as extremely few to date had raised a voice publicly on behalf of their Jewish neighbours. Many figured the Jews were finally getting what they deserved and said so, publicly and privately.

Judenrat representatives Leibovich, Katz and Kartun sheepishly followed Forster's heavy footsteps and stood in the open space by the gate.

The ever-dutiful Kartun announced, "If it is necessary, I will go," and stepped up, a little shakily, into the waiting truck. His colleague Katz followed him but when Leibovich joined them, an angry Forster ordered him off the truck. The Nazis still needed the Judenrat chair for a little while longer. Leibovich reluctantly left his friends and rejoined the crowd by the fence. Katz shivered a little as he awaited their departure; he wore only a light summer jacket and sandals. Similarly, Kartun, an old and sickly man, was also ill attired for a trip of any length. Children's doctor Uriah Razovski would join them later, after a search of his clinic unearthed a dozen hidden children.

Ephraim Gens, a former Lithuanian army officer turned Jewish police chief, dispatched his men. He ordered them to knock on doors and inform those who answered that the old, infirm and young should report to the gate immediately.

In Gens, the Nazis had the perfect shill. Most recently, he had worked as a chief accountant at a lace manufacturing plant but his proud days in the army left a strong impression on him. The 33-year-old Gens believed firmly that the military code of honour under which he served held sway over the SS. He rationalized that alone would prevent any harm coming to those taken that day. His brother Jacob held the same but more powerful position of police chief in the Vilna ghetto before its total liquidation. He too figured his policy of compliance would save more Jewish lives than it would lose. It did so for as long as the Jews had something to offer in return for their continued existence – cheap labour.

Most of the Shavl ghetto's Jewish police were less optimistic than their leader. Nevertheless, they agreed it was better that they deliver the bad news to the doorstep, rather than the soldiers on the other side of the fence.

Before the ghetto police had a chance to show up at the Kron household, Grandpa Shifman had put the Kron plan into action. As his daughter and son-in-law hoped, he had eyed the unusual early morning activity with great suspicion. As dawn broke, the previously restrained soldiers had noisily begun to laugh, joke, and smoke, no doubt bored with the hours of inactivity. Many chased away the morning chill with shots of vodka of the rotgut variety, which nevertheless had the desired effect of numbing them from the cold and preparing for the evil work at hand.

Moshe watched with bemusement as a group sang spiritedly to the accompaniment of a balalaika. There was a nervous excitement about them and that in turn made the senior Shifman anxious. He led his young charges by the hand, leading them swiftly out of the rear of their home, though not without a short struggle.

Ruta intuitively knew this was the eventuality for which papa had prepared her. She was suddenly seven going on 27. Ruta knew she must be quiet, unquestioningly obedient to grandpa and she encouraged her little sister to act in the same way. However, Tamara sensed the fear in her elders and hence resisted their insistence that she leave the safety of her home. Moshe dragged the reluctant Tamara, who protested loudly at her beloved grandpa's uncharacteristically rough handling. After the initial fuss, the thought of papa chastising her later for not obeying grandpa convinced Tamara of the wisdom of taking her sister's hand.

Moshe then rushed them not to the woodshed but out on to the street where he shooed them off as planned. He sought out his own refuge and Ruta took over the daunting responsibility of spiriting herself and her younger charge to safety.

On the way, Ruta watched her playmates scurrying in all directions like mice trying to escape the ghetto cats. She could hear the loud music playing.

Ruta was a step ahead, yanking Tamara, encouraging the little one to run as fast as her spindly legs would carry her. Using the same words Gita had often used to get her to speed up when dashing home out of the rain.

"Quick, quick, we'll be there soon," mimicked Ruta, using the same singsong delivery that so often cajoled her to pick up the pace.

Tamara kept falling, forcing Ruta to abandon the gentle persuasion approach. She found herself having to draw upon all of her physical strength to drag Tamara along. After a few strides, Tamara would find her feet and run a little more under her own steam before falling again on the sharp rocks that jutted from the potholed road. All the while, she screamed hysterically either through fear or pain or more likely both. This was no game of hide-and-seek. Ruta could not lose her or leave her. In a few seconds, Ruta had grown up and it is what her parents had expected of her.

After what seemed like an hour but was in fact only a few minutes, Ruta was relieved to see their hiding place. It was the very small, single storey home occupied by their mama's cousin Wulf, quite close to the ghetto gate. Gita had reasoned that as Wulf was a bachelor it was unlikely his place would be the subject of a serious search. It was wishful thinking.

Ruta pushed Tamara into a freestanding wardrobe then followed her inside. She was supposed to give a sleeping pill to Tamara and take one herself when her younger sister had settled down. She had forgotten them. Before pulling the door closed, she looked sternly at her sister and put a finger to her lips to warn her to be very quiet. In the darkness, she verbally reinforced that message, speaking in the softer tones of her mother. We have to be quiet until mama and papa come back," she said, finishing the sentence with a prolonged "hush."

Within the hour, the ghetto police had knocked on every door and delivered the bad tidings. Some who answered their knock obeyed their commands while many others slammed the doors shut, improbably hoping that would be an end of the matter. The mere trickle of compliant parents angered Forster, who immediately ordered the police to speed up the process.

In a desperate attempt to persuade others that there was nothing to fear, police chief Gens made a great public show of handing over his 10-month old baby daughter in a shocking demonstration of misplaced faith in the honour of the SS. It was something he would regret to his dying day. Gens had plenty of time to reflect on his folly after the war, when the Soviets imposed a 25-year sentence for his collaboration with the Nazis. His foolhardy sacrifice that day did prompt a few more to report to the gate as ordered but dozens more refused willingly to hand over their loved ones. It was about to get very ugly.

FINALLY, FORSTER'S QUIET fuming gave way to the utterance of the order all had dreaded. The soldiers burst through the gates and set about their search for those who would not surrender themselves. Armed with automatic guns and hand grenades, they spread out along the narrow streets of the ghetto. Systematically they worked their way through the area, surrounding buildings and then flushing out occupants hidden inside. If a shouted command did not entice their quarry to surrender then they battered their way through the flimsy doors that guaranteed no sanctuary to those on the other side.

They raced through every house, breaking furniture, ripping and scattering clothing as they ransacked every room in search of hidden children, leaving each already pitiful abode in a shape that suggested a cruel and merciless whirlwind had passed through. They strip-searched many of their victims, looking for watches, rings, or jewellery that would compensate them for their exertions on behalf of the Reich. They were sorely disappointed because the Jews' captors had already helped themselves to everything that sparkled in the many shakedowns they had conducted since the creation of the ghetto.

Some of the more drunken marauders and those who shared the Nazis, hatred of Jews rejoiced loudly in the discovery of the children's hiding places.

"Danya, Yure, come and see how many are here," shouted one as he found 12 children in an attic. With the help of his comrades, he herded them like wild animals to the open area. Soldiers subdued feistier youngsters by delivering blows to their heads with their rifle butts. They then grabbed their prey by the hair or any limb that came to hand to toss them on to the truck's flat bed.

The parents that had remained in the ghetto chased after their children, pleading with these monsters to let their children go. The assailants either silently ignored their pleas and went about their work or greeted them with contemptuous laughter. The more persistent parents found themselves beaten back with bare fists and the same rifle butts that had pummelled their resistant children.

While the soldiers were away and doing their worst, the Jewish police released some of the corralled children, shooing them away to find new hiding places. The leaders of the raiders beat without mercy those caught showing mercy. Though brave these were desperate and futile acts merely delaying the inevitable.

While ghetto police generally did all they could there were a few exceptions and one in particular. A man seen as an outsider, a German speaking Jew from Memelland, went about his assignment rather too zealously in the opinion of his fellow ghetto police members.

Much to their disgust, he boasted later about the 44 children he had personally caught. He would get his 'reward' later. His work for the Nazis did not save him from imprisonment in the Dachau Concentration Camp. There he was beaten and stabbed by some of his former colleagues with long memories and a score to settle. He survived the attack and now calls the United States home.

DENTIST POLINA TOKER, whose fate would soon entwine with that of the Kron family, was one of the mothers savagely victimized. She and some neighbours hid their children in their building's attic before crawling into the barn at the end of the yard with the remainder of their youngsters. In less than an hour, they were looking down the barrels of rifles waved menacingly within inches of their faces.

Without hesitating, Polina pulled out the money that was pinned to her stockings begging they leave her five-year-old daughter Adute alone. The money was accepted but no bargain honoured.

On the way to the truck, one soldier was distracted. Polina took the opportunity to grab Adute by the hand and briskly walked to the dispensary on Ezero Street – her workplace. Once there she gently pushed her child under a bed, used when the spot doubled as an impromptu medical centre. She was not alone in her choice. Other mothers also figured it was a good hiding place, unlikely to be the subject of a rigorous search.

They were wrong and the soldiers showed up shortly after. They manhandled Polina and the other adults out of the building but Adute remained under a bed. There was hope.

Polina cursed for not giving Adute some sleeping potion, not that she had easy access to such a drug. The distraught mother was among many held in check by armed guards and kept away from the Aktion.

CHAPTER TWELVE

And the band played on

Outside the Ghetto – The morning of Friday,
November 5, 1943.

THE CHEERY SOUNDS OF loud band music blasted from speakers atop trucks outside of the ghetto fence muffling the disturbing screams and the general mayhem within.

Perhaps the Nazis figured it would discourage the Jews' former neighbours from approaching the ghetto to see what was happening. If that was the intent, it was unsuccessful. The violent acts Ona Ragauskas witnessed shortly after arriving at the corner of Vilna Street and Ezero at 9 a.m. transfixed her. Shocked bystanders explained to the schoolteacher's wife that trucks had already ferried dozens of children and old folk out for an hour or more.

Ona had a clear view of what was happening from just 30 yards away. She may not have heard more than muffled screams, distorted by the cold breeze that blew, but she could see the hollow looks on the faces of the mothers and their animated pleas. She felt their pain and she knew very well the emptiness that would follow the cruel separation. She was still coming to terms with the loss of her toddler son to diphtheria nine months earlier.

For her own safety, perhaps she should have returned home or run away as others were doing. However, she had promised the Zilbermans she would take little Janina home and look after her as her own. She must stay, she thought, because there was still a chance they had managed to smuggle out their daughter. Perhaps they would find some other way of contacting her rather than risk exposing themselves in the street.

She paced the street for a while then left for an hour to seek the comfort of friends. They could not shed much light on the meaning of the frenzied activity at the ghetto, though one told her she had heard the railway station was the destination.

Ona returned once more before lunch. By then there were few non-ghetto residents watching, perhaps in fear of becoming embroiled. They learned through bitter experience to give the Nazis no excuse to punish the populace. Any sign of sympathy for the Jews in their midst might be perceived as treachery by their German occupiers. Ona was terrified and gave in to her fears. She walked around the town. The Aktion was the topic of chatter everywhere.

AT FRENKEL'S FACTORY, the Jews who worked by the windows alerted the rest of the factory to what was going on in the ghetto. Eighteen-year-old Leiba Lipshitz had a bird's eye view from his work-place by the leather sole stamping machinery on the fourth floor. At just 100 yards away, the motor man's sharp eyes could make out the contortions of the faces of the children dragged screaming from their homes and hiding places. He winced as he watched some children plunge from second-storey windows, forced out by unseen hands. Leiba's anger grew with each inhumane act he witnessed from afar. They were sights that would haunt him to his dying days 60 years later.

Yadja Perlov desperately tried to hold onto her son, repeatedly screaming, "You have enough prey… show us mercy."

None was shown: a grinning, loud soldier grabbed the young mother by the shoulders and pushed her in the direction of the ghetto gate, shouting "Walk, you Jewish swine."

A short time later he ordered her to stand against the fence and a squad of soldiers raised, their rifles as though ready to shoot her. Gleefully he shouted: "Say your last prayer to your God who has forsaken you! We are going to relieve you from all sufferings and your son will die in your arms."

Yadja wiped the crooked smile from his face when she calmly replied, "I thank you very much; you are very kind."

This act of bravado confused and angered her tormentor, who rained blows upon her head. The pain was unbearable yet she held on to her stunned son. She caressed the boy's head and gently pulled it next to her cheek, fearing this would be her last sight of her beloved child. He raised his face and gazed into her eyes, whispering, "Don't cry, mama." She squeezed him a little more tightly awaiting the inevitable.

"Wake up *Zydowka* (Jew). March on."

As Yadja approached the truck, Leibovich asked her in a soft voice to give up her child. He may have argued he was just a messenger but the ghetto newcomer did not see it that way. He was a collaborator in her eyes and she unleashed a vitriolic verbal attack, closely followed by a mouthful of spit. As the shocked man wiped the spittle from his face, she sank to the ground under the weight of the beating laid on her and lost consciousness. That would not have been the wish of the honourable Leibovich. When Yadja came round, her husband Berl was cradling her in his arms, which shook in time with his loud sobs. Their child was gone.

Throughout the day Georg Pariser, another German Jew from Memelland, who was married to a Christian woman, repeated and embellished the reassurance issued first by Forster and later by the gullible Gens.

"Children will be taken care of by their grandparents and fed fresh milk and good food," Pariser said with a smile on his face. By then, no listener was buying what he was trying to sell.

Some might have wondered why he was taking on this responsibility. He was not a member of the Judenrat and surely, he knew he was not a popular person in the ghetto. In fact, some suspected he might be an informant. The reasoning behind his attempts to impress the SS would become apparent soon.

Over at Frenkel's, very few leather boots were made that day for the Wehrmacht, fighting on the Russian front. The Jewish workers were too absorbed in their own thoughts. There were no attempts to break out of the factory because by this stage of the war, the futility of such an act was readily apparent and many had already had every ounce of resistance beaten out of them.

As the day wore on, remarkably, Ruta and Tamara remained undiscovered. For long hours, they hid in absolute silence, almost too frightened to breathe. Though the music blared outside, they could still hear the screams of their playmates and the barking of the vicious dogs that strained at their leashes.

It was so uncomfortable standing in the closet and so cold. The tiny four-year-old began to fret. Ruta squeezed her sister, desperately trying to warm her. She could feel every bone in Tamara's scrawny body as she embraced her. Tamara was not to be comforted.

This was the closest embrace they had ever shared. To Ruta, her sibling had been a source of annoyance since her birth. She had stolen the affection and attention of her mother. In her young mind, her birth had made mama very sick and almost taken her from Ruta. Tamara impeded her elder sister's fun in the ghetto. Ruta put that behind her. Now she knew it was time to grow up and protect her little sister at all costs. Despite the maturity she was demonstrating, Ruta was petrified, as one would expect of a normal child in her eighth year.

Perhaps a change of hiding place might calm her. Ruta tentatively pushed open the doors, shaking as the light of the room flooded into the closet. Timidly she stepped out and crouched by the low cot that served as Wulf's bed, peering into the safety of the beckoning darkness beneath. Once her eyes adjusted to yet another level of dullness they fixed on the floorboards Wulf had loosened to provide an alternative hiding spot. Ruta pulled at the nearest one and it came away easily in her hands, then a second plank soon exposed a space big enough to house the two girls.

Tamara crawled in first, closely followed by her big sister, who tugged at the threadbare cover to eliminate all light from beneath the cot. The shaft of light that did penetrate the confined space was just sufficient to enable Ruta to pull the floorboards slowly back into their original resting place, plunging the two girls into a blackness that would scare a child under normal circumstances. For the sisters this was an impenetrable cocoon that would keep them safe from whatever evil was going on outside. It even muffled the cacophony outside enough for little Tamara to fall asleep in her sister's arms. There would be only fleeting moments of sleep for Ruta though. Mostly she stared into nothingness, listening to her heartbeat, which raced every time Tamara turned in her sleep or made a sound that might attract unwanted attention.

By mid-afternoon only two places remained untouched. The searchers found a bunch of children in the dispensary and now the medical centre and the shoe repair shop were in their sights. Schlöf wanted the workers there to continue their work undisturbed, fearing this break in productivity would reflect badly on him. However, this was Forster's operation and he was clear in his orders, even if that meant disrupting the war effort.

The subsequent searches netted ten children hidden in the ghetto hospital attic. Still more children were found cowering in the roof space of the repair shop. Mothers broke through to the waiting trucks, begging to travel with their children. Four of the more vociferous got their wish.

Observers said later that Forster visibly enjoyed every minute of the Kinderaktion. He showed no favour to anybody, even the children he had made a show of playing with the day before. Among the children taken was the daughter of Dr. Luntz – Aviva. Berta Luntz threw herself on the floor and offered every family jewel she had hidden as the price for her daughter's release.

With a wicked smile, Forster waved Berta away assuring her there was nothing to fear. He reminded her that Aviva was a favourite of his. The wretched Forster, himself a father, threw Aviva on the back of the truck expressing his finer feelings as he did so – "Verdammt hübsches Kind" – damned beautiful child.

An unexpected plea from his comrade Schlöf to reconsider failed to sway him, prompted by an appeal from her father. In the near future, their roles would reverse and Schlöf would be looking for help from Dr. Luntz.

Forster remained equally unmoved by pleas for mercy for another child, a boy whom he once described fondly as a "two-year old blonde angel."

Simcha Brudno stood a few steps away from Forster, quietly seething. It crossed the mind of the 19-year-old that his childhood playmate now wore the same uniform as the SS man before him. Surely, he thought, Paul would not be as ruthless as this beast. For years, Simcha and Paul had played war games together, roughhousing their way through the summer. Simcha spent half his life at his friend's house across the street from his old home. The young Jew dined with the family on many occasions and even celebrated Christmas with them.

However, Paul's parents had never let him join Simcha's family for the Jewish holidays. They believed the so-called Blood Libels that periodically surfaced, which accused Jews of slaying Christian innocents to extract blood for use in the preparation of Passover Matzos.

Paul's father was of German origin from Memelland. Simcha shook his head as he recalled how everything had changed when Hitler came to power. The dictator's picture appeared above the mantelpiece. When Memelland returned to German governance, the family was one of the first to answer Hitler's call to return to

German territory. Their neighbours took advantage and offered little for the departing family's belongings, a story told repeatedly by other departing German families.

Shortly after the ghetto formed, Paul had returned to Shavl resplendent in his Waffen-SS uniform. Simcha was grateful they had not run into each other for it would have been difficult for them both. It would be decades before he discovered that Paul died in an ambush on the Eastern front shortly after that lightning visit. The compassionate Simcha would shed a tear when he learned of his playmate's demise.

Today, Simcha reserved his tears for the children. The bestial behaviour exhibited all around stunned him. He could take no more. With the bravado that comes easily to a confident teenager, the Krons' neighbour stepped closer to Forster. He did not speak but stared into the Bavarian's eyes, giving the kind of withering look of disgust that would likely elicit a violent response.

However, this arrogant young Jew would not distract Forster. The impetuous young buck would say later that it was like staring into the eyes of a crazed animal, like a wolf about to pounce on its prey. Despite the temptation to draw out his weapon and pistol whip Simcha, Forster was mindful that he was much more useful to the Reich without broken bones.

His mother Berta Brudno, a bookkeeper at Frenkel's, would have collapsed if she had known her son was risking his skin in this way. At the time Simcha was offering Forster a piece of his mind, she was consoling her friend Meyer Kron, who feared for the safety of his two daughters.

The families went back a long way, for she and her recently deceased husband had worked with Meyer's father when he was the chief accountant at the leather factory many years earlier. Meyer trusted the older woman. In happier days, he had regularly poured out his heart to Berta in her office, while chomping on his favourite boiled eggs as he did. Eggs were a rare commodity these days so Meyer settled for a chew on a pencil tip to ease his apprehension. Berta assured him all would be well as he exited, deciding getting back to work would help pass the day.

OVER AT THE DISPENSARY, the call of nature beckoned Adute Toker. As it now seemed quiet outside, the youngster crawled out from under the bed. She walked the two streets to her home unhindered. She took off her coat, grabbed the chamber pot and set about answering the call that had caused her so much discomfort.

Unluckily for her, a pair of vigilant soldiers made one final check of her home. While they dragged her away, half-naked, she pleaded, "Let me go. My mother paid you!" She never cried but continued to insist indignantly that they honour the bargain some of their comrades had made with her mother earlier in the day.

The Kinderaktion was almost complete and it seemed the younger Krons would live to play another day, perhaps even together. That would not likely be the happy outcome for the other youngsters, driven from the ghetto earlier in the day.

CHAPTER THIRTEEN

A ride in a big truck

The Shavl Ghetto – Late afternoon, Friday,
November 5, 1943.

ALL WAS QUIET ON the street outside the little house where Dr. Peisachowitz lived and the younger Krons hid.

Tamara awakened, disoriented and feeling somewhat claustrophobic underneath the planks beneath Uncle Wulf's low bed. Ruta's reassuring whispers calmed the little girl but soon Tamara began to fret and her tiny ribcage shook as the tears flowed.

Ruta tried to comfort her, repeating soothing words her mother used to calm her when she was younger and fretful. However, her mother's magic eluded her and Tamara continued to cry.

In the short breaks between sobs, Ruta strained to listen for any sign of activity beyond the thin walls of the shabby shack. As far as she could tell, just as young Adute Toker had mistakenly thought earlier, all was quiet outside.

Fleetingly, she recalled the words of grandpa about staying hidden until either he or another member of the family came to rescue the two of them. However, Ruta had to make a decision, one that would be an awesome burden for a person three times her age. She may have weighed the risks but it is more likely she feared Tamara's restlessness would attract attention and thus certain apprehension.

She decided they would get out from under the bed and look for somewhere else to hide if it were not safe to return home. Slowly she lifted the loose boards and pushed them aside. It was late afternoon and there was no longer much light in the tiny room. She listened for a few more minutes for any sign of trouble outside.

Ruta got out first and looked down at her little sister. Again, her parents' cautions ran through her mind. Tamara calmed down as she rose unsteadily to her feet and looked into the face of her sibling protector for further instructions. Ruta told her to remain quiet and they would run back home where grandpa would be waiting for them and maybe even mama and papa. The happy sounding, rising intonation of her final hopeful words made Tamara feel better just as intended.

With her sister's tiny fingers squeezed between her own, Ruta led her out onto the street. The fading light signalled that Shabbat neared but there would be no celebration that night. The encroaching darkness offered the two girls no protection: two guards on the roof of the adjacent red brick jail spotted the dishevelled youngsters. Ruta looked up to see the two distant figures a hundred yards away pointing at her and her sister. Her heart pounded. She stood transfixed like a deer caught in a car's headlights.

The Kinderaktion was by no means over. Within a minute, foul smelling, red-faced soldiers grabbed both sisters and pushed them into the street where two more soldiers, each with snarling dogs, frog marched them towards the green truck waiting by the gate.

THE 20 YEARS of maturity Ruta had acquired in an instant earlier in the day fell away and she became a frightened, screaming seven-year-old girl again. The two girls struggled to free themselves from their respective captors, without any success. The bigger and stronger Ruta kicked at the man, who had her in a vice like grip. She was nothing more than an irritant for the determined dog handler, whose canine companion growled and gnashed its teeth with each kick.

As they neared the truck full of bawling children, Ruta composed herself and drew once again on some of her recently acquired maturity. She decided to try another more reasoned approach. "Please let us go. We will be good girls." She could see that too was not having any impression so in desperation, she tried to grab the hand of the man and rain kisses upon it. It elicited a short and sharp response in German: "Shut up, get up and keep going."

Tamara was screaming hysterically. Ruta was crying also but was not about to give up and continued pleading with the big, bad men, undeterred by their cackling. Any hope of her pleas finding a warm spot in the chests of the soldiers disappeared as they reached the truck at the ghetto gate.

Just in front, a little boy of maybe five or six was making similar pleas for mercy as he was dragged along the muddy street. An exasperated soldier swung a large piece of wood catching the boy's leg on the downward swing. The youngster dropped like a stone to the ground. There was a split second's silence as the excruciating pain took its time to overtake the shock enveloping his young mind. Two soldiers lifted the boy up roughly and tossed him onto the back of the truck, his broken leg grotesquely swinging at an unnatural angle as he flew through the air.

The scene stunned Ruta, silencing her protests for a few moments. Tamara continued to cry, too absorbed in her own grief to take in what had happened to her peer.

ONA RAGAUSKAS WITNESSED the same act of cruelty from the other side of the fence. They are like animals, she thought, not for the first time that day. She turned away in disgust, just as Ruta and Tamara meekly scrambled on to the back of the truck. She composed herself and remained there, even more determined to wait until she got some indication of what had happened to little Janina Zilberman.

She did not have to wait long. Out of a back lane appeared Joseph Zilberman. He sobbed as he explained the soldiers had seized his daughter earlier in the day. Explanation done, he moved on quickly fearing that his presence there might endanger the brave woman, who had offered to save his beloved child.

It was the final straw. Oh, if only she had insisted the Zilbermans part with Janina a week earlier as originally agreed. The family had shared perhaps their last Shabbat meal ever, Ona thought. She began to cry. She felt guilty. She could not begin to imagine the guilt and remorse the Zilbermans would feel when the full force of their loss had sunk in.

Ona also walked swiftly away and knocked on the door of a friend across town. She would stay the night there. Her husband Antanas would not worry because she often stayed overnight in town if darkness fell before she had finished her errands.

Maybe the report of Janina's apprehension was a case of mistaken identity, she thought, and the morning would offer another opportunity for her to rescue Janina. There was no misidentification. She would get a second opportunity to save a Jewish child another day.

RUTA AND TAMARA were among a dozen or more children discovered late in the day by the search squads. Ruta did not recognize any of her fellow captives but then she was too busy trying to figure out how she could save herself and her sister. After all, that was what her parents expected of her. They would be extremely angry if they discovered she had led her sister into the arms of the Nazis.

As the minutes passed, she was occasionally distracted from her thoughts by more ugly, violent scenes. They did not look like daddies to her. Finishing this grisly assignment was their priority: there was more vodka to sup when this was over. They clubbed and slapped around any child that showed the slightest disinclination to board the truck. Amid the mayhem, Ruta stared expressionless from the back of the truck, holding on tightly to her sister.

DR. PEISACHOWITZ had dedicated his life to saving lives but he was powerless to help the parade of youngsters that passed by his current vantage point in the Judenrat office by the gate. Thank goodness, he had seen no sign of his cousin Gita's youngsters. They must have remained undetected at his place, he thought.

He looked forlornly at the truck starting up outside, just as he had countless times throughout the day. It seemed ready to go but, no, there was time to pack in two more passengers. In horror, he watched two thugs push Ruta and Tamara onto it. Maybe he could save these children.

Seconds later, ghetto policeman Wulf Levin looked up to see the respected doctor make straight for Forster. The 26-year-old man watched Wulf Peisachowitz bark something at the SS officer who stepped back, surprised by the outburst. Levin was himself surprised that the Nazi did not strike Wulf. Out of earshot, an intense exchange ensued.

Pointing to Ruta and Tamara, Wulf shouted: *"Kommandant, Das ist mein Blut."*

"I must remind you, doctor, you are a bachelor so how can they be your children?" Forster responded sarcastically.

Wulf fired back: "They are my illegitimate daughters and you must save them just as I saved you . . . you promised me a favour."

These were doctor's orders he was not inclined to obey. Forster's cool left him and the conversation became more animated with each man gesticulating in an exaggerated manner to emphasize his individual points. Desperate situations called for desperate measures and Wulf's lie about his cousins being his own spawn, easily disproved after the fact, worked. Well, partially.

Forster demonstrated many times that day that he was not in a charitable mood. However, when he weighed the possibility of being personally embarrassed, exposed as having received treatment from a Jewish doctor, he reconsidered his harsh dedication to removing every child from the ghetto. Then he muttered angrily: "The older one can stay because she can work but the other one must go."

Instantly, Wulf turned and made for the back of the truck, talking quickly to some of the adults standing by. Suddenly, Ruta noticed a bunch of men gathering in front of her and then a familiar figure walked into her field of vision. Whether it was the shock or confusion, it took her a few moments to realize it was the man they called Uncle Wulf. By the time her thoughts cleared, the men were tearing her away from Tamara's desperate grip. Now she was confused. These were not uniformed men but her neighbours.

Satisfied that the SS officer had ordered her removal, Wulf Levin had been among the first to help Ruta down from the truck. She almost fell over as she hit the uneven ground but immediately half a dozen hands pulled her upright. Before she was able to stand up properly and get her balance, Uncle Wulf grabbed her hand and dragged her away at a frantic pace. She struggled to keep up. The other men surrounded the two as they moved.

Tamara tried to join her sister but a guard restrained her so she began to shout.

"Ruta don't go . . . please take me with you," the little girl screeched repeatedly, her stick-like arms waving wildly.

Ruta slowed the pace as she stared briefly over her shoulder. As far as she was concerned, Tamara was the one leaving. She resented the fact that her sister and all of these other children were going to get a ride on a big truck. Ruta the child was back.

That did it. Ruta broke loose from the grip of her unexpected saviour and began to run back towards the truck. Friendly arms foiled her rescue attempt. Wulf took a firmer grip of her hand and, surrounded by other adults, they rushed back towards the Kron home. Long after they had turned the corner out of sight, Tamara continued yelling. Although she was no longer within Ruta's hearing, Tamara's earlier screams echoed in Ruta's mind.

Only the welcome sight of her grandpa at the door of their dilapidated shack temporarily halted the terrifying action replay. Wulf began to explain to the old man what had happened and why only Ruta survived. Ruta could no longer hear the explanation for Tamara's screams inside her head drowned out the words. Screams that would render some conversations inaudible for the rest of her life as she periodically recalled the last time she ever saw Tamara.

POLINA TOKER missed the dramatic rescue of Ruta because a squad of soldiers was holding her and a dozen others away from the scene. They released Polina just as the last truck left with Tamara aboard.

She ran straight to the dispensary to look for Adute. Before she got to the door, a woman stopped her and told her of her daughter's capture. She did not believe the bearer of bad news but once home she found her child's discarded coat. Alongside there was an upturned chamber pot, a puddle of urine spreading from beneath it onto the hard floor.

How would she explain this to her husband, a medical doctor? As far as she knew, he was fighting with the Red Army against these devils on some distant front but he would return one day. Until then she must do all she could to get Adute back.

Polina would not accept her daughter was lost. After all, somebody told her a little girl resembling Adute, had been removed from the last truck. She convinced herself it must have been Adute. Even the German soldiers used to laugh and point to Adute shouting "Ein Goldkopf" – golden head. Adute did not understand what they were saying and would run up to her mother pleading "Mama, hide me, hide me!"

Perhaps their admiration for her Aryan-like locks had persuaded them to let her go. After repeated telling, stories do change and sometimes offer false hope to those that hear only what they want to. Ruta's hair was, of course, the darkest brown.

WHEN THE WORKERS returned to the ghetto, Forster was still at the gate, following up on the tip offered by Siegel at Frenkel's. His men discovered a few more children with the returning workers and dispatched them to the same mystery location where the other children seized earlier waited. Babey Trepmann successfully re-entered the ghetto with her sister secreted beneath her coat.

Gita and Meyer Kron rushed home. There they found Grandpa Shifman and Ruta but no Tamara. Ruta was still hiding under the couch cushions with which Wulf and their escorts covered her. She had to be coaxed out, fearing she was about to be punished for her terrible mistake in a way she had never suffered before.

"Mama, is it my fault?"

She need not have worried but her seven brief years had not prepared her for this experience. She bore the weight of the world on her tiny shoulders that day. Instead of punishment, she received the warmest and longest of hugs. Unfortunately, Ruta's intense feelings of guilt overwhelmed her ability to accept the words of comfort and reassurance her parents offered.

All night long, the Krons could hear wailing from every house. They just sat there for hours, still in their dirty clothes and their shoes, caked with the mud collected on their way back through the streets to the ghetto. They were numb with shock. Gradually they began to think about what they should do with Ruta.

They plotted how they could get her out the next day because they could not risk exposing her to a second sweep of the ghetto. They had no inkling as to who might provide her with a hiding place beyond the fence. Maybe Jonas Jocius would come through in their hour of need – again.

A SHORT DISTANCE AWAY, Polina Toker was praying that Ruta was Adute. The screams of her neighbours penetrated the thin walls, one being the widow of Rabbi Aaron Baksht, summarily executed within days of the Nazi occupation. She screamed like a banshee for now she had also lost her granddaughter Janina. She wailed: "There is no God!"

Polina staggered into the street to ask a guard to shoot her but he just turned away. She ran to the dispensary and gobbled down all the pills she could find. She passed out but clinic staff found her and figured out what she had done. They saved her life.

Some anguished parents succeeded where Polina failed and took their own lives as they pondered an existence without their children. Strange scenes of extreme anguish played out throughout the whole ghetto as the enormity of what had happened became apparent to all. Few if any lit Shabbat candles that night in the Shavl ghetto. There was darkness everywhere: in the streets, in the homes and in parental hearts.

It is not clear how many were taken in the Kinderaktion: Yerushalmi recorded that the Komandant claimed 816 people were removed. However, the Judenrat scribe speculated that the number was nearer 1,000 as the trucks had made 21 return trips during that dreadful day. Some documentation showed up in later years and testimony about the event received at various trials and inquiries. How much of it is trustworthy is up for debate. The smallest number is 570 children but others claim that in excess of 700 of Shavl's children were taken, with the remainder made up of seniors and the sick.

The ghetto census of 1942 offers a clue as to why a larger number may have been taken. At the time of the count, there were more than 1,000 children under 12 years of age. During the Kinderaktion in November 1943, they would all have been targets for removal. In the intervening year, some of those children were undoubtedly smuggled out to safety. Others may have moved with their parents when they were reassigned to another work camp following the closure of the Kaukazas ghetto weeks before the Kinderaktion. Others may have perished when the Nazis simply moved their parents out and shot them in the nearby woods.

Some, like Ruta, survived the round up and stayed in hiding until a safe house beyond the fence could be found. In light of all of this, a transport of more than 700 children to Auschwitz seems very plausible in the absence of trustworthy documentation.

At the station, 100 or more of the captives were loaded into each of the 30-foot long, seven-foot wide wagons before the heavy doors shut. There was no air, little food and water and the daylight barely penetrated the narrow slats high above the hard floor.

What happened to them? After the war, there were gruesome unverified stories, published in the Russian controlled press. Survivors recall some newspapers reported the Germans drained the children's blood in order that casualties returning from the battlefront might receive transfusions. The Russians had their own nefarious reasons for spreading such tales of inhumanity. It seems unlikely given the Nazi aversion to anything Jewish.

Answers that are more realistic are in accounts offered by witnesses to the train's departure and a lone observer at the destination. At nightfall on that terrible day, railway workers returning to the ghetto reported seeing a powerful 52-series German locomotive build up a head of steam before pulling cattle cars full of human cargo out of the station for a destination that remained unannounced on the crackly public address system. However, Jewish workers in the maintenance yard recalled seeing the name Auschwitz daubed on some of the cars but the destination did not mean anything to them at the time.

Shortly after the train steamed away, the snow that threatened earlier began to fall, covering all traces of the evil that had blackened the rundown streets of the ghetto.

The train likely picked up more passengers on the way before reaching its final destination in Poland, more than 700 miles distant, two or three days later.

The train's last stop was just outside the rural Polish community of Oswiecim, where barking dogs greeted its arrival. Hundreds of similar transport trains had made this trip and the pattern was always the same. On arrival, the dogs padded along the frozen platform, their handlers bringing them to heel with clipped commands.

The doors opened and those within were ordered to jump the three-foot drop to the ground. The weary travellers' first sight of Auschwitz-Birkenau was the savage dogs and their equally savage SS masters. Any child searching for a fatherly smile among the uniformed men would be disappointed.

Some older children among the hundreds lined up along the trackside might have sensed doom. The younger ones, such as Tamara, would be too frightened and bewildered to have any sense of foreboding. It was beyond their comprehension.

New adult arrivals underwent a selection process in which the able bodied arbitrarily picked by SS peeled off to the left while those deemed disposable would pass to the right.

There was no selection for a transport of children and seniors. The man in the uniform at the head of the line simply told them all to get undressed in the room ahead. They then proceeded quickly to the place he described as a shower room. The dogs growled and snapped at the heels of the youngsters.

Inside, a *Sonderkommando* – a Jewish prisoner forced to work in the camp's extermination centre – later wrote about his brief conversations with the children from Shavl.

An older girl, perhaps only months away from the age of 13 that would have saved her, knew what was happening, thanks to the warnings shouted by adult prisoners lined up behind the fence. She cursed the hunched man in the striped pyjamas.

"Go away, you murderer! Don't touch my little brother with your hands soaked in the blood of your own kind."

Her words showed a maturity one might not expect from one so young. It is impossible to confirm if the diary entry was verbatim, but it clearly conveyed the substance of the angry remarks that would haunt the writer to his grave.

The thoughts he frequently shunned returned: he lived on because he was willing to do the Nazis bidding. Was his life so precious that he was willing to do this to draw breath for another week, a month or maybe a little more? That was not his thought but a question posed by a young boy from among the Shavl children.

The youngster's words hung in the air as he and the other children walked into the gas chamber to draw their last breath on a bitterly cold November day in 1943.

Tamara and the others perished inhaling the poisonous gas created by the crushing of Zyklon B crystals. The German industrial giant, IG Farben, for whom her own father Meyer Kron worked in the happier times of 1929, owned a significant share of the company that manufactured Zyklon B.

The practice was for the SS to bill Jewish community funds for the cost of transporting their loved ones to the death camps. The railway company – the *Reichsbahn* – charged 0.04 Reichsmark (RM) for one adult per kilometre, half price for children and those less than four years old travelled free. However, at this time business was so brisk that the SS got a 50 percent discount rate when a train carried at least 400 people. The parents in Shavl were spared official confirmation of their children's deaths. The normally efficient SS bureaucracy overlooked the billing.

CHAPTER FOURTEEN

The little schoolhouse

Shavl ghetto gate – early Saturday, November 6, 1943.

IT WAS WORK AS usual for the ghetto inmates the day after the Kinderaktion, though some parents did not show up at the gate.

The invaders would round up those absentees later, once they were missed at their place of work. In the meantime, children, who had survived the Kinderaktion, replaced them in the exit line, hidden among the adults.

Minutes earlier in the comparative safety of their ghetto home, Meyer and Gita had explained their plan to Ruta, reassuring her that she would be safe so long as she followed their instructions. Ruta nodded exaggeratedly to show she would follow their orders to the letter. Not as she had failed to do the day before. The images of Tamara screaming out and waving from the back of the truck began to cross her mind but in slow motion. She pushed them away, not allowing the scene to replay in so slow and painful a way.

There were no hugs from papa. Romantic and as physically demonstrable as he was with his bride, that was not his way with his children. Meyer tapped his remaining daughter's shoulder gently, telling her to be brave. Gita's eyes teared up and she swallowed loudly to force back a sob. Such a show of emotion would not be helpful this moment. It might make Ruta fearful of what lay ahead, especially during the next few minutes.

The head count at the gate was sloppy that day, something the likes of the Krons were counting on. The smallest youngsters hid beneath the coats and skirts of their parents. In Ruta's case, adults surrounded her and she was able to walk out unnoticed by the guards.

Once at Frenkel's factory, Meyer and Gita created a hiding place between piles of sacks in the building next door to the laboratory. It was an unpleasant place at the best of times but made more so at this time by the stockpiling of the most vile glue. Ruta was dutifully quiet. She stayed there motionless for hours without any thoughts of venturing away from the safety of the stacked sacks that surrounded her.

Gita returned at the end of the day, clutching some ragged blankets. She would stay with her for as long as it took to find a hiding place beyond the confines of the factory. Ruta pulled closer into her mother as the rats ran over them in the darkness, nipping at their legs and toes. This was to be the pattern for the next few nights as the Krons desperately tried to find a safe haven.

Meyer tried to contact Jocius but he was out of town, no doubt doing one of his deals – hard cash in exchange for food he came by illicitly. This time the amiable big man would not come to the rescue.

THE DOOR TO Meyer's office opened and hope was born out of despair.

"May I see you for a moment, Mr. Kron?"

Meyer turned to see who had invaded his thoughts on what to do next to save Ruta. It was Felya Zilberman.

"Err, yes, come in," responded Meyer uncomfortably.

He tried to smile but it was more like a grimace. They both moved to the corner of his office-cum-lab, looking around to make sure no one was watching. It was a paranoid response because it was not out of the ordinary for them to consult during the day. Everybody was extra edgy this day. Fighting back the tears, she made a remarkable offer.

"We have lost our little one to these monsters but there's no reason you should lose yours and she deserves a chance to escape. I think I can help."

She commanded Meyer's full attention, who now desperately wanted her to say what she wanted to say. He said nothing, feeling guilty that he could be so impatient with this grieving mother. He nodded for her to continue.

"We found a place for Janina and the woman came to get her yesterday but it was too late. Ruta should take her place."

She looked ready to burst into tears and Meyer worried she might alert others. What was he thinking? – As parents gave vent to their innermost sadness, there were many tears shed throughout the factory that day. Meyer now had a tear in his eye and a lump in his throat as he listened.

"Her name is Ona Ragauskas and she is married to a school teacher. She is a good Catholic woman and I am sure she would take Ruta. I don't know how to contact her now but I'm sure you have people you know and trust that could approach her on your behalf."

"Yes, yes, I'm sure we can ask for help in that regard," he answered very formally just in case somebody was listening and he could say he was discussing a work problem. She left immediately, her shoulders heaved with her sobs.

Now the Krons really needed Jocius. How much longer would he be away? Meyer approached one of the few sympathetic Lithuanians in the factory. The message would reach the ears of their friend. This time the response came quickly.

The factory was quiet at dusk when Gita settled Ruta down for the evening, telling her that mama had to go on an errand and she should be silent. Gita then removed her yellow star and walked out of the back door of the factory, striding out purposefully into the street. Jocius was pleased to see Gita, expressing his sadness for her loss but his joy for Ruta's good fortune. He agreed instantly to arrange a meeting with Ona, suggesting it happen at a neutral location.

"Yes, yes, we will do whatever you say Jonas," said Gita, shaking her head for emphasis. He was Jocius to everybody else but she always liked to address him by his chosen name. He liked that.

"But please arrange it soon because I don't know how much longer we can remain in the factory without being discovered.

Jocius smiled his broadest smile and told her not to worry. He knew she would worry, but what else can one say in such dire circumstances? Gita did feel reassured because the man had come through many times before.

BACK INSIDE THE ghetto, the population had only one question: "Where did they take them?" Nobody was familiar with the name Auschwitz. The official Nazi answer to the ghetto leaders was that it was something like a children's camp or colony.

A wave of mysticism washed over the ghetto. People tried to invoke spirits of ancestors, the most popular method being that of staging a séance. Even Meyer participated on one occasion, desperate to discover Tamara's fate.

Four people sat around a small table and put the palms of their hands on the surface. They then challenged it with simple questions such as "Do I have one brother, two brothers, or three brothers?" The table answered by tipping the appropriate number of times. If the answer was correct then those present figured it was reliable and the serious questions began. Meyer's description of his experience to Gita confirmed why it was a one-time experience.

"It was amazing how the table always gave correct answers to the simple questions," he said, with a wry look. "All answers to our questions about Auschwitz were optimistic and that gave us a little relief."

It was easier now for Meyer to be cynical as his second daughter at least had a chance of survival, whereas most of his neighbours had lost all of their offspring to the unknown.

THE HORSE AND cart pulled up outside the little schoolhouse in Amaliai. Ona Ragauskas, who had spent the last half hour peering out from behind the curtains, emerged nervously. She looked all around her as she climbed into the buggy. The large man who visited her the day before told her he preferred not to identify the woman who wanted to meet her. As they moved slowly down the lane, she wondered if it was Felya Zilberman. Perhaps Janina was safe after all.

Half an hour later they pulled up at a small house on the edge of Shavl that she did not recognize. She was taking a big chance. She did not know this man but something told her he could be trusted. Jocius let her into the house where his wife, also called Ona, excitedly showed her through to another room and then left.

The schoolteacher's wife fixed her eyes on the glamorous, blue eyed, blonde woman sitting on the couch, her beauty spoiled only by the red blotches around her eyes, evidence of recent crying. Her tailored clothes had seen better days but even so, it was obvious they were not cast offs. They were stylish and fit her perfectly. As soon as she made eye contact with Ona, Gita quickly got up from the couch and immediately fell to her knees.

"My baby was taken by the Nazis but Ruta her older sister was spared by a miracle," sobbed the distraught mother.

"I beg you please take my child please."

Ona was embarrassed and tried to pick up the woman. There was no need to beg.

"I too have lost a child but to disease and I know the pain," Ona responded sympathetically. "I would like to help but I can't make this decision on my own. I must talk to my husband."

She felt guilty about making the woman wait but she must talk to Antanas. Between sobs, Gita explained how she was a Shifman, a name familiar to farm folk such as Ona. Her own father used to sell grain to Papa Shifman.

"Yes, I think my husband went to school with Iudite Shifman."

Before she could say more Gita pounced on the remark.

"Yes, yes, that is my sister. She left Shavl before and settled with her husband in Italy."

Ona was warming to this woman and she gave Gita cause for optimism.

"Bring your daughter here tomorrow so that I can meet her and I will tell you then if I can help."

Ona figured the surviving child must already be out of the ghetto, so bringing her to the home of Jocius would pose no great risk. Gita did not enlighten her to the fact that Ruta was hiding between the machines at Frenkel's. She was thrilled that this woman had offered her more than a glimmer of hope.

ONA LOOKED DEEP into her husband's eyes over the kitchen table, held both of his hands, and poured out a heartfelt plea.

"Antanas, I want to save her . . . it is the right thing for Christians to do," she said.

"I saw the hollowness in the eyes of the mothers who lost their children when the Germans came for them that day. We know what it is like to love and lose a child."

The good-looking teacher's eyes dulled a little as he recalled how diphtheria so cruelly took Rimantas from them nine months earlier. Now all they had left was a memory and the hope that their one-year-old daughter Grazina would remain healthy.

"You know the mother's sister, Iudite," she added.

"Yes, she was a bright girl and an even brighter woman," he said. "The Shifmans are a good family. I don't believe I ever met her sister Gita though," his brow furrowed as he tried to remember any encounter.

"She's blonde," Ona announced, not referring to the rest of Gita's appearance.

There was no need to, for it was code. Mother like daughter, they both thought. It would be far easier to look after a blonde girl than a dark haired girl, which matched the description of most of the ghetto's former young inmates. Neither had counted on the influence of Meyer Kron's genes on the looks of this child.

"I agree we should help." He would deny his beloved wife little. He gazed at the woman with the lovely long brown braided and curled hair and big eyes. He snapped back to reality.

"You know, after what we have seen and heard in these past months it is quite likely the girl's parents will not survive the war."

Ona worried he was about to withdraw his consent so she was relieved to hear him continue.

"We have to be prepared to raise this child until she is an adult. I will love her as our own child."

Her smile lit up the room and that was a remarkable sight, thought Antanas. How could he refuse?

THE NEXT DAY RUTA left the factory with the garbage. The truck was used often either to take out children or bring in food. Immediately after the Kinderaktion, the guards closely scrutinized it for illegal cargo but now they had returned to their old ways. Who wanted to dig through all of the foul smelling garbage? Besides any child who survived surely must be long gone four days after the event.

Ruta hated the smell too but she knew this journey would give her freedom to play, as every little girl should. Less than half an hour later Jocius was retrieving her from the depths of the wagon. His wife made sure her first stop was the bath. Gita left the factory for the last time, as Ona Jocius began lathering Ruta with as much black market soap as her husband could lay his hands on.

Later that night Gita would return to the factory knowing her daughter was in safe hands and would be in still safer hands within a day or two. Nothing else mattered. She did not allow herself to think of the consequences of a negative answer from Ona Ragauskas.

She dashed across Vilna Street and entered the field that led to the Jocius home. At about the same time, the schoolteacher's wife wheeled her bike out of the shed and began pedalling in the direction of Shavl.

AN HOUR LATER, they were all in the same room. Ona looked at Gita's blonde hair then looked at little Ruta with her dark hair. She repeated these back and forth glances a number of times as though she was playing for time so she could think of something to say. Gita's heart sank. She knew exactly what was going through Ona's mind.

Then Ona fixed her gaze on Ruta who had not taken her eyes off the kindly woman since she entered the room. She is like a frightened little rabbit, thought Ona. The youngster remained quiet but, to Ona, her eyes spoke loudly and clearly – "take me, take me."

Ruta sensed something was wrong and sprang into action.

"I can recite a poem," she said. She then proceeded to deliver the lines in Lithuanian but in the strongest Yiddish accent imaginable.

Ona smiled as she finished the verse and looked down at the floor for a few moments. It gets worse, she thought. Her appearance is one thing but that accent . . . oh, my goodness.

She turned back to Gita: "How can I hide her, she is too Jewish? I hoped she would look like you."

Before Gita began to plead, Ona held up both her arms and said, "Alright, we will take her and keep her safe."

If Gita had hugged her any more she would have fractured the ribs of this angel. They arranged the exchange.

When she got home, Ona told Antanas about Ruta's appearance but he did not change his mind.

"The Lord will help us," he assured his wife, before quoting her own words back at her. "Besides, as you said, it's the right thing to do."

RUTA WAS FAR from happy in her new temporary accommodation. It was a cold night, even inside the Jocius household. Ruta lay in a narrow bed in the corner of a long dark room. At the other end, beyond a wooden table that cut the room in half, her hosts slept in two beds warmed by the pot-bellied stove between them.

Ruta could not sleep. She tossed and turned, hugging her own body in a bid to get warm. Oh, how she longed for the arms of her mother and father about her. She drifted off only to wake again minutes later with a stomach cramp and a burning sensation in her bladder. She needed to go but she was too scared to move for fear she might wake Jocius and his wife. The white chamber pot was close to the ends of their twin beds.

"I am a big girl," she said to herself, "I can hold it until mama and papa come back to get me."

Her thoughts wandered into dangerous territory as she pondered the notion that they may not come back. Perhaps they had brought her here to punish her for allowing the Germans to take Tamara.

"Please God bring her back so mama and papa won't be mad at me," she prayed in a whisper, heard only by herself and the Almighty. Tears rolled down her cheeks. A few barely detectable sobs issued forth. She learned how to cry quietly when she and Tamara had hid in Uncle Wulf's room.

Her bladder filled a little more. She was bursting to go but she could not do so in front of these strangers. "Forgive me, mama," she pleaded in a louder whisper, as the trickle spread down her thighs. At last, she was warm but also wet and the temporary respite from the cold would give way to an overwhelming feeling of shame for what she had done.

Ruta decided that if she moved around, wriggled, twisted and turned for the rest of the night, she could dry the large wet spot. They would not be able to punish her as it would be dry and nobody would be any the wiser, she rationalized. As the cock began crowing outside and daylight flooded in the small windows, she chanced a touch of the wet spot with her toes. It was dry. "I did it, mama," she exclaimed excitedly to her absent mother.

There was a stir from one of the beds at the end of the room. The pungent smell of urine hit Jocius's wife as she approached the little girl curled up in the bed but she managed to maintain her smile. She whisked Ruta away to the kitchen for breakfast. While she chomped into a heel of bread, her host returned to the tiny bedroom to strip sheets and do what she could to rescue the mattress. It would be almost 15 years before Ruta realized that she had not fooled Ona Jocius. It came the day she cleaned up after a bedwetting by her first daughter Marilee. All the events of that scary night flooded back and she marvelled at the kindness and sensitivity shown to her.

∽

THAT EVENING THE rendezvous with Ona was to be at the medical office of Dr. Domas Jasaitis, in his yellow painted, single storey home. This same man had made it possible for Gita to bury her mother. He was coming to her aid again as he had many times for other Jews seeking to escape the clutches of the Nazis.

The Shavl hospital director began his non-medical, lifesaving, mission shortly after the arrival of the Nazis when an appeal to reason spectacularly failed. Dr. Jasaitis, Father Justinus Lapis and another respected citizen received short shrift when they attempted to intervene on behalf of the Jewish community. A second meeting with the Lithuanian authorities met with the same response. On that occasion, the Nazi dismissed Jasaitis with a chilling warning: "If you, Sir, meddle in this matter, you will lie in the same grave with the Jews."

It did not stop Jasaitis from continuing to defy the Nazis at every opportunity. It would be decades later before the brave doctor was recognized for his heroism, long after his move to the United States.

GITA PICKED UP Ruta from the Jocius household at twilight and wrapped her in a blanket as though she were suffering from some serious ailment. No acting was necessary, as Ruta was not the picture of health.

The doctor's wife Sofija greeted Ona Ragauskas warmly when she showed up a few minutes after her first pair of visitors. She showed her to the waiting room. Once seated, Ona could just make out Gita through the door to the doctor's office, which was ajar. Gita was talking quietly to Jasaitis. After a minute or so, the doctor turned his head and they exchanged glances.

Gita wrapped her arms around Ruta and squeezed her gently. She released her seconds later and backed up a step to look down into Ruta's eyes. "Be a good girl and do as you are told," she said, as though she was merely dispatching a child to school. There was no time for speeches and besides Gita doubted she could hold back her tears much longer. Gita walked away and let herself out of the side door, not looking back at the child she feared she might never see again. She was returning to the ghetto this night instead of the factory, sneaking in with the last work party of the night. She was going home to her husband and an uncertain future but at least her child was safe.

Seconds after Gita had left, Jasaitis appeared in the waiting room with Ruta. He was nervous and did not hug the stranger before him as he might have done in any other circumstance. He

patted Ruta on the head and shooed her towards to an equally
nervous Ona, who rose quickly from her chair. She reached for
the child's hand and headed quickly for the door. Just like Gita
moments earlier, she did not look back for an instant. Now she
was frightened.

Just as Jasaitis promised, the carter and his horse were waiting
for the mother and her 'new' child at the roadside. She got into
the back of the cart quickly and without saying anything to the
man upfront. Ona was grateful of the cover, as a light snow was
falling. It also sheltered her from prying eyes, if any cared to pry
on this winter night.

Ruta leaned into Ona. She felt safe but dared not speak. As they
pulled away from the town, the darkness enveloped them. By the
three-mile mark, there was no longer anybody on the road. By
seven, she could see little and all she could hear was the sound
of the wheels clattering over the ruts that protruded through the
snow that cushioned and quietened their ride. With just a few
more miles to go, Ona recognized some of the landmarks in the
gloom. Her stomach turned over. Maybe he was going to hand
her over to the Gestapo for money.

The driver heard her call the second time. "Drop me off at the
station, please."

That was not the destination he had in mind but if that is what
the woman wanted that was fine with him. As she scrambled the
last 500 yards towards her schoolhouse home, Jonas Jocius watched
her, wondering if she had not recognized him.

Antanas was playing with Grazina when Ona and Ruta
came through the door, a cold draught following closely behind.

He turned to smile at his new daughter Ruta. Before him was
a dark haired little girl dressed in dirty and torn clothes.

Ruta's clothes were full of lice as was her pretty head of hair.
Ona gently removed her clothes and threw them on the fire.
With Grazina on his hip, Antanas hauled the bathtub to a spot
by the fire and filled it with water. He had already begun to heat
up the water half an hour before they arrived. This would be a
scene repeated nightly as they rid the youngster of the dirt of
the ghetto.

"I'm going to be safe here," thought Ruta, "these are nice people."

CHAPTER FIFTEEN

Ruta's Closet

The little schoolhouse, Amaliai -
Friday, November 12, 1943.

R IDDING RUTA OF THE lice that feasted and nested on her tender scalp was a thoroughly unpleasant and seemingly endless task. However, ridding Ruta of her unmistakable Jewish accent was a bigger challenge for Antanas and Ona. Though Ruta understood Lithuanian fairly well she spoke only Russian at home. Ona started what became a daily ritual of teaching Ruta to speak Lithuanian like her neighbours. She was amazed at the youngster's stamina, her tireless repetition of the trickiest pronunciations.

"Again, Ruta," she would say, almost singing the request and making sure she rewarded her pupil with an appreciative smile.

Ruta never complained but complied with her tutor's requests to recite and to repeat those long Lithuanian words that left her tongue-tied. Saying *Rs* was particularly difficult. Ruta watched Ona's lips and mouth shape intently, trying to imitate her teacher to please her.

Ona possessed the patience of a saint. As the lesson proceeded, she would carry on with her food preparation or baking, occasionally banging out the rhythm of a word with a ladle or spoon.

Unlike the pupils in the next room, who sat at desks, Ruta squatted on the floor for her lessons. She leaned up against the open door of a closet into which she knew she must jump instantly if told to do so. Ona had one ear listening constantly for a knock on the side door entrance or for any sign of one her husband's pupils straying through to the kitchen. If she had the slightest suspicion, she would spit out the word for the closet: *"Spinta!"*

For most of the time, nothing interrupted Ruta's lessons but one evening, while working in the kitchen, Ona heard the crash of somebody barging their way through the side door to the school, just a few yards away. Instinctively, she made straight for Ruta, ushering her up into the attic above the kitchen. The closet was too far away on this occasion. Ona's hands left an impression in flour on the back of the youngster's cardigan as she pushed her into the darkness of the roof area. Once there, Ruta retreated behind a large wooden box and remained as quiet as the mice that sometimes scurried across the floor.

Ona returned quickly to her spot at the table, dusting off her apron, just as the uninvited guest came through the kitchen door. The pounding of her heart gave lie to her external calm as she took in the sight of the large German soldier before her. He was shouting something at her but she knew no German. He was sweating, slightly out of breath and was scanning the room as he yelled.

Luckily, Antanas had already spotted the intruder from the classroom where he was setting out papers for the next day's lessons. In seconds, Antanas was in the doorframe, his arrival heralded by his repeated shouts of "What can I do for you?" in German. It was a smart move; it let the agitated soldier know he was approaching, therefore reducing the chance of him shooting without asking any further questions. He had already pulled the trigger minutes earlier when a young lad failed to halt and submit to questioning.

The German had spotted the youth run in the direction of this building. Antanas exhausted his rudimentary German trying to calm the man. It seemed to work. The uniformed officer clearly figured he was wasting his time searching the place. He walked by the closet, where Ruta usually hid. Doubtless, he figured it was too small a hiding place for the tall youth he was chasing. For a few moments, he pushed open doors but left as abruptly as he arrived, prompted by a shout from an unseen comrade outside. His suspect had run by the schoolhouse and continued to the fields beyond the orchard.

Ona and Antanas were shaking. This episode reminded them that no matter how careful they were, the actions of others could inadvertently put them at risk of detection. Ruta remained so quiet that the couple almost forgot she was in there as they calmed down. They began to laugh in that nervous giggling way that people often do after a shock. They opened the attic door, lighting the space where Ruta sat cross-legged. Seeing smiles all round, Ruta grinned, wondering what the joke was. There was no punch line to share.

The couple often marvelled at Ruta's strong sense of survival. As Ruta prepared for bed that night they reflected on how sad it was, that one so young should need to have such a finely defined instinct of self-preservation. There was no carefree childhood for this youngster.

Antanas returned to the schoolroom to finish his preparation for the next day once Ruta was in bed safely. That was when Zophia, the widowed mother of Antanas, who had stayed in her room for the duration of the incident, decided to cover some old ground with Ona.

"You see ... I told you, you are killing your family doing this," she scolded.

Ona was never disrespectful but she no longer hesitated to put her mother-in-law in her place.

"Mother, as I have told you it is a decision we made together to save this child and we are not abandoning her now. This changes nothing. She is a guest in this home just as you are."

It was a brief exchange. Zophia flinched at the last remark, as did Ona, regretting for a moment that she had now said what she had only previously thought. Ona's next thoughts pushed away the regrets. Zophia had never made Ruta feel welcome. The youngster scooted out of the room whenever Zophia entered.

Zophia could see that yet again she was getting nowhere with her headstrong daughter-in-law. She was not confident she would get support from her son, despite the fright they had all suffered. She only ever raised this thorny issue when he was absent.

In the past, Zophia had tried many times to play the 'poor me' card without success. She frequently repeated such remarks such as, "You are risking my life too. Why don't you respect me? You are warm to that child and so cold to me."

Ona never overreacted or allowed her mother-in-law to draw her into a war of words. At first, she said little, likely because she was a young bride, unsure of her position in the household. She recalled similar conversations with her own parents, who lived on their farm a short distance away in Kairiai. The difference was that her parents, Juozas and Ona Kupaitis, raised the cautions without malice. Her younger brothers Vacys and Leonas said nothing, though in the near future the latter would play an important role in ensuring Ruta remained safe.

It seemed Zophia did not want the younger Ona around in the first place. Perhaps she viewed Ona as a poor replacement for Elena, her son's first love, who tragically died of a heart problem after only two years of marriage. At least that is what Ona imagined. To be fair, although the woman made many wounding remarks, Zophia's acid tongue never formed such words.

As Ona became more confident in herself and her relationship, she became more assertive but held back her innermost feelings and temptation to lash out. The 30-year-old woman had matured beyond her years since the war broke out and a recent response to her mother-in-law demonstrated that.

"It was my good fate to get married to a person who feels exactly the same way as I do, mother. Your son Antanas has the sensitivity and heart to embrace people and the desire to help those in need. You should know that, he's your son."

It should not only have been that day's conversation's stopper but one to end any further discussion on that topic, Ona had hoped. However, this latest exchange following the German's intrusion showed that notion was somewhat optimistic. As always, after Zophia had left the room and Ona had cooled down from her uncharacteristic rage, she thought more charitably of her mother-in-law. Zophia was a frightened old woman, concerned about the safety of her own flesh and blood. She was not a bad person.

Ona could hear Antanas moving desks around in the next room. That was her husband. He was again totally focused on the 40 youngsters who would be there tomorrow eagerly feeding on the knowledge he served them.

She indulged in some reminiscing, a warm buffer against the harsh reality they now faced together. There was the key; they faced it together. Nothing could touch them.

Ona met the dashingly handsome, curly-haired Antanas – that is how she always described him – when she was a girl of 18. It was 1931 and he had arrived at the Amaliai schoolhouse with his new bride to teach grades one through four. Ona sang in the choir at Father Adolfas Kleiba's church, which the family had attended since their return to Lithuania in 1914.

As she reflected a little more on their love, she pressed the steam iron a little more firmly on her husband's shirt. If she had stayed in the United States where she was born, she would never have met Antanas or been able to save Ruta. Her family returned to their native land to get away from the labour strife that had struck the

Michigan copper mines in which her father worked. Nevertheless, her father did return with enough cash to buy their dream farm.

In 1934, almost two years after Elena died; Ona and Antanas went out on their first date. They then both sang in the choir and Antanas played the piano for the entertainment of himself and his friends. He made brave efforts to tackle classical music. However, he particularly liked to play his versions of songs made popular by the singer and comedian Danielius Dolskis, a pioneer of the Lithuanian pop music of the time.

Ona most admired his dedication and sensitivity. She once proudly told a girlfriend: "While many men chose to sit next to a beer at night, Antanas prefers to sit next to the piano."

They saw each other socially for the next few years but there was no talk of marriage. Antanas was still suffering the loss of his first wife so young. He needed time to heal before considering marriage again.

The impetus for him to focus on re-marriage came in 1937 when Ona went off alone to the States. She was 24 and travelled to New York to stay with a paternal uncle. Her relatives accepted her enthusiastically when she arrived but soon lost interest in the young girl, who could speak only Lithuanian. By October 1938, she was sailing home with a wedding dress in her suitcase and on January 1, 1939, she was exchanging vows with Antanas before Father Kleiba.

Antanas had missed her. She smiled and recalled her triumphant return. "He was my first love and he will be my last love," she thought as she hung up his shirt and began folding some of baby Grazina's clothes. The spell was broken when Antanas appeared at the kitchen door.

"Time to sleep," he said. There was no resistance from Ona.

SLEEP DID NOT come so easy in the ghetto. Within days of the Kinderaktion, the Krons moved to another house a short distance away. It was just too painful to stay in the same place.

The accommodation was no roomier than the little house on Ginkunu Street, as they shared with ten adults. Most of the tenants were old friends and they spent their evenings playing gin rummy and poker, often late into the night until sleep finally came. They took it in turns acting as a lookout as gambling was illegal and they were anxious not to attract any uninvited guests in authority.

On the rare occasions when the Krons were alone, the conversation always turned to the same topic – escape. It usually followed a discussion on the latest news from the Eastern Front. Wulf was the best source as he overheard much in his job at the local hospital.

Ghetto radios were becoming rare as they either broken down or were seized by the authorities. Some of the Jews heard the latest news from their Lithuanian colleagues at the various workplaces beyond the gates. Others, who cleaned or repaired the houses occupied by high-ranking Nazis, heard just how badly the Germans were bogged down in Russia.

The Nazi retreat was good news in a way, but the continued movement in their direction surely also signalled the end of the ghetto by the removal of its populace – either by execution or a march to some other godforsaken camp closer to Germany.

"We really must have an escape plan for ourselves," said Meyer during one of their few times alone. "Ruta is safe now. We know Barbora will take care of your father if we can get him there."

"Papa has to go first," said Gita, cutting off Meyer in mid-sentence.

"We will have to take our chance when it arises. He is much older and would not respond well to such a sudden exit."

Her husband agreed: "When we go we will have to be light on our feet. So, let's concentrate on finding a way to smuggle him out and while we are doing that perhaps we can figure out where we might go when the time comes."

Gita nodded, staring through the window to look for signs of a return by one of their roommates. She doubted they would find a safe haven so easily, based on her bitter experiences trying to retrieve belongings from their former friends and neighbours in their continuous quest for food. She turned back to Meyer, who offered his further thoughts on their departure.

"The Germans won't miss papa but they will miss the two of us, which will endanger our friends here. They will make an example of them, saying they aided and abetted our escape.

"When the end comes there will be public disturbances throughout the ghetto. Some will go quietly but others will put up a fight. There may be even a fully-fledged riot when people figure out what the Nazis might have planned for them.

"We will be of no use to them here; we would be a liability. At the first sign of such trouble or upheaval, we must be ready to go.

In those circumstances, none of these good people would be held to account for our absence. They would be fleeing themselves."

Gita went to their hiding place behind the sink in the kitchen. She strained to reach down to the little cloth bag that now held the last of their worldly wealth.

Meyer would have offered help but his arms were too big to fit down the narrow gap between the basin and the wall. Her eyes watered a little as she made that final stretch and felt the material snag a nail on her right hand. She retrieved the sack, smiling as though she had hooked a huge fish.

It was Meyer's turn to check the street. As he did, she tipped out their assets – some gold, some jewellery, and some cash. It was not clear what use the Lithuanian currency would be; nevertheless, they divided the contents and hid their individual shares on their persons. The treasure would remain on them until they smelled the sweet air of freedom or the Nazis found their stash. If the latter were to be the case, it is doubtful they would live long enough to regret their actions.

WULF'S CLOSE FRIEND and colleague Luntz and his wife Berta could no longer stand life in the ghetto after losing little Aviva. They were determined to escape by whatever means.

They had a doctor friend in Telz and through Wulf, they were able to convey a message that they would soon be on their way to him. Like Wulf, Berta also had a permit enabling them to leave the ghetto to assist in the treatment of patients and she took full advantage, of it getting not only herself out but also her mother Eugenia Nurok. Her husband left separately a short time after, escaping through the tannery with the help and guidance of Meyer Kron, who knew every gate and entrance.

AT THE TIME the Luntzes were making their escape bid, Polina Toker was contemplating the same. In the weeks following the Kinderaktion, she wandered around in a daze, still hoping her seven-year-old daughter was the child taken from the back of the last truck out of the ghetto. Nobody she encountered had told her it was Meyer Kron's daughter Ruta. Maybe she did not ask for fear her hopes would be dashed.

If only her husband Chaim were there, she thought, they could flee together. He was fighting on the Eastern Front, or at least she hoped he still was. To lose Adute was so painful that to lose him also would surely cause her to question whether life was still worth living.

Early one frigid morning in the first week of December, she ripped the yellow star from her coat and slipped out of the gates with an early work party that left the ghetto. She ducked down an alley, returning to the snow covered streets minutes later. It was a risk to be there but there were people already about, heading to their workplaces. Their heads were down as they tried to avoid the sting of cold delivered by the swirling sleet that now drove almost horizontally into their faces, no matter which direction they were walking.

Polina, like Gita, trusted none of her gentile friends for they also proved unhelpful in finding a hiding place for Adute during her earlier forays out of the ghetto. While some were clearly frightened, others were downright threatening, saying they would call the Gestapo if she bothered them again.

As she walked, she recalled the name of a Catholic priest called Vincas Byla, who her night school class students talked about so lovingly. They told how, during catechism classes, he daringly expressed his displeasure about the German treatment of the Jews. He may not hide her but he would surely not betray her.

The mere act of getting there was fraught with risk for the rectory was adjacent to the German administration office and the guards outside just might be suspicious of a woman at large at 6 a.m. Fortunately, they had called it a night and were supping on a drink inside waiting for their relief.

Polina knocked on the priest's door with knuckles blue with cold. She did so with a confidence she cannot have felt within but if seen by guards, she did not want to appear timid or out of place. To her great relief, the housekeeper opened the door almost immediately. The woman responded quickly, hoping the Father would not awaken from his slumbers by the rapid rapping on the door. She also feared it might be one of those dreadful Germans, though they rarely extended the courtesy of knocking.

The housekeeper looked up and down the handsome yet shabbily dressed woman in front of her. She noted the visitor's coat was stylish but tatty and what she could see of the garments beneath suggested the ghetto was where she called home. It was not the first time she had answered the door to a Jew in distress. She would not turn this one away either, though she was often tempted in the past. The Good Father made it clear that all comers were welcome. She asked herself for the hundredth time why he would take such risks.

After listening to Polina's request for an appointment with the cleric, she responded precisely: "Please come back at 9 a.m. By then, Father Byla will have awakened, said his prayers and has eaten his breakfast."

Polina pleaded: "But I've nowhere to go, can I at least wait here for him?"

The housekeeper reluctantly agreed, leaving the door to the corridor ajar as she returned to her duties. There was a concession, if she got worried, she could push the door open and wait inside.

As the appointment time neared, German soldiers began walking back and forth past the dishevelled woman. She became increasingly uncomfortable. At the time she was ready to push her way in, the housekeeper reappeared. She led Polina to a large rectangular, sparsely furnished room. In fact, the only item she noticed was a small table on which a telephone sat.

From the reception area, she spied the priest's office beyond. In the anteroom, she saw a tall, lean man in a black cassock standing behind a simple desk, a typewriter perched on one side. He looked up and smiled at Polina, beckoning her with a sweep of his arm to join him.

He said nothing, waiting for her to introduce herself. Here was a careful man, always on the alert for somebody who might be trying to trick him into exposing himself and thus putting a whole network of rescuers at risk.

For once words failed her. After a short, awkward silence, she introduced herself: "I am the wife of Dr. Chaim Toker. I am on my own. My husband is with the Red Army."

The priest, now confident this was no ruse, responded: "I know what happened at the ghetto. We tried to persuade the Germans that we would take care of the children but they would not hear of it."

He studied the paper on his desk for what seemed like an hour before continuing with a single sentence that set Polina's heart racing.

"A little girl was removed from one of the trucks and is now in the care of a couple with good Christian hearts near Kuziai (Kuzh)."

Polina stared at him, thinking he would identify the rescued child. Instead, he suddenly walked around the desk and towards the door. Panic overtook Polina, not caused by the fear of hearing what she did not want to hear but the thought that he may be calling the Gestapo. It made no sense that he would but nothing made sense anymore. She was relieved to hear him shout for the housekeeper: "Marija, Marija!"

He returned to the desk and dashed her hopes.

"Where was I? Oh, yes, the little girl was the daughter of Kron the engineer at Frenkel's."

Before she was able to register her disappointment the housekeeper appeared at the door. She was not that surprised but she had hope until that moment.

Father Byla gestured towards Polina: "This woman is the wife of Dr. Toker. Take her to your room, close the curtains and give her something to eat."

For the next week, Polina stayed at the rectory, under the noses of the Nazis. Marija, who turned out to be the priest's sister, brought food and a whole sack of stockings for Polina to fix! It was a distraction.

She did not see the priest again. She was puzzled at first but her connection with the outside world told her the good father was too busy taking care of business, parish duties and the important job of finding a safe place for Polina.

At the end of the week, another smiling priest showed up at the rectory. He invited her to climb aboard his small horse-drawn wagon. He was Father Adolfas Kleiba, the Ragauskas family priest at the Holy Virgin Mary mission church in Kuzh. The tall, balding priest, with the misfortune to share the forename of Hitler, introduced Polina to his household as a new maid. She was the wife of a Lithuanian military officer exiled to Siberia, he told his helpers. They did not believe him but decided to play along.

Polina felt safe in this caring household among a ragtag bunch of fellow Jews also rescued by the jovial priest, who was unafraid of taking any risk to perform what he believed was his Christian duty.

JUST AS IT was in the Krons' household, playing cards was also a popular pastime outside of the ghetto. There was little else to do socially as the occupiers looked with suspicion on any gathering. Every week, Antanas and Ona would travel by cart for three miles to play cards with Father Kleiba.

Ona's 22-year-old brother Leonas, a strong young man who worked on the railway, would give his beloved sister a break by taking care of Ruta and his niece for a few hours on Sunday evening.

On one occasion, three weeks before Christmas, the couple wrapped up warmly and made their way to Kuzh for the social highlight of their week. Ona was shocked when a familiar face, but one totally out of place, opened the door to the old farm estate house. The couple walked in quietly, Ona unable to take her eyes off the woman. The priest greeted them warmly as always and introduced his latest 'guest'.

"This is Polina. Her husband is a military man and was exiled to Siberia by Stalin."

Ona smiled and the priest knew his cover story was not convincing. His face reddened a little.

"We have met before," said Ona, turning directly to the bemused woman, who knew she should know this woman but could not quite place her.

"Your husband is a wonderful man. He told my sick aunt in Radvilishok that she had a very serious bout of influenza and would die if she did not go to the hospital! He took her there in his own coach and he saved her life."

It was Polina's turn to blush. Father Kleiba chuckled. He should have known better than try to keep his guest's identity from this young couple. However, his belief was that what they did not know could not hurt them in the event of questioning by the Nazis.

Polina thanked Ona for her kindness in recognizing her husband's dedication to his patients. Ona noticed Polina swallow uneasily as though trying to remove the lump in her throat. Tears welled up in Polina's eyes.

Father Kleiba relieved the awkwardness of the moment.

"Come now, let's have tea and get down to the business of the evening . . . a friendly game of cards."

As they moved into the other room, another familiar face appeared but this time it was no surprise.

"Father Lapis it is so good to see you," said Antanas, clasping the right hand of the priest from St. George's Church in Shavl.

Lapis was a tall, handsome man with an easy manner. If he had not chosen a celibate life – he would deny he did the choosing – there is no doubt the women of the parish would have considered him a catch.

The Jesuit priest was an extremely important person in the loose network of rescuers in the region. There was nothing formal about the organization of mainly church people but the likes of Lapis always seemed to know who to go to for help.

Lapis was also skilled at forging birth and baptismal certificates. He would provide documents impressed with an official seal for completion, often using names of deceased children whose age matched that of the Jewish child. The baptismal forms bore the names of fictitious priests or even deceased priests. If a birth certificate were needed, an insider at the records bureau assisted him.

Lapis was all business on those occasions but tonight he was there just for fun. For the next couple of hours the card players dealt and bluffed, with no wager at stake. As the evening progressed, Polina retreated to the corner of the room and Ona excused herself from the table. Nobody heard, as the men's laughter drowned out her good manners. Father Kleiba noticed. He was grateful for her intercession. It was so hard, as a man and especially as a priest, to talk to Polina about her tragic loss. Kleiba would comfort his flock with the message of the scriptures. However, what use were Christian platitudes to a daughter of Abraham?

Ona talked quietly with Polina about Adute's capture. She bit her lip when the distressed mother explained that she had only recently discovered that the child saved in the Kinderaktion was Meyer Kron's daughter and not her own Adute as she had long hoped. Ona was not about to reveal that she was Ruta's rescuer.

The two women spoke in no more than a whisper. Ona thought she had said the right things. She explained how she too lost a child and that made her even more determined to rescue any child she could.

The conversation ended with Polina sighing: "You could have taken my child."

Polina seemed to have taken some comfort from their private conversation. On the way home, Antanas asked what she and Polina discussed. She told him in some detail but omitted Polina's final words.

THE NIGHT OF playing cards at Father Kleiba's three days earlier put Ona in the Christmas spirit. Though ingredients were hard to come by, Ona was determined to do her usual festive baking. She spent a large part of the day before scouring the stores and the pantries of family, friends, and neighbours.

"Oh my, we don't usually get those tasty sližikai until Christmas Eve," remarked Antanas as he watched his wife and Ruta mixing up a batch of the cookies in separate bowls.

"How do you know that's what it is?" Ona quizzed.

"Well, the first clues were the poppy seeds Ruta has managed to spread across the table top and the second was the flour moustache she has. I won't ask where you got the seeds in the first place."

Ruta looked at him, not sure as to whether he was reprimanding her or not.

"We're making sweet biscuits," she said, trying to win him over with an equally sweet smile.

"Yes, I can see, my little one and I'll bet they taste good," he replied.

"Not that you will taste before their time," teased Ona.

Antanas feigned a hurt expression.

"Tomorrow you can try mine, papa Antanas," offered Ruta; now certain she was back in his good books.

"This is Ruta's first Christmas with us and I want to make it memorable," advised Ona.

Antanas laughed, his head falling to one side.

"Have you heard yourself?" he asked in a mocking tone.

Knowing exactly what he was getting at, she swiftly responded: "Well, yes, but there's no reason why Ruta shouldn't enjoy Christmas with the rest of us."

This part of the conversation sailed over Ruta's head. Ona's voice lost its jovial tone when she quietly observed, "Only God knows how many she will spend with us. Let's start off the right way, at least."

"Quite right, quite right, quite right," agreed Antanas, his voice trailing off with each repetition.

The latter remarks were also lost on Ruta, who promptly dug deep with the ladle and helped herself to a dollop of the mixture. The treat was unbaked, but it sure tasted good to the little Jewish girl, for whom Christmas was a completely new adventure.

The lighter banter returned with the comical sight of a child with a face caked with biscuit dough. It was just like a normal day in peacetime. Just as Antanas finished dabbing the remains of the ingredients from Ruta's face there was a sharp knock on the side door.

Ruta knew what to do and headed for the closet, while Antanas went to open the door. Ona checked to make sure there were no giveaway signs of them having one more youngster than they were supposed to have. Grazina just gurgled in the corner playing with a felt dolly.

Antanas was surprised to discover it was not a neighbour or member of the family but a beautiful young woman. She was tall, blonde-haired and he guessed in her early 20s.

"My name is Olia and I have been told you can help me," she announced, the words tumbling out before Antanas could say anything.

Antanas puzzled as to why a confident, well-dressed, young girl like this one would need their assistance. Curiosity and courtesy, probably in that order, demanded he invite her in.

He beckoned her to follow him through to the kitchen where Ona was removing her apron in anticipation of greeting a neighbour. She tried to hide her surprise by instantly pulling a chair from beneath the table for the girl to sit on, as though it were a common occurrence to receive uninvited guests. Olia thanked her politely and sat down as Antanas introduced her.

The young woman began the lines she had practiced all the way from Radvilishok, where in better times her father operated a successful shop that satisfied the hardware needs of all of his many customers, Jews and Christians alike.

"I need somewhere to hide. I am Jewish and my parents are gone."

Olia did not say where and neither Ona nor Antanas asked. It was self-evident they were shot in one of the early roundups.

She did not say who had referred her to them, which worried them. Was this a trap? She looked like a Gentile not a Jew.

Maybe she had encountered one of Father Kleiba's new 'helpers' while they worked in the fields. After all, he had directed his Jewish guests to go there in the event of an emergency. Surely though, they would have sent her to Kleiba first and he would have contacted them ahead of time.

It occurred to Ona that as Polina was also from Radvilishok she would know the girl. Maybe she sent her to them. She puzzled why, then, the girl did not use Polina's name if that were the case. Oh, what she would have given to have Polina there at that moment. She would have known if the girl was a fraud. They would have to go with their instincts.

"We really have no room," cut in Ona, who was wary of attracting any more attention to the schoolhouse.

"Oh, please, I won't take up much room. I will sleep anywhere. I will be helpful around the house. Besides, I speak Lithuanian very well and no one will think I'm Jewish."

A little arrogant too, thought Ona, sizing up the self-confident young woman. Nevertheless, Antanas wanted to help. Ona looked at him. That was her Antanas, never one to turn away somebody in need. He was a good judge of character and clearly believed the girl's story. What was she thinking? For better or worse, the two of them would make it work. Maybe a lot of this girl's boldness was mere bravado.

Zophia was more accepting of the new lodger. Maybe she spotted a potential ally in Olia. She welcomed her warmly and told her to consider herself part of the family. Ona cringed.

Ona went for the closet door. Olia was visibly shocked when out stepped Ruta. She took an instant dislike and did not attempt to hide her animosity. Yes, she would be a good ally for Zophia.

"Who is this?" she asked, clearly flustered.

"This is Ruta," explained Ona.

Ruta performed a little curtsey out of a desire to impress this stranger but Olia was very much unimpressed.

"She's Jewish," said the newcomer, stating the obvious.

"And she sounds Jewish."

It was as though she was thinking aloud, unwittingly giving voice to her fears, thought Ona. Surely, somebody would not be so rude after spending only ten minutes in the household. Well, that confirmed it anyway. This behaviour convinced all doubters that she was on the run. An undercover agent would not have voiced such concerns about Ruta.

Ona eyed Zophia, half expecting her to nod her head in agreement and add a few not so well chosen words to add fuel to the fire. No, Antanas was there, so she would doubtless save any comments for a quieter moment with Olia, out of earshot of the rest of the household.

"She could get us all killed," the young woman sneered. No sooner had the words left her lips, than she realized that in pointing out these obvious dangers she might have jeopardized her own place in this hiding place. Her next words were somewhat more conciliatory

"I'm sorry. I do not know what came over me. I'm just so frightened."

Zophia felt there was no need for any apology; she could not have put it better herself. However, she bit her lip. If she must sleep under the same roof as one of those people, she would rather it be Olia, or whatever her name was.

Olia began to sob but Antanas stepped in to ease her fears.

"Ruta is learning to speak Lithuanian as well as you do. You will be safe here."

The Luntzes were far from safe. Within days of their escape, somebody had betrayed them. The Gestapo arrested them and imprisoned them in the red brick jail.

Berta and her mother Eugenia Nurok shared a cell with 20 others considered criminal by the Nazi administration. Doubtless, under any authority, most of the inmates would have earned their incarceration. There was the odd accused communist, but most were thieves and prostitutes. Joseph was enjoying similar company in the male section.

To the women's great surprise, Father Lapis appeared at their cell door one morning, grinning and offering a freshly baked loaf to them.

"Thank you father but you must take half and give it to my husband," said the ever courteous and polite Berta.

"No, no, this is for you, he has already been taken care of," he said, looking over his shoulder briefly before leaning in to the bars of the cell.

"If there is anybody specifically you should wish me to tell where you are I will do so."

Wulf and the Judenrat should know but this would not be news to them because the grapevine was already vibrating with the news of the Luntzes' capture.

The guards were kind to the family; doubtless Dr. Luntz delivered some of their offspring into this world during happier times. The two women went to the sewing workshop each day where they worked alongside their cellmates, who also seemed to respect the Luntzes and left them alone. Through the prison infirmary, Berta even managed to get messages to and from her husband.

A feeling of unease began to swell to virtual panic in the women's section one day as one by one the occupants observed what was going on through the cell windows. They could see their captors loading male prisoners onto trucks. They would face a firing squad and that story was soon circulating the jail, courtesy of the least kind of the guards. Berta wondered if Joseph was among those executed. The guards were not so free with that information.

A couple of days later, the two women moved to a part of the prison full of Jewish women. Fear and the continuous recitation by their fellow inmates of the Psalms kept them awake all night.

In the morning, a woman jail supervisor approached their cell and asked, "Why don't you smile?"

Berta and her mother's faces remained blank.

"Soon you'll smile, because you will be taken back to the ghetto."

She left without further explanation, her keys jangling as she disappeared down the corridor. The two women did not believe her: she was either teasing them wickedly or trying to settle them down until their date with destiny arrived. Either way, they wanted this mental torture to end. A few hours later, the guards put them out of their misery. The Luntzes and sixteen other Jewish prisoners transferred, not to the forest, but to the ghetto jail.

They were later ushered into a room where sat a fuming Schlöf. He ripped into the three of them with such ferocity, the women again feared for their lives. Making an oblique reference to the rest of the ghetto residents, he began by stressing their importance in maintaining orderliness:

"What should the soldiers do if the officers run away? You are important in ensuring the welfare of your community and your place is here."

Schlöf continued in that vein for some time but the more he said the less convinced they were that he was sparing them for the good of the ghetto. He told Berta she could repay the people of the ghetto for abandoning them by sweeping the streets. The calluses had barely begun to form on the new street cleaners' elegant hands when the real reason for their pardon became clear. Schlöf summoned Dr. Luntz to attend his home to examine a woman and confirm her condition. That done, Schlöf demanded Dr. Luntz perform an abortion.

"I cannot do that," he responded nervously.

Schlöf sneered: "Why? You were not so reluctant when you and Dr. Peisachowitz terminated the lives of dozens of little Jews in the making."

The gentle doctor countered, a shade more assertively: "According to your regulations I am permitted to perform such procedures only on Jewish women."

Schlöf's expression changed to the thunderous look they saw back in the cells some days earlier. He repeated his order, making it clear he would brook no further opposition.

This was his mistress. She was the superintendent of the military hospital. The abortion was urgent because she had just learned that her husband, an army captain, was about to get some leave and reunite with her after a year apart.

On December 20, 1943, an SS staff car whisked the Luntzes and Wulf out of the ghetto to Schlöf's abode. The doctors performed the abortion on the dining room table.

The smirking German handed Luntz his fee – a parcel of food. The Jewish gynaecologist handed it back and left the Kommandant with these words to ponder.

"My fee will be my life and the lives of my family, which you have granted me."

Schlöf could not be sure whether this Jew before him was referring to his recent act of clemency or one expected in the future.

CHAPTER SIXTEEN

No safe hiding place

The Schoolhouse - Christmas Eve, 1943

R UTA'S NEW FAMILY CELEBRATED Christmas as grandly as they could in a time of such scarcity.

Christmas Eve is the time Lithuanian Christians celebrate the coming of their Lord and Saviour. This year it coincided with the start of Shabbat but this little Jewish girl would spend Friday evening enjoying the spirit of Christmas.

The day was one of comings and goings, visits from Ona's parents Ona and Juozas, and her two brothers Vacys and Leonas. Leonas was Ruta's favourite: the skilled carpenter had carved a doll for her.

December 24 is the shortest day of the year in Lithuania and therefore visitors ensured they were home before night descended. All were most anxious not to take the risk of running into a trigger-happy German patrol.

Ruta watched anxiously as the mound of baking that she and Ona had lovingly produced in the days before seemed to be disappearing before she got her share!

This occasion reminded Ruta of the Jewish high holidays, when all of her family came around to celebrate. So far, her first Christmas was fun. They all – with the exception of Olia – spent hours that week cleaning, just as grandma did before the Shabbat meal. By the time they all sat down for dinner, there was not a speck of dust anywhere.

One meat they never ate at a Shabbat meal was pork, for a reason unknown to her. Her papa said Jews do not eat pigs. Maybe she would get to try some soon, though she was not too sure she really wanted it. Antanas and Ona's brother brought a pig home one day and just spread it out on the kitchen table. She watched its slaughter

215

and the way they cut into it and made sausages! However, this day, Ona told Ruta, they would have a special supper – Kūčios – devoid of any meat, as tradition dictated.

Zophia assisted in preparing the food ahead of time. In fact, Ona made the most of it as a way of involving her mother-in-law more in the family.

While Zophia chopped the vegetables, Ona fulfilled another tradition by changing all of the bed linen, with Ruta in tow. Between questions from Ruta, Ona thought how much she regretted the rocky relationship with her mother-in-law. Zophia had lost her husband Adomas to diphtheria 33 years earlier when Antanas was just six. What a cursed disease this was, she thought as she plumped up the pillow on Ruta's bed. Perhaps Zophia's disposition would have been different had he lived. For one thing, they would have lived under a different roof!

As the sky darkened, Antanas drew the heavy blackout curtains and turned his attention to preparing the table for what would be a feast in the imagination but somewhat less in reality.

"Why are you doing that, papa Antanas?" questioned Ruta, who by now had grown tired of watching Ona strip yet another bed, especially as it was the one occupied by Olia.

Antanas was sprinkling a handful of hay over the pure white tablecloth, hay that he thoughtfully secured at harvest time and stored for this family occasion. He turned to face his inquisitor.

She fired another question at him before he could explain this strange behaviour: "Won't mama Ona be mad at you for dirtying the cloth she has just ironed?"

Antanas laughed and knelt down, "No, no, we do this to remind us that Jesus was born in a stable."

"Will I meet him?" asked Ruta innocently. He was tempted to say that Jesus would be at their table that night but decided against it.

"No, not this Christmas, but soon you will come to know him if you wish."

"Yes, I would like that," she said, surprising Antanas a little with her quickness to agree. Ruta was fast learning that it was important to fit in with these people and that meant doing what they did. She was beginning to turn her back on her heritage: being Jewish meant suffering.

Possibly, in a month or so, it would be less risky for Ruta to move among locals and she would be able to go to church with the family. Already her accent was softening and the torrent of questions was testimony to her rapidly improving comprehension of the Lithuanian language.

Of course, that would pose a new challenge: finding a way to introduce Ruta to friends and neighbours without raising suspicions among those that might be disposed to calling the Gestapo in exchange for some bauble or extra food ration. However, that was a problem for another day.

Having finished that job, he extended his hand for Ruta to grab and led her to the bedroom he and Ona shared. He closed the door behind them and ensured there was no stray light shining before pulling back the heavy curtain. The last thing they needed was a police officer knocking on their door to tell them they were breaking the blackout.

He hoisted her up to sit on the windowsill, holding her steady with his right hand. She looked out into the gloom. She could make out only the dark shapes of the trees in the orchard.

"Look up, little one. What do you see in the sky," urged Antanas.

Ruta saw nothing until her eyes got used to the fading light.

"I see the sky."

"Yes, but what do you see in the sky," he prompted.

"Nothing, papa Antanas," she replied, disappointed because she so dearly wanted to please him.

"Over there above the barn," he pointed to a spot immediately above the roof.

"It's a star, it's a star," Ruta shouted with joy, delighted with her powers of observation but more pleased by making papa Antanas happy.

"That's right, little one, and that is the first star of the night and the signal that our supper can begin."

"Oh," said Ruta, now lost in thought. She recalled that night before the Germans came when she and papa lay in the field all night and he pointed out all of the constellations in the sky.

Minutes later, they each took their places at the table for their supper by candlelight. Ruta counted the six wafers that lay on the plate in the centre of the table. She was just checking. She did not need to ask what they represented because she had asked that question when Ona brought them home from the card game last Sunday and unwrapped them in front of the wide-eyed Ruta.

Ona explained: "Little one, they are *Dievo pyragai* – God's cakes. On Christmas Eve they will sit on a small plate at the centre of the table and there will be one for each of those present at our table."

At the time, Ruta seemed satisfied with that explanation and remained quiet until she took a closer look at them and noticed the pictures etched delicately into their surface.

Anticipating her curiosity, Ona continued: "Those are scenes from Bible stories. We are very lucky to have these. Father Kleiba kept these just for us."

The wafers, identical to Communion hosts in shape, were a little stale, as the good father had held onto them for some time past what today would have been referred to as their 'best before date'. That did not matter: it was an honour to receive such a gift for their table.

"Is there one even for baby Grazina?" asked Ruta.

"Yes, even for Grazina, for the Lord loves us all whether we are big or small," said Ona with that smile that so pleased Ruta. That smile told her this woman – her new mama – loved her. She thought about her real mama for a moment and then went to play on the rocking horse made by Leonas for the little boy Ona had lost. Ruta combed and braided the hair of its tail, pressing her cheeks against it. It felt good. It was something she did regularly as she thought about her old life and wondered what her parents were doing at that moment.

Everything felt good here, she thought, except for Zophia and Olia. She put such thoughts out of her mind until Olia took the chair opposite her at the Christmas Eve celebration. Zophia sat next to Ruta, opposite a vacant chair where Ona would take her place after serving the food and securing Grazina in a higher chair next to Antanas, at the head of the table.

"Who are these seats for?" asked Ruta, sitting on her hands, her head bobbing from side to side. She noticed Antanas lighting the candles earlier and wondered why she did not have one. Spread out between them, around the table, were five empty chairs opposite single plates on which small candles burned.

Ona began to explain: "Those are for my mother and father and my two brothers, who cannot be with us tonight because it's just too dangerous to be out at night. That's why they came to see us during the day."

There was no use hiding that sad state of affairs; Ruta was very aware of the dangers that came with the darkness. Ona's voice faltered as she looked toward the fifth chair next to Ruta. Antanas spotted the tear in her eye and finished the explanation for her.

"The chair by you, little one, is for a little one we have lost . . . Rimantas, who was taken from us by sickness to be with Jesus.

We do this to remember him and show to him in heaven that he is still in our hearts."

There was also a tear in Zophia's eye as she silently recalled not only the tragic loss of her grandson at the tender age of three but also of the passing of her beloved husband to the same wretched disease many years earlier.

The war had crushed this time of family bonding throughout the country. There would be many thousands of empty chairs around tables for family members who had died since last Christmas and others kept apart by curfews and other travel restrictions imposed by the Nazis.

Ruta knew a little about Rimantas but sensed this was not a time to ask more. She would learn more in a few short months in a most surprising way. Ona and Antanas both looked at their young guest, knowing Ruta would have wanted to have asked more and appreciating the fact that she did not. Her maturity for one so young continued to amaze them.

Antanas reached for one of the wafers and handed it to Ona.

"Happy Christmas, my dear," he said, staring into her bright eyes.

Then he turned to the rest of his guests: "God grant that we are all together again next year."

Secretly, he prayed Ruta would not be here but reunited with her parents in happier times. It was a silent prayer shared by Ona, who then offered a wafer to Antanas, in keeping with the tradition.

Ruta watched intently as he in turn offered the wafer to his mother and wished the rest of the table his blessings for the Christmas season. Ona followed with a similar heartfelt blessing and then began the exchange of greetings and morsels from each of the wafers by the rest of the table guests.

Ruta caught on quickly. Olia also opted to take part, managing not to show her reluctance. She was not fond of what she saw as pagan rites. The next stage reinforced that belief. Ona reached into the bowl of apples, picked a couple of months ago from the orchard behind the schoolhouse, and began cutting one to produce almost six identically sized pieces.

She handed the first piece to Antanas, re-enacting the fall of man when Eve picked an apple from a tree in the Garden of Eden and urged Adam to eat despite the Lord's order not do so. Just as Adam did, Antanas bit into the juicy piece of apple. The rest of the table joined him, munching on the crispy crop, perhaps the tastiest food of the meal.

Traditionally, the twelve different dishes served represent the twelve apostles. This night they would eat well but not as richly. Other than the Christmas biscuits Ona and Ruta made, most of the menu consisted of whatever food was available. Some herring would have been nice but they made do with some Carp caught in Talsa Lake, near the ghetto. There were also boiled potatoes and dried vegetables, some of which Ona tried to rehydrate just to provide some variety. Oh, how Antanas would have loved some of that kisielius – cranberry pudding – but it was not to be at Christmas 1943. He wondered just how long it would be before they could again enjoy such a traditional feast after a daylong fast. Ruta did not like the look of some of the watery vegetables and shook her head when offered.

"You must, little one, you must have a little of everything," said Antanas in a gentle voice.

Ruta began to sob.

"No, you must," he insisted, a little more firmly.

She screwed up her face and reluctantly obeyed. With every chew, her facial expression soured more as the juice hit her taste buds. She was puzzled because her new papa had never been so forceful before.

As she obeyed, his smile dressed up a look of relief. This is where paganism meets head on with Christianity. The ancient belief is that the person who skips one of the dishes will not survive until the next Christmas Eve. Neither Antanas nor Ona, believed such a superstition but they would take no such chances with their little Jewish guest.

The rest of the meal passed without incident while they enjoyed their meagre rations. Ruta noticed how quiet it was and not just because eating took precedence over conversation. It was a solemn event, not like Shabbat meals. Olia had the same thoughts but did not share them with her fellow Jew – the biggest threat to her life in her mind.

Once finished, they all left the table at the same time and each retired to their room with barely a word spoken. Antanas and Ona stayed up a little later and talked about Christmases past. Both wished they could have gone on to midnight Mass or, as they called it, Berneli miðios – Shepherds' Mass. Christmas might have been seen as something of a letdown as there were no material gifts to exchange but the family didn't see it that way because they had each other and that's all that mattered. It was a priceless gift in these dark times.

❦

Ruta was never happier than when she was in the kitchen with Ona. She never took her eyes off her rescuer and when Ona scooped up Grazina in one arm, Ruta insisted on the other spare arm going around her.

"What shall we do next, my little shadow?" Ona would ask.

"Let's make Gogol Mogol." Ruta would reply most frequently.

"Oh, you always want to make that."

Then Ona would generally search out sugar and eggs to mash together and bake. Ona made an extra effort to trade rations among neighbours just so she could always please Ruta with her favourite sweet dish.

As January passed, Ruta's fluency in Lithuanian improved and those Rs were no longer such a challenge. Ona noted that in her efforts to get her little mouth around those consonants it could look unnatural to an observer. She would have to speak more naturally. That would come.

The sooner the better, as Ona feared the risk of discovery grew every day Ruta remained hidden. A fact she was regularly reminded of by her mother-in-law and her 'other' guest. It was a constant source of friction in the household.

Ona did not know how much longer she could put up with the bickering. She feared the psychological damage it was inflicting on Ruta could be devastating. The little one was clearly aware of the unhealthy atmosphere. In fact, Ruta had asked a number of times: "Why don't Zophia and Olia like me?"

What could Ona say? – To date, she had told Ruta she was mistaken but she could tell this bright child was unconvinced by her assurances. She did not want to continue avoiding a direct answer. The danger was the youngster might begin losing trust in her and lead to Ruta becoming fearful. No, Ruta's wellbeing would not be sacrificed, at any cost.

❦

FATHER KLEIBA HAD JUST finished his catechism session when Antanas appeared at the schoolroom door and dismissed the children.

"Antanas, my son, let's chat for a while," he said, as the final pupils filed out and of the room and headed for the exit into the early February snow that showed no signs of melting.

The rare frown on the priest's face indicated this was not going to be a light exchange. Antanas braced himself for what he figured would be another serving of the daily dose of bad news. He moved a little closer because the priest was speaking softly while impatiently beckoning him to move in.

"The Germans are carrying out surprise searches looking for saboteurs and Jewish children," said Father Kleiba, giving a warning passed on by one of his priestly brethren. There were advantages to Father Byla sharing accommodation with the Nazi administration.

"These things never last long because they quickly lose their element of surprise but I think it would be wise for you to bring Ruta to me for a few nights."

Antanas was about to question why the Germans would target a humble schoolmaster, when his informant revealed something that stunned and frightened him.

"I understand that a 'teacher' in this area has come up as a person of interest. People talk and if they are desperate they talk to the wrong people."

Out of Christian charity, Father Kleiba did not say that talking to the wrong people usually meant the messenger would benefit materially from such a conversation. It was irrelevant anyway.

The priest left and Antanas walked briskly to the family quarters at the rear of the schoolhouse. He was shaking when he passed on the news to Ona.

"We have been so careful," she said, puzzled as to how anybody could have singled them out.

"Yes, but not careful enough," said Antanas. "We should act immediately before all of our lives are at risk."

Zophia overheard some of the conversation, misinterpreting her son's final sentence. She resisted the temptation to repeat her concerns about Ruta's continued presence when he began talking about hiding Ruta at another location temporarily. However, Olia showed no restraint with her comments when she came in a few moments later.

Ona snapped back at the outspoken young woman: "You are like a knife through my heart, Olia."

Olia stepped back, stunned by the sudden outburst from a woman she had never heard raise her voice. Zophia was glad she had kept her own counsel.

"You have to find somewhere else to live. You have papers now and you can pass for one of us."

Antanas had not seen this side of his wife for a long time. He was shocked but he would not intervene because he knew she was right. This girl was poisoning the household. He suspected his mother was not helping matters but they could not throw her out.

Ona continued: "Antanas will arrange for a cart to take you to the woods . . . the people there will find you somewhere else."

She was referring to the resistance bands operating in the forest near Kuršėnai. It would do this girl good to spend a few nights outdoors. It might be the making of her, thought Antanas.

Olia argued for a few minutes but realized she was getting nowhere and stormed out of the room to gather her belongings. Antanas and Ona heard her sobbing long into the night but ignored her. Their lack of response not only surprised Olia but also themselves, both suppressed their natural tendency to forgive and forget. It did not sit well with either of them but this was a time to remain steadfast for the sake of the family and Ruta.

A carter would pick up Olia the next day and transport her to the forest, where she would spend not just a few nights under the stars but the rest of the war with the partisans. The anger of her former hosts subsided and in the days that followed, they dismissed the behaviour of Olia as that of a frightened youngster. Her confidence would serve her well in her fight to survive and she would doubtless become a fine person.

Leonas arrived on his bike shortly before dusk that evening. He planted Ruta on the handlebars and whisked her off to Father Kleiba's via a circuitous route through fields and little used trails. The Ragauskases lay awake for hours, tossing and turning, worrying that a German patrol might have intercepted Leonas and Ruta. They need not have worried.

LEONAS DISMOUNTED before arriving at the rectory gate and performed the delicate balancing act of holding up his trusty steed while removing his passenger from the handlebars. Ruta giggled but stopped abruptly as Leonas pressed a finger to his lips. He passed her the makeshift overnight bag Ona had packed and then led her by the hand to the front door.

Juze the housekeeper opened the door before Leonas could knock. She was expecting them and had stationed herself at the front window, peering from between the drapes looking for the first sign of them. Leonas kissed Ruta on the head, patted her back, and assured her he would be back for her when it was safe. With that, he pedalled off, disappearing quickly across the road and into the field opposite from which they had emerged only minutes earlier.

Ruta had never met Juze before but she felt safe with her, clutching her hand as she followed into the entrance hall. She smiled as she heard the familiar voice of Father Kleiba coming from another room.

"Who do we have here?" he asked in an exaggerated manner as he caught sight of Ruta entering the room.

"It's Ruta," she said, needlessly answering his question.

"So, I see," he said closing a big book that looked a bit like papa's bound copy of the Torah. The other four adults at the table excused themselves and left.

"We will read more tomorrow," he said, distracted briefly from his warm greeting of Ruta. Ruta noted that the two men looked to be of a similar age to her father. The younger of the two women was very pretty, Ruta thought, and, like the second woman, looked like a Lithuanian or a Gentile as her father called them. The second lady reminded her a little of her own mother. She was the last to leave the room and, as she closed the door behind her, she smiled at Ruta.

The smile was soon gone. Ruta made Polina think of her own daughter Adute, who was gone, never to return. She did not ask from where the child had come. She knew better than that, for such information would only be supplied 'on a need to know basis,' to use the terminology of today. The name Ruta was not familiar to her. When Father Byla had told her of the rescue of Kron's daughter, he had not supplied a given name. It would be another 60 years before she learned the identity of the child when she told her personal story of survival to one of the authors of this book.

Father Kleiba flipped the cover of the large Bible, allowing it to fall closed under its own momentum. He was instructing his four Jews in the Christian faith. He hoped they might convert but knew that was doubtful. Nevertheless, he had fulfilled his duty to spread the word and it might stand them in good stead if they must flee and pose as Catholics.

He chatted to Ruta for a while, repeating Leonas's early assurance about her returning to the schoolhouse once it was safe to do so. Ruta liked this man in black frock, he reminded her of the rabbi that disappeared before they moved into the ghetto.

Juze reappeared with towels, bent down, crooked her forefinger and wagged it. Ruta knew what that meant: bath and bed. The housekeeper returned her employer's smile and chased Ruta upstairs. She admired his bravery, though she was a late convert to his mission . . . to the Jews.

When the Jews first started arriving, Juze accepted the father's explanations that they were either relatives or friends of friends. It became obvious quickly that they were Jews devoid of the skills needed to pass themselves off as farm workers.

The scholarly Dr. Juozas Pasvaleckis was a gentleman in the truest sense of the word but his fellow workers in the field thought of him merely as a useless fool. They were the fools, she thought. She was reluctant to admit to herself that she too had told the Father how useless was "this labourer from some God-forsaken corner of Byelorussia". She felt herself blush as she recollected using those words.

"May God forgive me for saying that and taking the Lord's name in vain," she said aloud.

"Forgive you for what?" asked Ruta, as she wiped soap bubbles from the area of her mouth.

Juze snapped out of her thoughts: "Oh, nothing . . . I was just thinking out loud about something."

"How do you do that?" countered the sharp youngster.

"What?" the confused housekeeper asked.

"Think out loud."

"It's just an expression."

Ruta decided this line of enquiry was unlikely to bear fruit so she abandoned the questions and played quietly with the sorry looking rubber duck Juze had given to her.

Juze returned to her thoughts about the doctor as she dried off Ruta and pulled a vastly oversized nightdress over her head. He had almost given himself away to his co-workers with his practice of bathing every morning.

"Why all these ablutions like some kind of Jew?" asked one labourer, who intended his smart remark as a good-natured joke. Fortunately, thought Juze, the man never knew how true a word he had spoken in jest.

Others suggested that he was so inept because he was a woman in disguise! The doctor's practice of bathing alone and his refusal to join them in the communal steam bath at the end of the week's work prompted that remark. Several times, they tried forcibly to remove his clothes but by then they were drunk and the struggle was half- hearted. Exposure would not have revealed womanly attributes but his circumcision.

Juze sat by Ruta's bed to make sure the child did not fret and could get to sleep. She grinned when she thought about Judke Levitan, the first to show up at Kleiba's. He was blond and blue-eyed but he could not go out in public because his accent was of the kind only heard in the Jewish neighbourhoods before the war.

It was months before Father Kleiba decided to come clean and introduce Juze to the guest in the loft at the top of the house. The arrival of Jadze, who fled the killing fields of Zhager, and later Polina Toker, began to confirm her suspicions. For a time, Polina periodically snuck upstairs to feed Judke and keep him company.

Now Juze knew all of them and worried about them, especially young Jadze, who never revealed her full name. The massacre she witnessed traumatized her. She never spoke of her experience.

Father Kleiba surmised her would-be executioners left her for dead but she had crawled out of a mass grave after they left. Juze thought that such an explanation was preposterous at first. Then she began to hear similar stories from family members, some of whom she suspected collaborated with the Nazis.

The doctor appeared to have a soft spot for Jadze. The optimistic servant thought there was a good chance that romance would bloom for those two once this mess was over.

Keeping quiet and helping these people was her way of going a little way towards making up for the sins of her brethren. She would have been less hopeful if she had known how many Jews had perished and the role some of her friends and neighbours had played in their deaths.

Now there was this little one. Juze wondered what her story was. She left the room as she heard the soft, rhythmic breathing of a child asleep to the troubles of the world around her.

"Good night, Father," she said moments later, as she popped around his study door.

"Is there anything more you need before I retire?"

"No my child, good night and God bless," he said, pulling off his large reading glasses and giving his baldpate a habitual scratch.

As she climbed the stairs to her garret, as she called it, she whispered to herself.

"No, God bless you, father, for you are more worthy than I of his divine blessings."

She moved in and away from the family home because she felt secure and useful here. Even before the war, she had admired him.

The old church burned down in the first war and he masterminded its rise from the ashes in the shape of an old-fashioned wooden building. It did not match the beauty of the city's churches but it was a holy place and one in which all the congregation was proud to pray.

The next day the household went about its business and Polina took care of Ruta. She volunteered to entertain her for the day. She marvelled at how the bright, playful child had lost her Jewish accent and now spoke Lithuanian well.

LESS THAN 24 HOURS later, Ruta returned to the little schoolhouse. The teacher targeted by the Nazis was not Antanas but a noble fellow in another village. Fortunately, when the Germans arrived the youngster was spirited away to the safety of another hiding place. That child would remain there for the rest of the war, as it was clearly too risky to return to the original rescuer.

CHAPTER SEVENTEEN

History repeats itself

The Schoolhouse – February 16, 1944.

THROUGHOUT LITHUANIA, PEOPLE NORMALLY celebrated this day of their nation's independence, proclaimed back in 1918.

In the privacy of their homes, they could now only remember the freedom they once enjoyed, for now independence was but a distant memory. At first, many saw the invading Germans as an opportunity to regain that independence from the Russians. Others relished their arrival as a chance to seek vengeance on the Jews. They were convinced their Jewish neighbours had formed the mainstay of the Russian tyranny.

In the schoolhouse, there were no such nationalistic thoughts. This day a year earlier that Ona and Antanas had buried their first-born, Rimantas.

Neither of them recognized the symptoms of diphtheria. Antanas had been only a child when his father died 30 years earlier so he had no specific recollections. His mother had figured at that time that the nagging cough, sore throat and resulting difficulty her husband had in swallowing were merely the symptoms of a fever. In this baby's case, Rimantas did not exhibit the same signs; the red blotches on his baby's skin were no more than a rash to their eyes.

Diphtheria is a highly contagious disease but miraculously spread no further than the little tyke's bedroom. It could have taken the lives of all of the schoolchildren Antanas taught.

"It will not strike here again," said Antanas, comforting his weepy wife in the kitchen. "Grazina is healthy and so is Ruta."

Ruta stared at Ona. She had not seen her cry before. Ona could see her tears were troubling the youngster. She dried her eyes and sat herself alongside Ruta. Ruta soon had the answers to the questions she had withheld at Christmas.

WHEN THE RED spots appeared on Ruta's throat a few days later, there was no doubt that history was repeating itself. How she could have possibly contracted this disease was a mystery to them and one that would remain unsolved. Perhaps one of those in hiding at Father Kleiba's home, where she had taken temporary refuge, was a carrier.

Regardless, a doctor had to diagnose Ruta's condition properly. If their suspicions were correct, she would have to receive treatment quickly. Ona would never forgive herself if she lost another child. Ruta narrowly escaped certain death at the hands of her sister's ruthless captors; now an invisible natural killer threatened her.

They could not run the risk of calling in a local doctor for fear of betrayal. Leonas cycled over to see Father Kleiba, who dispatched Dr. Pasvaleckis instantly to confirm their worst fears. Once diagnosed, Ona pedalled to the hospital in Shavl to see Wulf.

"Return to me tomorrow and I will have the serum for the doctor," said Wulf. "He will know what to do. I will give you the syringe he needs to administer the anti-toxin."

Ona just nodded, she was in a daze. Words such as serum and anti-toxin meant nothing to this simple woman. She would risk anything to save this child. So would Wulf. He had saved her life once before and was not going to allow a mere disease to take her now.

Meyer's shopping list during the start of the Russian invasion was now looking inspired. While everybody was rushing around like headless chickens emptying the store shelves of food, his beloved cousin's shrewd husband sought out razor blades and diphtheria serum. Meyer might have suggested it was just a wise precaution and his accomplishments demonstrated such a claim was not boastful. It did not matter whether it was good luck or good planning; the means were at their disposal to cure Ruta.

Wulf headed back to the ghetto to pick up that lifesaving little vial. Meyer fell to the floor in prayer, on hearing the news. Ever the pragmatist, Gita went to their hiding place, a cool spot, and retrieved it. It was among the last of their treasures stored behind the sink, but it was more valuable than any gold baubles bartered for food. Neither man expressed any fear it might be ineffective because of its age. It was Ruta's only hope.

DR. PASVALECKIS ADMINISTERED the treatment and Ruta was confined to bed for three weeks. All prayed it had not lost its effectiveness. Ruta was in a feverish, delirious state during the days that followed. Ona would mop the youngster's brow, soothing her with the gentle words of the caring mother she was. As she did, she prayed for the young life in her care and asked that her daughter Grazina not catch this horrible disease. It was on one such quiet occasion that she heard a gentle tap on the side door.

What should she do with Ruta? Antanas and his mother were out and she was alone with the two children. It could be somebody with an important message for Antanas from the education authority or delivering a warning about impending danger. The knock on the door had to be answered. She closed the bedroom door quietly as she left, continuing her silent prayer, asking that the visitor be either a friend or neighbour.

She was shocked to see Meyer. She ushered him in, looking up and down the street to see if her visitor was attracting any unwelcome interest. He apologized for surprising her in this way and explained he was doing an offsite errand related to his work. His senior position at the factory placed him in the 'trusted' category and enabled him to leave unescorted sometimes.

Nevertheless, he took a big chance in straying so far from the railway station where he claimed to have business concerning a regular shipment of chemicals that in the past had been delivered to the wrong location. There was no need for any explanation or apology. Ona guided him to Ruta's room.

"My Ruta, how are you?" he whispered into her ear. Ruta stirred, her eyelids flickered, but she did not awaken. Her peaceful breathing was enough of an answer and he left confident she was on the mend.

"I will come again whenever I can," he said as he made off into the darkening late afternoon. It was a promise he would keep a few more times before he ran out of excuses to leave his post. Ona wished him well.

One night a week or so after Meyer's appearance, Ruta awoke with a start to the sound of a persistent tapping on her bedroom window. She was frightened but sat up in bed, her little heart pounding. Through blurry eyes, she looked up at the frozen pane of glass. A small patch in the centre began to melt. Something she could not make out on the other side appeared to be rubbing it in a circular motion. As Ruta's vision cleared, the moonlight beyond illuminated what was now clearly a hand wiping the glass. With each movement, the ice and snow that obstructed the view from both sides of the window melted away.

Ruta was now more curious than frightened. Within moments, the hand moved out of sight and a familiar face replaced it. She was staring at her mother. Their eyes met and Gita greeted her child with a smile warm enough to melt the rest of the ice. As a larger area of the window cleared, Ruta again saw the hand but this time it was shaking a string of coloured glass beads. The beads knocked against the windowpane and the moonlight caught them as they rotated, sending flickers of colour into the darkened bedroom. The heavenly body also illuminated the carved wooden cross that swung slowly like a pendulum from the bottom of the Rosary. Ruta was now familiar with this aid to Christian prayer. She had watched attentively as her rescuers used it to worship their God.

Ruta read it as a sign that she had her mother's approval to go to church and become a Catholic. It meant survival for her. She was very wary now of anything Jewish. Being Jewish meant pain and suffering while Catholicism meant safety and security.

There was much talk prior to Ruta's illness between Ona and Antanas about the rights and wrongs of educating Ruta in the Christian faith. They vowed that they would not attempt to convert her or have her baptized without her parents' permission. They conducted much of the conversation on this topic in hushed tones but Ruta missed little of what they said within earshot.

Did she imagine her mother's nocturnal visitation in her fevered condition? Ruta fell back to sleep, with no doubt in her mind.

THE TREATMENT WORKED. Ruta soon recovered and within a couple of weeks, she was out of bed asking questions, indicating that she was on the road to a complete recovery. When she ventured into the kitchen she spotted the Rosary her mother brought, hanging by the fireplace where the flames lit up the beads as it flickered in the draft. It was tangible confirmation that Ruta really did not need.

Gita had removed her star and left the ghetto in the usual way as part of a work group a couple of times to see how her surviving daughter was progressing in her recovery. On the last occasion, she had brought the Rosary given by a Catholic friend before the move to the ghetto. She knew it would come in useful one day. She and Meyer had talked at length about how they must allow their daughter to blend in by learning to be a Catholic, even if that meant losing her to another faith.

PRIOR TO THE diphtheria scare, Ruta's rapid-fire examination of Ona about every little aspect of her new life was wearing at times even for the ever patient Ona. Now every query posed in her native Lithuanian delighted her rescuer. Ruta's stumbles over the language were no worse than any made by a child her age.

Ona was grateful to her God for ensuring she did not lose another child. It signalled that Ruta was getting ever closer to making her first public appearance, in the guise of a distant relative. At least that was the ruse Ona and Antanas planned to explain away the child's presence. A short time later, that day appeared to have arrived a little too soon for their liking.

Ruta scrambled out of the kitchen before the second knock on the outside door. There was no time to get to her usual daytime hiding place in the closet or above in the attic, so she made for the nearest ground floor room and hid beneath the bed.

No adult would come in, she thought, unless it was a German soldier. The friendly greetings and conversation she heard through the thin wall relieved her of the latter fear. Visiting Ona was Konstancija Gabshevichius, a teacher colleague of Antanas. With her was her three-year-old daughter Giedre.

Ruta's relief was short-lived. It did not take long for the energetic sprite in the other room to become bored with the adult nature of the conversation. The adults were lost in their discussion when the mischievous mite rolled out of their sight into the corridor. She helped herself to Grazina's bright green ball and threw it against the wall. The open door to Ruta's temporary hiding place was irresistible.

Ruta's heart picked up a beat as she heard Giedre enter the room, talking to herself in the singsong way small children do. She proceeded to roll the ball around the room. Seconds later, it bounced off a wall and shot under the bed, closely followed by the little girl. Her eyes almost popped out of their sockets as they met Ruta's equally wide orbs. They looked at each other for what seemed like an eternity for both girls.

Ruta wet her pants immediately but remained silent and frozen to the spot in her shock. Giedre instead hauled herself out of there at great speed, never taking her eyes off Ruta as she retreated. She ran from the room yelling: "Mama, mama, there's a girl under the bed."

Ona and Konstacija's conversation abruptly ended when the whirling dervish burst into the room, knocking the door against the wall as she entered. The little girl's eyes were still wide with wonder and she was bursting to tell her mother of her amazing discovery.

She repeated her claim about the girl under the bed but mama was dismissive. The woman's face reddened to match that of her blushing host. Giedre tugged on her mother's skirt to no avail. Ona thought her friend's lack of response unusual but perhaps her inquisitive daughter had stumbled onto something she should not have.

"Just a moment, mielas," said the child's mother kindly but firmly. "Can't you see we are talking?"

"But, motina, I have seen a girl. I was in the bedroom and I lifted up the sheet. There was a girl under the bed."

Ona's heart sank. Her guest turned to her.

"Ona, I'm so sorry but my daughter has a vivid imagination."

Ona forced a smile. The child continued her tale as Konstancija rose from the chair.

"It's time to go," she said, before even looking at her watch. A social faux pas but not one that would cause affront to Ona, even if she had noticed.

"Do you have to?" Ona politely asked somewhat belatedly and unconvincingly, picking up the child's coat without waiting for an answer. The story Ona hastily concocted minutes earlier about Ruta being a visiting relative would not face the plausibility test that day.

Giedre looked back to the house as they reached the corner on their way home. The girl under the bed was not a figment of her imagination, whatever mama meant by those big words. She slowed as she scrunched up her eyes looking for a sign in the window of the little girl with the dark, bushy hair and big eyes.

"Come on, now," said her mother forcefully, pulling the child round the bend in the road. Giedre slipped her tiny hand out of her mother's and skipped down the street. Konstancija decided against calling her back to her side. All was forgotten.

For the rest of the way home, she thought of other teachers she knew who had taken in children. Ona and Antanas were just the kind of people to rescue a child. She wondered if she and her husband could ever do the same. After all, just like Ona, she thought it would be the right thing to do if the opportunity arose. As she closed the gate, the front door opened and Giedre leapt into the arms of her loving father, screaming as she did.

There was the uncomfortable answer. Konstancija really could not even contemplate such an act with a child as noisy and nosy as her own, who would doubtless expose their secret to the first neighbour she encountered. That would be the death of them all.

BACK AT THE SCHOOLHOUSE, Ona retrieved the sobbing Ruta from her hiding place. She stripped the youngster down and gave her an early bath. Between reassuring Ruta that all was now well, she thought again how remarkable this youngster was. She stifled her cries throughout the period of danger.

Whenever she hid during these trying times, she remained as quiet as a mouse. In fact, that is how Ona and Antanas sometimes explained away to visitors any slight movement made by Ruta when she was hiding in the attic. Most people seemed to accept the explanation but their closest friends were less than convinced by the rodent story, praying no ill would come to Ona and Antanas.

Ona's thoughts then traced a well-worn path of sadness that Ruta had to endure such traumatic events and fear that such experiences would come back to haunt her in later life. Ona would have given anything to be able to treat the whole incident as a fun game of hide-and-seek and encourage the two girls to continue their game while she and Konstancija finished their tea and chat. Her mood lifted instantly as Antanas took her in his arms, dropping one to ruffle Ruta's dishevelled hair with a soft hand.

"So, how was your day, ladies?"

A WEEK LATER, the couple finally decided it was time to introduce Ruta to the world outside the schoolhouse door. It was an evil place at the time, but paradoxically, being able to walk its streets would make it a safer world for her.

"Why are you doing this?" questioned Ruta, as Ona rubbed in the homemade hair dye she concocted from the chamomile that grew in the back by the barn.

"It is time for you to join the family at church and to do that your hair should be lighter in colour so that people don't ask as many questions as you do!"

She laughed as she explained, dabbing Ruta's nose with dollops of the dye. The youngster giggled and Ona gently pressed her head down again over the sink so she could apply some more chamomile into the roots of her hair on her neck. The sink hid Ruta's now more serious expression. She was a little worried about going 'out there'. It was a worry shared by the woman massaging her scalp but she never let it show.

Antanas came home and withdrew a sheaf of papers from his case. Among them was a perfectly forged baptismal certificate for somebody called Irute. It would be easy to get used to calling Ruta by that name in public.

Now Ruta was reborn and she had the papers to prove it to any Nazi or collaborating local bureaucrat that demanded to see something of an official nature to confirm her identity as a good Catholic child. The signature was the same as that which appeared on dozens of other baptismal records, concocted years after the birth of their holders, including Benya Gotz, the last baby born in the ghetto now living and growing up under a new name. It belonged to Father Justinas Lapis, friend and colleague of Kleiba, whose name appeared on hundreds of documents. He was, after all, the parish priest.

THE STORY PLANTED judiciously among friends and neighbours was that Ona had a very sick relative in Kaunas. Ona was Godmother to the woman's daughter and therefore insisted she take care of the child.

The drozhki arrived at the back of the schoolhouse, with a familiar figure at the reins. Ruta was ushered into the back of the cart where she lay still under a large cloth, used to tie down cargo. It smelled of pigs. Contraband pigs if it were anything to do with Jonas Jocius.

Ona climbed alongside the carter and they were on their way to pick up the Godchild. A few hours later, after killing time on the back roads, they returned with Ruta sitting upright in the wagon. This time the cart pulled up at the front and prying eyes from behind curtains watched as Antanas made a show of lifting the child from the cart and hugging her as though he had not seen her since she was knee high to a grasshopper. Among the watchers there were some who would do them wrong if they suspected the new arrival was anybody other than Ona's Godchild.

"WE ARE NOT trying to convert her, Ona, we are making it safer for her to stay with us," rationalized Antanas, in another round of the recurring family discussion about the role the church should or should not play in the life of their little Jewish guest. It was not that Ona was raising any objections; it was just that she felt uncomfortable. She needed reassurance from him again and she sought to justify herself in her response.

"Yes, we must prepare her, because it will be expected that she has seen the inside of a church many times before back at her home in Kaunas."

"I can think of no person better to instruct her," smiled Antanas, "for there is no more righteous a person in this house than you my sweet."

Ona grinned and mockingly swung an open hand in the direction of his face, as if to prove that she was not such a goody two shoes. She was flattered, in truth. This was praise indeed. She had always believed Antanas would have made a wonderful parish priest had he not chosen to explore life's highways with her.

So began Ruta's more focused instruction in the rudiments of the Christian faith and specifically the practices she would encounter in a Roman Catholic Mass. Ruta's natural curiosity made her a good learner. Her desire to survive made her an expert imitator of somebody who had faith in this new Saviour. Maybe she just wanted to believe.

"She is a good prayer," Ona often told Antanas.

"I only ask her to pray for her mother and father though," she would invariably add.

Her concerns about exposing Ruta to the Catholic rituals while her parents were still alive would continue to haunt her. Ruta soon learned every prayer and devotion willingly and enthusiastically. She worked her Rosary beads like any good Catholic child.

∾

IT WAS A chilly but bright Sunday morning in March when Ruta attended her first Mass at St. George's Church in Shavl. There would be many people there so she would not attract undue attention if she made a mistake in her worship. Ruta would go to the family church in Kuzh in the future but not now. There were too few people at the much smaller church where everybody knew everybody else and, more to the point, everybody knew everybody else's business.

The towering figure of Father Lapis caught Ruta's eye as he strode past her in the direction of the front of the church, stopping only briefly to shake hands with worshippers in the pews. He had such a kind face. He winked at her as he went by. Ruta had no idea who he was but the priest knew exactly who she was. Her secret was safe with him.

She took the hands of Ona and Antanas as they made their way to seating at the rear. She heard a little dog-like yelp from Grazina, who followed behind in the arms of her grandma Zophia. She turned to make sure nothing was wrong and Zophia gave her one of the cold stares. Ruta was used to them and ignored them.

Once seated, Ruta's eyes scanned the magnificent structure. She loved the splendid awnings that lined the walls and the colourful glass in the windows. Everybody sat together; men and women. She was too young to attend the synagogue, but mama told her that when she was older she would sit with her, away from papa. If she ever saw mama again, she must remember to ask why that was.

A hush descended on the gathering. Ruta was in awe of the procession that floated as one body towards the altar. The brightly coloured vestments worn by the priest were nothing like the dowdy gowns she had seen the rabbis wear around the town.

So, began Mass of the Catechumens. She craned her neck to see what the priest was doing. He seemed to be messing with water. Ona gently placed a hand on Ruta's leg and whispered to her to sit still. This was not supposed to be the child's first Mass and she did not want to draw attention. Other children seemed bored by the whole ritual, something the bright newcomer observed and thought odd. On this one occasion, Ona would have preferred it if the inquisitive child had appeared as bored as the rest of her peers present that day.

Lapis sprinkled the liquid around the altar. That must be the Holy Water Ona told her about, she concluded. The priest mumbled a lot. How could the people other than those on the front row hear what he was saying? The priest must have been reading her mind, she thought, because suddenly she could hear him clearly and she sat bolt upright in shock. Again, Ona touched her gently, creasing her brow as she did to convey the need to remain quiet and attentive.

"Confíteor Deo omnipoténti, beátæ Maríæ semper Vírgini, beáto Michaéli Archángelo, beáto Joanni Baptístæ, sanctis Apóstolis Petro . . ."

Ruta looked around to see if she was the only one unable to understand a word spoken. Nobody moved. Not even Ona or Antanas batted an eye. Ruta mistook the congregation's uniformly rapt attention to mean they understood the strange words that tumbled from the priest's mouth.

The truth was few among them understood the Tridentine Mass delivered almost entirely in the long dead Latin language, save for a few words of Greek and even a little Hebrew that likely only Ruta among them might possibly recognize. They were not required to understand.

Nevertheless, the service captivated Ruta and she was reluctant to leave with Grazina and some of the other young children when Lapis prepared to say the Mass of the Faithful. It was for the baptized and those who had publicly confessed their faith.

Ona explained baptism was a bit like the Jewish tradition of Bar mitzvah, the ceremony at which boys at age 13 take full responsibility for their moral and spiritual conduct. Ruta was not really any wiser though she had heard her parents talk often enough about such religious practices. In the Roman Catholic faith, Ruta would have been old enough to experience her first Communion at seven.

As Ona returned to take her place next to Antanas in the pew, she thought about her rationale for absenting Ruta from a part of the service so dear to her and her husband. How could she explain the complexity of her reasons to a girl of such tender years when she still felt so conflicted herself about her decision. She smiled at Antanas, who turned to face the front while she continued her inner conversation. It would have been against the practices and traditions of her faith for Ruta to ingest the body of Christ, she had reasoned some days earlier while discussing it with her beloved and faithful man.

Ona's position was rooted in guilt though she would never confess such a reason. She was uneasy at Ruta participating in the rites of a religion whose adherents included so many anti-Semites. They justified their cruel treatment of Ruta's kind as a God-given right to punish Christ's executioners. They even gained succour from the rites for Good Friday liturgy, which described Jews as perfidis – faithless – one of the few Latin words understood well by these people. Even some of the clergy disgraced themselves by siding with the fascists who supported the Nazi occupiers. Ona was devout but the horrific activities of some of her neighbours and some of those ordained as men of God shook her very soul, if not her faith. Thank goodness, the priests known to Ona were saints in waiting, the backbone of the informal rescue network that saved hundreds of Jews.

Ona refocused herself on the Sacrament of the Eucharist soon to follow. In an anteroom, Ruta remained quiet among the other children, disappointed at not being able to share with her rescuers what they called the Bread of Life.

THERE WAS A darker and more worrying side to Ruta's new-found devotion to the Christian deity that would have a profound and long lasting effect on her.

In the quiet of her room, she would stare at the crucifix her mother brought. As she gazed at the figure on the cross, she wondered about her parents. She wanted to see them but then again she did not. She was confused. She missed them but being with them was dangerous. She crossed herself as her thoughts strayed in that direction.

However, ambivalence towards her parents was not the source of her greatest anguish. The mystery of what happened to her sister Tamara and the rest of the children of the ghetto tormented her. She prayed for forgiveness for allowing the Nazis to take her little sister. When nothing tangible resulted, she would blame herself again because she feared her prayers were not strong enough. God, who either did not hear her prayers or just plain ignored them, was punishing her.

She would then slip out of bed, take off her nightclothes and drop onto the floor on her knees to pray. To which God should she speak? Perhaps her Jewish God would be offended that she was on her knees because she knew enough to be sure that Adonai, the God of the Hebrews, did not approve of such gestures. Perhaps that is why her bony knees hurt so much on the cold, stone floor, she thought.

Mama had made it clear to her the night when she crept up to her window during her illness. Despite her tender years, it was obvious to her that by dangling the crucifix she had made it clear that she must pray to the Christian God. Her young mind was very befuddled. She prayed alternately to Adonai and to the new God – Jesus Christ – to whom her rescuers were so devoted.

One night, Ruta decided she must pray harder for longer and ignore the shooting pains in her knees. She believed now that in order for God to hear her she must suffer more. She shook and shivered in the cold, becoming numb as the time passed. Her teeth chattered while tears streamed down her cheeks.

This was the only way she would earn forgiveness, she told herself. No assurances from her own parents or her rescuers would convince her of her innocence. When Ona looked in on her much later, she found Ruta passed out naked on the cold hard floor.

CHAPTER EIGHTEEN

The living corpse

Near Shavl – late February 1944.

IN THE FIVE MONTHS that had passed since the liquidation of the Vilna ghetto, 17-year-old Misha Shabsels had lost all of his nearest and dearest.

At the outset, the Nazis put his mother Golda, grandmother and his sisters Mira and Gita on a train to a destination unknown. He and his father Baruch had been taken immediately to Vaivara Concentration Camp in northeast Estonia and then on to a smaller labour camp. From dawn to dusk, they worked on the railroad and dug anti-tank ditches. They performed this backbreaking hard labour in the harshest of winter conditions and on a daily ration of only 200 grams of bread and vegetable soup.

During the cold evenings, Baruch tried to cheer up Misha, surmising the war was going so badly that the supposedly indomitable German army was in retreat. Clearly, the Germans were expecting a tank-led attack from the Russians.

Baruch was a proud man and once a wealthy member of the community with a large store in Vilna. The tall, handsome blonde boy before him was his rightful heir to this fortune. His heart ached. Maybe after the war the whole family would reunite.

In December, Misha contracted typhoid from bad water; the dreaded disease ran rampant through the camp with its appalling conditions. The teenager recovered quite quickly but a month later, the same enemy felled Baruch and he quickly passed away.

Misha's good looks began to disappear beneath a mask of pain, equal parts mental and physical. The death of his father devastated him. He was alone in life. He did not share his father's optimism about the survival of the women folk in his family.

243

Dysentery was a fact of everyday life in the camp but other ailments sapped away at the youth's depleted reserves of strength. His swollen feet sealed his fate. He could barely hobble from his shared bunk to the latrine. On February 18, there was another of the dreaded twice-monthly selections, during which he and all of the other inmates who had fallen down on the job were weeded out. The next stop was a train platform in a nearby station.

As the cattle car rolled along, Misha looked around at the other people sharing the ride. He wondered if the train was on the same route the women of his family had taken months earlier. He hopped from one pained foot to the other. He was determined not to sit, as he feared he would suffocate beneath the sorry mass of humanity crammed into the carriage.

He distracted himself by trying to count heads. He reached 80 before losing count. Somebody fell to the floor in a heap. Misha wondered how many would leave this mobile cell alive. What a horrible way to die, alone among strangers. Was a worse death awaiting those that did arrive at the unknown destination? Did his grandmother, mother and sisters meet that death he no longer wanted to ponder?

Wherever they were going, it was via a circuitous route. Some children were picked up somewhere along the way. He could hear their wailing; no doubt, they were wrested from arms of loving parents. He contemplated from what monstrous species these persecutors had descended. He had lost everybody important in his life.

The train arrived in Latvian capital of Riga after what he calculated to be four days. Maybe it just seemed to take that long, as it was hard to distinguish between night and day in the current mode of transport. He only knew where he was because the man standing next to him had hauled himself up to an opening at the top of the car. He recognized the station from happier times.

Suddenly, the car was flooded with light. It was not daylight but an array of artificial light reaching into every corner from flashlights. As his eyes adjusted to the dazzle, he could see the controllers of the beams were uniformed men. They were members of the Estonian SS division, collaborators and volunteers for the Reich.

The frantic prisoners cowered and backed still further into each other as though that would save them from those they feared would be their executioners and their snarling dogs. They need not have fretted just yet.

Under orders, they yielded their dead, who were hauled off as they were nought but dead meat. Those lucky enough to continue their journey received a piece of bread and water. The ravenous Misha wolfed his down.

Just before the train began to pull away from the station, he overheard two German guards on the platform say they were going to Auschwitz in Poland. At this rate of speed, they would not be there for another week, he thought. Poland was a great distance from home, he knew that much. Misha was determined he would not be there when the doors opened at this place called Auschwitz, wherever it was.

Many hours later, the train again rolled to a halt. It was time for the train engineer to load up with coal and water for the steam engine. While they waited for service, the hot tea warmed the driver and his breath gushed like smoke into the night as he exhaled. None of his passengers would enjoy such comforts. Bouts of coughing emanating from within the cattle cars broke the stillness of the night. The sounds of long, drawn-out groans also travelled along the tracks to the driver's perch in the engine. These sounds of the sick did not penetrate his inner ear any more.

When the train stopped, Misha figured they must be across the border in Lithuania. To the amazement of those around him, Misha summoned all his remaining strength and tore a loose plank from around the ventilator window. He pulled his emaciated body through the hole. He climbed down on the trackside of the train and leapt towards a pit full of water.

He was so horror struck, the coldness of the water barely registered and he did not even shiver. He remained motionless for what felt like an eternity. That eternity ended about ten minutes after he had caught sight of the train leaving the rural station. He climbed out of the pit on all fours and attempted to stand but he could not. Now he did begin to shiver. The swellings that covered his legs and feet throbbed and rendered him incapable of normal movement.

He crawled almost half a mile, stopping only briefly every few minutes to catch his breath for now he was numb to the pain. He saw a light in a hut and dragged himself there. He must have given the peasant inside a shock when he saw Misha's contorted face in the window, alerted to its presence by a knock on the glass.

Misha recognized the colourful language of the man who dragged him indoors; it was Lithuanian. Why did he feel relieved? Well, he was home, even though there was no welcome mat. The man angrily told him he would not hide him but would allow him to spend the night there. He explained the Shavl ghetto was only about 15 miles away. The man's face wore an expression of distaste as he informed Misha that there he would be able to get help from 'his own.'

It was hopeless. He could not get there without help. In despair, he told the man to hand him over to the police. If the man did not say "with pleasure," his body language did.

Before daybreak, he was in the town jail. For three days, he shared a cramped cell, though not as cramped as the cattle car, with the lowliest of crooks, who left him in no doubt how unfavourably they viewed Jews.

The authorities there handed him over to the Gestapo for interrogation. Despite regular beatings, the young man maintained the story that he did not escape from the train. He claimed, somewhat unconvincingly, that he had been allowed to disembark in order to get water but was left behind accidentally. The interrogators did not believe him. No such courtesy would be extended to the quivering Jew before them.

Misha was taken to the ghetto, where he was housed in a cell normally reserved for the likes of thieves who stole from their 'own kind,' as the peasant would have put it. It was a cellar without a window and offered only a hard plank bed.

A small deputation from the Judenrat arrived with food and some wood for the oven. They too asked him to repeat his story for their benefit. The frightened young stranger could not help but think that they did not trust him. Maybe they thought he was a Nazi plant, put there to learn about whatever they were doing that they should not be doing, under this hard regime.

He was hurt in a way that people of such tender years and inexperience are when somebody casts doubt upon the veracity of what they say. Even his 'own kind' no longer trusted him, he thought, mentally slipping into the same parlance as the man in the hut. He had better start making escape plans.

Dr. Peisachowitz, accompanied by a nurse, entered. The doctor's smile suggested that he was more trusting of the young man from Vilna. The two medics worked on his legs for a long time, removing the temporary bandages applied back in Estonia many days ago. By that time, the bandage material had glued to the wounds. Their painful removal elicited only whimpers. He had withstood much pain in recent memory. Peisachowitz re-bandaged his infected legs and feet and Misha felt immediately brighter and better, risking a smile and a nervous "thank you." Wulf also chanced a smile again, though he too was a little suspicious. He just hid his apprehension better than did the wise but worried men of the Judenrat.

For ten days, the good doctor returned every day to treat Misha's painful skin condition. He diagnosed a bacterial infection called Erysipelas but he did not share that with his patient. All Misha needed to know was that he was getting better.

Peisachowitz brought him a prayer book and a bag with phylacteries and then told him to pray. The doctor's actions led Misha to suspect his end was nigh. When he heard some women talking about a freshly dug grave in the courtyard that was all he needed to hear to convince him of the worst. When the jailor appeared at his cell door, he was ready to scream anticipating his imminent death. Misha was shocked to discover he was moving to the tiny ghetto hospital to undergo intensive treatment. What was going on?

∾

THE JAIL INTERROGATORS HAD made their report about Misha's escape from the Auschwitz-bound train and turned it over to the Nazi administration. Schlöf informed the Judenrat that the young man would be executed once fit. Schlöf dismissed the inevitable plea for mercy.

"You don't understand military discipline. This is an order from higher up which must be carried out," said Schlöf, leaving without further discussion.

Schlöf had other ideas as to what role this group of argumentative Jews would play in the future. However, that was for another day when he had tightened his grip still further on their daily lives.

The council met in private to discuss what kind of bargain they might be able to strike. They would invite Wulf to help because he dealt with Schlöf during the normal course of his duties and the German appeared to like the doctor, or at least was able to get on with him.

When Wulf did their bidding, he got the answer he expected. "I know why you are coming to me," said Schlöf, clearly irritated by Wulf's approach. "Don't waste my time and I won't waste yours. I can't do anything about it."

The SS officer walked across the room, pulled open a drawer and walked back in Wulf's direction armed with a piece of paper. At least it was not a Walther P38, thought Wulf.

"You see, this is an order from the highest S.S. official in Kaunas," he said, pointing at the signature. He handed it to Wulf.

"Here, see for yourself. You read German."

That instant, his secretary interrupted and called him away to take an important phone call. Wulf expected a prompt dismissal but kept his head down peering at the paper. Schlöf hesitated but decided to leave the doctor alone.

Wulf read the order at the bottom, which required *Sonderbehandlung* – special treatment. Wulf knew that to be a euphemism for execution. The method would be left to the recipient of the order. A scribbled note at the bottom, which assigned six SS men to this duty, suggested a firing squad.

Then his eyes went to the beginning of the letter and they alighted on something that fired the doctor's imagination. There was a description of Misha, which noted a distinguishing characteristic – a gold crown on a tooth in the right corner of his lower jaw. A germ of an idea was forming. It was a dangerous idea but one that was irresistible to a born risk taker.

The war was not going well for the Nazis and there was a desperate shortage of vital supplies for the forces at the front. When Schlöf returned to the room, Wulf would use this knowledge to lay the groundwork for a grand deception.

"If the shooting is carried out in public, as was the hanging of Mazovetsky, all the workers will become very nervous and their productivity will fail," said Wulf.

The last four words hit home. The ghetto workers manufactured warm clothes and boots for his fighting colleagues, who faced the ravages of a Russian winter. The hospital in Frenkel's mansion was full of wounded soldiers, some missing limbs not lost to manmade ammunition but frostbite.

After a few moments, he responded: "I must obey orders without question."

Schlöf pondered Wulf's words a little more. "Our local guards will not carry out the shooting. The execution will be performed by six of my men at the airport, away from the eyes of your people in the ghetto."

That was not the concession Wulf was seeking for it benefitted only the Reich, not the ghetto.

Wulf said, "If there is no choice and it has to be done, let it be done quietly."

"Well, that's what I've just suggested," said Schlöf. "How do you think it can be done any more quietly?"

Wulf pounced. "Give me the boy and you will get his corpse."
Not much shocked the SS officer, but this did.
"Are you really serious?"
Wulf did not squirm or prevaricate. There was no point. Just
a simple "yes" was his response. Schlöf took time to weigh the
pros and cons of this strange offer. Wulf's stomach turned over.

The Nazi pursed his lips. "I could not decide such a thing."

Abruptly he left the room, raising his hand to make it clear Wulf
should stay. The confident doctor – perhaps over-confident – told
himself the boy's life was as good as saved.

He would worry about the details in the comfort of his room.
Fifteen minutes later Schlöf returned.

"When can you do it?"

Wulf had to think on his feet.

"Give me a week or ten days, so that I can prepare the other
patients. I will tell them that the young man has a sick heart and
could die at any time."

Wulf was making it up as he talked. Fortunately, it did not
seem that way to the listener. It did not seem to have occurred to
either Schlöf or the superiors that he had just consulted that on
the surface there was nothing in this deal to benefit either Wulf
or the ghetto. Wulf left a few minutes later not knowing whether
to laugh or cry . . . with joy.

Wulf did not intend to do the devil's work. If successful, his
daring plan would save a life though it would jeopardize his own.
Wulf would indeed deliver a dead body but it would not be the
young man from Vilna. It would be a corpse with a gold crown
in its mouth, acquired during some delicate post mortem dental
surgery. Now all he needed was a suitable body.

WULF MET WITH senior members of the council to select
some candidates. Who was near death for there were no bodies currently in the makeshift mortuary? The families of each
person on this 'critical' list would be approached and asked for
their cooperation. Perhaps one would have to be 'helped' along
their way earlier than the Lord had intended. The Judenrat had
played God before, making decisions about the lives and deaths
of individuals for what it considered to be the greater good of
the ghetto.

Every day the Nazis pressed Wulf for a body and each time he stalled. After a week or so, Wulf had to make a choice. Wulf brought his cousin Shmoil Verbalinski, the dentist, to the clinic. Earlier, Wulf had rejected the first patient to die in the clinic. In the spot where Verbalinski would have to put the crown, the dead man had two missing teeth and one broken tooth. A second man who died shortly after was just too big.

Wulf ushered his cousin into a darkened area and pointed to the corner, where a third body lay beneath a sheet. This young man had arrived at the clinic unannounced hours earlier. Wulf explained he had subsequently died of a heart attack.

Wulf did not volunteer the name of the dead man to Verbalinski at the time. In fact, he kept the name secret from anybody but a few Judenrat members for decades. In later life, he would reveal it was the severely disabled son of Moshe Shimser, the carpenter. Arye Krupnik had smuggled him into the ghetto in a coffin shortly after its formation. The man whom Wulf identified as Isaac Shimser appeared normal physically but he had been inanimate throughout his life. The Nazis would have forbidden him entry to the ghetto if they had known of his infirmities, hence his unusual method of entry. Only the family would notice his disappearance. Misha Shabsels would become Isaac Shimser.

MEANWHILE, MISHA WAS feeling much better physically but still puzzling about what was going on. Clearly, the grave in the courtyard was not for him and his death was not imminent from the ailment that was now clearing up. He noticed how nervous the doctor was when he came in. Wulf leaned into Misha and in a whisper told him to get out of bed. He then led the young man to an attic.

Misha was introduced to Verbalinski, who to his amazement told him he was about to have some dental work done. A little ether goes a long way but it was not a painless encounter. His eyes watered but he stifled a scream as Verbalinski removed the telltale crown from Misha. The dentist worked skillfully to ensure his patient suffered minimal discomfort. As he did, he wondered how Misha had held onto the gold crown, given the SS proclivity for removing anything of monetary value from the Jews in their charge.

Verbalinski left the room leaving the young man to nurse a sore jaw. He went immediately to a second room and transferred the crown to the chosen corpse.

Not one to leave anything to chance, Wulf called in a favour and persuaded a former theatre make-up man to work on the corpse. The dead man was some years older than Misha. He soon looked years younger in death. Would it be enough to convince the Germans that the corpse before them was the one on their execution list?

The next day Wulf reported the three deaths to Schlöf and the Kommandant announced his intent to carry out a personal inspection of the corpse.

Suddenly, Wulf was not so confident. He thought about how difficult a situation he had created. As he walked back to the ghetto hospital, he kept repeating some chapters of Psalms, which he knew by heart. He began: "Out of the depths have I called Thee, O Lord" from Psalm 30 – and concluded with Psalm 102, "Hide not Thy face from me in the day of my distress; Incline thine ear unto me; in the day when I call, answer me speedily".

When Wulf had encountered extremely dangerous situations in the past he had read those words from the Book of Psalms many times. Never had he recited those words with such depth of feeling.

Wulf sought the comfort of familiar and sympathetic faces in the office of the Judenrat. Smiles greeted him but they would soon disappear. When he told them that it was mission accomplished, fear smeared their faces. They had supported his plan but did not think even Wulf would be able to pull it off.

One stoic senior member, who had lived to tell the tales of shocking pogroms against the Jews long before the devil's latest incarnation goose-stepped into Lithuania, snapped the tension.

"We should all start saying Psalms," he quipped, following it with a clipped laugh. There was some nervous laughter from around the room but for once, Wulf was not laughing. He was soon out of the door and moving as quickly as his gimpy leg would allow.

SEVERAL HOURS LATER Schlöf arrived with another now familiar face at his side, Forster. A medical student from the German military hospital and two handlers with their sniffer dogs joined them. Peisachowitz had shown great foresight. Prior to their arrival, he had run around dabbing ether over parts of the room to throw any dogs that might appear off the scent of the secret patient above in the attic. A more liberal dose of it may have eased the pain of Misha in his impromptu dental chair but this was a better use for the small quantity Wulf smuggled out of the town's hospital. It worked.

Wulf quickly realized that neither of the senior SS officers nor the young German medic had met their victim. That was good. Their body language and fidgety movements clearly showed they did not want to hang around to carry out a closer inspection. How interesting that these men, who had prematurely shortened the lives of many innocents by their orders and likely had shot others in cold blood personally, were so squeamish around dead bodies. Schlöf motioned the junior medic to go about his business immediately. He went straight for the mouth, peered in and nodded to Schlöf and Forster. Wulf suppressed another smile but a warm glow was burning unrestrained inside him.

"Our business is done, Herr Doktor," said Schlöf, who left without making any further observation.

MISHA SHABSELS COULD not believe his ears when Wulf explained the subterfuge. He fingered the yellow identification card in the name of the dead person, whose place he had taken in life. He broke down crying uncontrollably.

The next day, on a very cold March morning, he was smuggled out of camp to a location many miles away where the truly deceased was unknown. Isaac Shimser was a name he would answer to for the rest of his life, he vowed.

Days later, Wulf decided it was safe to tell the story to his nearest and dearest. Meyer and Gita listened with amazement as he played up the drama, as he so loved to do. He omitted to name the family who donated the body of their dead son. Moreover, he protected young Misha's real identity, referring to him merely as Yitzchok Wilner – Isaac of the Vilna ghetto.

CHAPTER NINETEEN

A day of miracles

The Shavl Ghetto – June 1944

Rumours of Red Army advances during the spring of 1944 met with great trepidation in the Shavl ghetto.

The reported dramatic progress on the battlefield suggested that the Red Army would soon liberate Lithuania. Though the Shavl Jews loathed the governance provided by Stalin, it was a better prospect than that offered by their current masters. Conversely, they recognized that the Nazi retreat would likely signal the closing of the ghetto. The bigger fear was that such an action might go well beyond their mere evacuation.

Meanwhile, there was also apprehension among their captors, whose future wellbeing was also in limbo. The SS took out their frustration on the ghetto inmates, choking the supply of food and laying a beating on anybody that so much as looked at them in the wrong way.

The arrival of Jews in the ghetto from work camps situated near to the front confirmed the advances of the Soviets. The first to arrive were almost 500 exhausted slave labourers from a camp in Joniskis, north of town and close to the Latvian border. They erected fortifications under the direction of the Organization Todt, the Reich's civil and military engineering group, named after its founder Fritz Todt, an engineer and senior Nazi figure.

Shortly after, the infamous Bruno Kittel, liquidator of the Vilna ghetto, arrived by motorcycle. What did his arrival mean? The Judenrat were relieved to see the Gestapo officer leave, leading two trucks bearing the sign 'Mail'. Actually, 50 of the strongest males remaining from the Joniskis camp were aboard. Their assignment was to burn the corpses of their fellow Jews executed at Fort 9 in Kaunas.

The ghetto inmates were also nervous about the direction of the Judenrat. Schlöf grew tired of the meddlesome and outspoken group and though his wish would be to disband the body, it did have its uses. He stripped Leibovich of his leadership and placed Georg Pariser in that position in April 1944. This was the same Pariser, who worked just a little too enthusiastically to encourage his fellow ghetto residents to give up their children during the Kinderaktion. Pariser continued to live in the ghetto with his wife Eliza, their teenage son Hans and four-year-old daughter Inga. Somehow, his youngest survived the Kinderaktion. His wife could have divorced her Jewish husband and have the children declared Aryans, as did other women in her position, but she remained with him. How long he would survive in this exalted position was anybody's guess.

WULF RETURNED TO the ghetto daily with the most reliable information gleaned from conversations with the Gentile doctors, who happily supplied every detail from the BBC foreign language newscasts they listened to in the privacy of their own homes. Wulf also listened alone to the radio in the hospital basement when it was safe to do so but those occasions were now severely limited. He feared somebody observed his every move.

The June 6 broadcast from London told of the massive Allied Forces invasion of occupied France after a daring channel crossing. Hitler was now fighting on two major European fronts and the Soviet offensive picked up speed. The good doctor was bursting to break the news to the Krons and the rest of his family.

Now the time was surely coming for Papa Shifman to make good his escape. Timing would be extremely important and choosing it would depend on a combination of gut instinct and the news from afar, though the latter was fast becoming the near.

Meyer was confident that he and Wulf would have a strong sense of when the ghetto's days numbered in single figures. Both men talked about it and considered the progress by the Russians almost as though they were accomplished military strategists. They figured it was a few weeks away; perhaps July would herald the end.

THE ARRIVAL OF 3,000 Jews from Ponevezh offered more evidence that the ghetto's end was nigh. Most of them were originally from the Kaunas and Vilna ghettos, saved from a trip to Auschwitz only by their ability to carry out tough physical labour. They were sent to Estonian and Latvian camps the previous year.

Among them were also 240 Jewish women from Hungary who were drafted to dig trenches on the Eastern Front. Wulf had a firsthand encounter with three sick members from that particular group. He was astonished that the SS allowed these strangers to be treated for their ailments rather than just shoot them. It was unlike the Nazis to be so humane: there must be an ulterior motive, thought Wulf.

Confirmation came after a few minutes' examination of the three women, who resembled scarecrows in their dirty, ill-fitting tattered clothes. Their ills were relatively innocuous, being more to do with exhaustion and malnutrition, but the patients were of good stock and slave labour was at a premium.

The small ghetto hospital was full but Wulf made space in the reception area for the most feverish of the women. He would place the other two in a larger bed in the same area currently occupied by a man injured at work.

Once the accommodation arrangements were completed, Wulf turned his attention to the sickly woman. He sat on the edge of the narrow bed. There was no room to stand and then bend over to examine her without butting the wall. He gently moved her head from side to side, looking for signs of rashes or growths. He carefully broke away the dirt encrusted around the stubble that poked through her scalp. All the while, she sobbed. It did not seem to be a reaction to pain, he thought. Maybe it was shock or simply relief at being temporarily away from the Devil's spawn.

He stared into her red tear-filled eyes and she stared back, still sniffling but trying desperately to compose herself. The skin hung from her bony hands, which clearly had not always been a feature of this woman. Her hands and arms were criss-crossed with inflamed cuts. Unsightly scabs had formed over half dried, older wounds. She bore all the dreadful hallmarks of hard labour performed by somebody unused to such work. Beneath the grime, he discerned a distinct elegance about her, the way she sat upright, the softness of the skin on her upper arms.

They exchanged no words until Wulf decided to try out the languages at his disposal. He knew she was Hungarian but the language of the Magyars was not familiar to him. He wondered what she was doing in Lithuania. He heard on the BBC news that thousands of Hungarian Jews were in transit to camps inside Poland and Germany. After a few minutes, he tried German, the language of their shared captors.

A change of expression indicated she understood him but perhaps feared she was in the hands of the enemy. He sought to reassure her, explaining he was a ghetto doctor and member of the Judenrat. She smiled a little. It was not one of joy but obvious relief. She was cautious at first; still a little worried that Wulf may be the enemy, despite his acts of kindness.

Wulf gained her confidence and she realized no uniformed men would return while she told her horrendous story. She told how she and her husband Matyi were taken from their hometown of Ungvar and transported to the Auschwitz concentration camp, near Krakow, in Poland. They were separated from their children, Koka and Tibor, whom they never saw them again.

That camp's name had reached Wulf's ears many times in recent months. By now, everybody in the ghetto knew it was the destination of the children, spirited away the previous November. They heard rumours about its purpose but prayed they were just fanciful, wild stories. The woman before him, Reska Weiss, dispelled any doubts Wulf had about what had happened to his little second cousin, Tamara Kron. He would not share the exact nature of what was going on at Auschwitz, as described by this woman, with his cousin Gita and Meyer.

The last numbing blow for Reska was the final separation from her husband at the trackside in Auschwitz. She told how those sent to the left entered the gas chambers. A man that she later learned was the infamous Dr. Josef Mengele sent her to the right. He told her she had good feet and they would serve her well, as they would the Reich.

Thousands of Hungarian Jews were arriving each day to face execution, she revealed in a whisper. The SS spared her and shipped her out a few months earlier to work in camps in Latvia and more recently Lithuania.

Her storytelling came to a grinding halt. It was as though she suddenly thought she was saying too much. Maybe she could not stand to listen to the sound of her own voice telling how she was almost buried alive. Guards had forced her to dig a pit along with a group of fellow captives. Initially, she thought it was for an air raid shelter but soon learned it was her intended grave.

Miraculously, the firing squad missed her. She fainted and fell into the pit and soil fell over her and the corpses around her. Darkness fell and the Nazis' henchmen did not complete their job very thoroughly. Later that night, she crept out and returned to the nearby camp, mingling successfully with the inmates.

Wulf thought she was just tired. He had let her talk uninterrupted for an hour. He got up to go. His mind was racing but he managed to extend a courtesy that came as second nature to him when leaving the bedside of a patient.

"Is there anything I can get you?" he asked.

"Really, I have everything, except my French red wine," she said, a smile creeping across her thin face.

The next day, a nurse delivered a bottle of fine French wine, one that Wulf had hidden in the cellar of the hospital. In later reminiscences, he would explain, with some ambiguity that the wine was intended to "ease my eventual departure." Did that mean from the ghetto or, more chillingly, from this world? He never clarified his explanation but anybody who knew Wulf would think the latter was unlikely, for he was made of sterner stuff.

The Hungarians left by train transport to a destination unknown 12 days after their arrival. Reska found a way of taking the wine with her – to ease her own departure.

WULF WALKED AWAY FROM the Hungarian patient's bedside and straight over to the Krons' home a few blocks away. Gita and Meyer agreed and decided it was time to get papa out. They re-established contact with Barbora and Pranas Jakubaitis and set a date for his escape in a few days.

Meyer enlisted the help of close friend Dov Fabelinsky, who knew every door, window, and gate in the factory. The arrangement was that Meyer would get him out of the ghetto unseen and Fabelinsky would make sure the senior remained undetected while hiding in the factory grounds.

Meyer figured the exit from the ghetto perhaps posed the most risk but consoled himself with the thought that papa looked like the farmer he was and spoke Lithuanian perfectly. The plan went like clockwork. Under cover of early morning darkness between guard shifts, Meyer assisted his father-in-law through the wire.

From there he watched old Shifman move more swiftly than he had seen him move in many a year! He was soon through the small gate that led into a quiet, overgrown corner of the factory grounds. There he would wait behind the bushes for daybreak.

After an hour – the time dragged – he heard a gentle tapping on the gate, which moved only slightly so light was the knock. "Here goes," he thought. A nervous smile on a familiar face greeted him.

The older man blended in perfectly with the passing crowds heading to their various workplaces. He chatted in perfect Lithuanian as they made their way to the Jakubaitis farm. When the safety of his new temporary home was in sight, their pace picked up and under his panting breath he prayed in a whisper for an early reunification of what was left of his family.

FEW PEOPLE FOUND hope in news of the front moving ever closer to them. The sounds of low flying aircraft and exploding bombs nearby created great anxiety. It became very tense as the Jews wondered just what drastic measures the SS would mete out.

Some took desperate chances to escape and paid for their bravado with their lives. Among the fortunate ones was Nathan Katz, who took off with his young wife Sima when an opportunity presented itself. Benya Gotz's uncle Yankl Ton fled too, but his parents and grandmother remained, unable to escape. Yankl's partner Esther Ziv and her daughter Haviva had found refuge outside of the ghetto following the Kinderaktion, aided by sympathetic locals allied with Father Kleiba.

On Saturday, July 8, rumours of the impending dissolution of the ghetto and the marching of its remaining occupants to the forest for execution spread like wildfire.

That day Meyer was working in his lab at Frenkel's. Around mid-morning, while gazing through the window overlooking the gates of the ghetto, he noticed frenzied activity among some young soldiers. They were all young at this stage of the war, he thought, just cannon fodder for Hitler's maniacal folly. He recognized some of them as messengers from the administration.

He went downstairs to check out what was happening. There Fabelinsky repeated the rumours within earshot of other workers. Within minutes, the thousand Jews working there were soon anticipating the worst.

The first part of the rumour was true. The messengers Meyer saw were ferrying communiqués back and forth from the Nazi administration to the Judenrat. The members were ordered to prepare their people to be shipped out by train.

The fiery rumours swirling around made the warm day hotter. Meyer took off his jacket, which contained some money and some documents, including a false passport under a Lithuanian name, and left it hanging in the lab. He put on his work coat with the two big yellow stars - one on the back and one on the front. Then he closed the door and passed calmly through several different departments, heading in the direction of the main gate. Everybody seemed confused, chattering excitedly to each other. By the time he arrived at the front gate, he had made his decision. This was their time to go.

Gita was working in the front area on the third floor. When he appeared there, their eyes locked instantly. Meyer said nothing. His wife understood the situation immediately. She stepped away for a few moments to retrieve the girdle she had hidden, which was loaded with their remaining valuables. She slipped it on and the two of them left without uttering a single word.

On his way over to pick up Gita, he saw Siegel, a senior German staff member, by the gates with a gun in hand as though ready to shoot the first Jew who made a wrong move, which he would later do. They slipped through a corridor to another area that bordered the orchard that surrounded old man Frenkel's original family home.

The new controllers of the factory were unaware that a small door, hidden beneath brambles, provided a connection between the factory and the garden. In happier times, the original owner tripped back and forth between his home and the prospering business next door. Fabelinsky knew of it and so did Meyer, who had a key made for it.

As Meyer and Gita made their way to the door, they heard shooting in the compound as people tried to get away. They each guessed it was Siegel and the German guards opening fire. They stopped in their tracks.

"Should we go back to my lab and pick up my coat?" asked Meyer, speaking for the first time.

"There's no time. We have to go now," Gita responded without hesitation, already stepping away, tugging on his hand.

As they approached the gate, Meyer noticed friends, Bertha Pochmil and Naum Gold, at his shoulder.

"Quick, quick join us," invited Meyer, after overcoming the initial shock of seeing them almost breathing down his neck.

"No, no, we have to return to the ghetto to pick up something," said Bertha.

Meyer was speechless. They could only be returning for valuables to barter. How foolish, he thought, and they would discover that to their great cost within the hour. A cost immeasurably greater than the value of any trinkets they would retrieve from the ghetto.

Meyer had a pocket full of loose keys and miracles, apparently. He pulled out the correct key instantly. Meyer would use the word miracle many times when later describing that day's events. At no time was its use an exaggeration.

They passed through the gate and entered the now overgrown garden where they discarded their work clothes bearing the Star of David, a mark they were determined never to wear again.

That was the easy part. Now they must pass by a sentry at the gates. As they neared the entrance, a little boy appeared and threw a ball to the soldier standing guard. By force of habit, the young German kicked it back to the boy. During that split-second distraction, Meyer and Gita hurriedly passed through the narrow gates. Another miracle.

Their hearts were pumping hard as they began to cross Vilna Street. They almost stopped beating as both saw an open top German staff car approaching them. They froze in the gutter, only a step away from the curb. There, large as life in the front passenger seat, was one of the German directors. Kaiser and his chief tanner made eye contact. Kaiser was one of the two Germans in charge of the factory, the other one being a nasty specimen by the name of Reinert. Meyer respected Kaiser and clearly, the feeling was mutual because as the car passed them, Kaiser turned his head away and distracted the driver, who would surely have recognized Meyer. Another miracle, thought Meyer, who prayed their luck would not change now.

Gita was white. Meyer was shaking. They picked up their step and their hearts picked up a beat. They glanced at each other incredulously, squeezed each other's hands and crossed the rest of the way.

They walked into the adjacent field, where the grass was parched and browned by days of exposure to the hot summer sun. Down the hill that lay before them and across the field was the house where Jocius lived. They doubted he would be there but his wife might be and she would help any way she could; they were confident of that.

They dropped out of sight from the street as they descended the slope. Meyer smiled broadly. It was not in response to their good fortune but rather the recollection that he once feared Jocius would be his nemesis rather than the saviour he turned out to be. No sooner had he finished that thought than who should appear within their eyesight? Galloping towards them, aboard a horse drawn buggy was the man himself!

Jocius had returned early from one of his little forays out of town in search of good produce for his black market dealings. He was sitting with his feet up pondering potential profits when he was jolted from his daydreams by the shots fired near the ghetto, a short distance away. The moment he exited the front door he spied his friends crossing the road; he would recognize their familiar outlines from any distance and especially Gita's blonde hair. The horse was out and harnessed so he leapt onto it and headed in their direction.

The Krons wore no jackets and truthfully had no need of outer clothes given the blazing sun. However, their worn attire was a giveaway. After brief greetings, Jocius thrust light peasant's coats into their hands and gestured to put them on and quickly. He also gave Meyer a gun. Meyer gulped but made no protest and thrust it into his pocket.

Jocius voiced his next order: "Let's go!" His passengers scrambled towards the back of the cart. Gita had springs in her heels and did not need much of a hand from her husband to get aboard. Jocius tugged at the reins and yelled at the horse. The cart took off back towards the road. The horseman could see that his choice of route surprised the couple.

"Everyone will be running out of the city. Let's turn into the city." Police stopped them twice along the way across town but they were just routine cursory checks by men too hot and bothered to ask more than the simplest of questions. Besides, none was expecting to find anybody running away . . . into the heart of the town. The Krons decided earlier that if they were able to get away, they would go to where Papa Shifman was hiding. They offered directions there to Jocius once they hit the town centre. He took a route across town where the roads were now quieter, with little traffic in evidence. Jocius steered the cart off the paved roads and began to follow country tracks towards the farm. He slowed down so as not to attract unwelcome attention. As they passed other carts heading in the opposite direction, the threesome took time to smile and wave as country folk do.

It was a beautiful summer day and the wheat was high in the fields, a day that makes one glad to be alive. Gita thought that under any other circumstances she would be preparing for an after-work family picnic.

The cart bumped to a sudden stop. Jocius suggested they get out and wait in one of the wheat fields and then head to the farm nearer nightfall to avoid nosy neighbours. The Krons agreed it was a wise precaution and jumped down. Gita this time accepted a hand from Meyer to step down. Jocius would go ahead and warn Barbora and Pranas that they were on their way.

Meyer and Gita crept beneath the wheat in the direction of the house as planned. Then they would just make a run out of the field and to safety at the appropriate time. They felt safe now and had no fear of betrayal. The brother and sister needed to keep them all alive if they were to receive their reward: all of the property owned by Papa Shifman.

They were perhaps being over cautious waiting for nightfall, as the nearest neighbours were more than a stone's throw away. Once alerted by Jocius, Barbora sent her brother out immediately to find them. Before they got much closer to the farm, the Krons heard him coming in their general direction across the field. However, they feared it might be someone else working in the fields or perhaps even a German officer.

Thinking quickly, Gita stood up in full view of the approaching Pranas. She surprised both men: Pranas stood back and Meyer, shocked by her move, tugged at her leg. He quickly realized she had a plan and he retreated on his knees a few yards further into the wheat. Pranas had never met Gita and never imagined her to be blonde anyway. Gita did not know what Pranas looked like either.

"What are you doing here?"

She answered calmly, with a dirty smirk on her face: "Waiting for my boyfriend, a German officer," raising one eye in a way she imagined a woman of loose morals would.

Pranas beat it back to the farm, not wanting to encounter a member of the occupying force. He burst into the house.

"What's wrong," asked his startled sister.

"Well, there's a woman out there in the field but it can't be Gita. It's a prostitute waiting for her Schwab boyfriend to show up."

Back in the field, Meyer congratulated his wife for her ingenuity with a kiss.

"You do that really well but I'm not sure I like it," he said, laughing.

She swatted him affectionately. They remained there for what seemed like hours. Finally, they decided a little more play-acting was in order and might help them get undercover sooner.

She mussed his hair and then undid the buttons of his shirt to expose his chest. Then they stood up and put their arms around each other. They began singing as they walked slowly, acting like young lovers. It was not play acting but such public demonstrations of love were not the norm. They strolled through the little village and closed in on the Jakubaitis homestead. Barbora was at the gate. Unlike her brother, she did recognize Gita and motioned the couple in, looking in both directions as she beckoned. They needed no further invitation. When Pranas appeared, there was a sharp intake of breath from all sides. They all burst out in laughter as they realized the previous charade had not been necessary.

MEANWHILE, OTHER FRIENDS of the Krons were fleeing the ghetto. After telling Riva Kibaasky they were leaving, another Kron family friend Arie Lurie directed her to seek out some rescuers by the name of Antanas and Ona Ragauskas.

Her journey to safety was to be perilous. As gunfire and confusion filled the air, Riva sneaked out of another factory gate and just ran along with a crowd of non-Jews, frightened by the shots. She slowed her pace as she reached the rural roads across town.

After a short time, she encountered a man from her distant home village of Alite, who threatened her with betrayal to the Gestapo. She handed over her gold wedding ring, which she had hidden under clothes for this very purpose, though she never expected having to use it for a bribe so quickly.

After he had taken off, she came across an older man in a horse drawn buggy, who offered to take her home and hide her . . . if she would "keep house" for him. In the moment, it seemed like a good idea so she got up alongside the kind man. Minutes later her heart skipped a beat as she noticed her old neighbour ahead at the crossroads talking to man on a bike. Their second meeting was tense and she urged the old man to leave, fearing he would be in danger.

Riva prepared to hand over the rest of her belongings and throw herself at the mercy of the two men. The man on the bike surprised her.

"Your need is much greater," he said, shaking his head and waving off her offer. "Where are you heading to?"

Riva did not trust the man who accepted her earlier bribe and was now looking sheepishly at her. He had not told his acquaintance about the transaction. She told the man she hoped to meet somebody near Amaliai. Without further ado, the cyclist directed her across fields and via quiet paths towards her destination. Many hours later she staggered, exhausted, towards the old schoolhouse.

Ona quietly welcomed her at the side door, while a little girl behind her tugged at her dress. If Riva had known the identity of the youngster, she could have told her that her parents Meyer and Gita had escaped at the same time as she. Riva joined the other Jews hiding out in the barn at the rear of the Ragauskas home, one of whom was Lurie who had directed her to this sanctuary.

Ruta returned to her play in the back yard, aware of the eyes peering out at her from the cracks in the wall of the wooden barn. She did not stare back, despite her curiosity, or venture across the threshold. She knew they were in hiding just as she was and that meant dangers. Besides, Ona had told her she must stay away from the dilapidated farm building.

Bored with her imaginary playmate, Ruta returned to the house in time to hear another knock on the front door. Ona's next guests arrived in relative style. Ida and Isya Shapiro arranged to meet a non-Jewish friend in the event of the ghetto's closure. He agreed to take them by horse and buggy to their hiding place. Just as the Zilbermans guided the Krons to seek refuge for Ruta with Ona and Antanas, they also offered the same advice to the Shapiros.

By the end of the day there were 14 escaped ghetto inmates hiding in the barn behind the schoolhouse. The Zilbermans were not in a position to follow their own advice.

CHAPTER TWENTY

The liquidation of the ghetto

Jakubaitis family home, Shavl – July 1944

THE KRONS WERE SURPRISED to see that they would not only be
sharing their hiding place with Papa Shifman but also another
family of three from the ghetto.

The home's front door opened into a central area that housed a
large wood-fired oven and doubled as a kitchen and dining area.
Flanking it were two small bedrooms, one occupied by Pranas
and the second by Barbora. There was no upper floor but there
was access available via a ladder to straw covered areas above
each of the ground floor bedrooms. The Krons took one side of
the open attic while Girsas Reis, his wife Leja and 12-year-old
son Mendel took the other dark and uninviting area beneath the
slope of the roof.

Fortunately, the brother and sister did keep to themselves and
entertained few visitors. A curious visitor would surely see or hear
something that would reveal their hidden guests. The two families
remained motionless for most of their waking hours.

It was a very difficult and stressful time for the Krons. Their adult
neighbours constantly bickered and fought with their unruly boy.
Added to that was Papa Shifman's dreadful smoker's cough. He had
always suffered from a dry rasping cough but the poor substitute
tobacco made it considerably worse. It was called Mahorka and
it was made from the broken stems of the tobacco plant, which
were pressed into a newspaper to form a small pipe. With each
cough, no matter how muffled, everybody would jump. It was a
very tense time and they felt constantly at risk of detection.

In the rear yard, water was drawn from a well not just by the
house residents but also by unwelcome visitors from a German

265

military unit stationed nearby. One older looking German soldier would come several times a day with a horse and a barrel. He would drop the pail down and very slowly wind it back up in his own sweet time when it was full of water. No doubt, he was a volunteer for this task. It gave him a chance to while away some time having a peaceful smoke on those hot sunny days. He could also put behind him the hardships of war in a strange land and think of his family back home in Germany. It may have eased his stress but it contributed greatly to that suffered by the unseen eyes peering down at him through the cracks in the wall of the house less than 10 yards away. The Jews in hiding lay frozen, barely breathing for fear of the uniformed smoker hearing them.

In the evenings after dark, the two families would descend for a few minutes and go outside to gulp the fresh air. They did so as desperately as the German officer had earlier quaffed several tin cups full of the cool water following his exertions hoisting it to the surface. For 19 days, the tension mounted.

There was neither radio nor any newspapers to pass the time. Pranas would climb the ladder occasionally to deliver the news to his guests. They were never sure that his information about the progress of the Red Army was accurate. There were many times when they prayed it was not, particularly when he repeated rumours of a counter offensive by the occupying force.

Barbora's smile brightened their days, especially when it accompanied a bread delivery. It was often stale and never substantial enough to feed them but at least it was something to quell their hunger pangs. The milk she brought helped wash down their meagre rations, even though it was often sour. The Krons would not dream of either complaining or asking for more. Unfortunately, that was not the case on the other side of the roof beams. Goodness knows what kind of service they expected in hiding but they sure complained a lot to their hosts.

The lack of toilets probably posed the biggest domestic challenge to them outlasting the hostilities. There was an outhouse in the yard but, of course, that was out of bounds all day. Some clay flowerpots stored in the attic certainly came in useful during times of desperation. However, Gita once suffered the great indignity of cutting herself badly during a nocturnal visit. It was very painful and frightening as they tried to stem the endless flow of fresh blood. After beating the odds in their escape, it was unthinkable that something as stupid as this could lead to their capture and possibly worse. Barbora's limited nursing skills, nevertheless, came to the fore and the danger passed, though Gita would suffer an unpleasant reminder for days to come whenever she sat down. It was no laughing matter but as is the case often in such situations, the event that causes such horror later becomes the subject of dark humour. Meyer described it later in his diary as an example of 'adding injury to insult', a cheeky play on the words of a much cited saying.

∾

DESPITE THE ANNOUNCEMENT to the Judenrat, it would be another week before the evacuation began.

In those seven intervening days, many Jews tried to escape and some paid with their lives. During the first day's panic, others followed the Krons' lead, breaking through the fence into the mansion grounds. Siegel, the factory's German chief of production, seen by Meyer Kron with gun in hand during his escape, soon put that weapon to use. He shot two women dead while one of the local jail wardens, visiting the workplace, killed two youths.

Most of those that made it beyond the gates, long after the Krons left, were intercepted by the SS and their cohorts and returned to the confines of the ghetto. Some escaped and showed up at hiding places similar to the haven offered by Ona and Antanas Ragauskas.

Even when the liquidation began on July 15, the first to leave by freight train were the most recent arrivals – the 3,500 from Ponevezh and Joniskis. Four days later another 1,990 followed from the satellite camps but still the ghetto's original inmates remained, petrified that their exclusion could only mean bad news. The tension became unbearable.

That tension was shattered on July 21 with the deafening blasts of Russian bombs exploding over Shavl at the start of what would be two nights of intense aerial raids. Explosives fell in the ghetto area, killing some inmates including Judenrat member and former leader Leibovich, Gita's cousin.

Finally, on July 22, 1,500 long-time residents got their marching orders. The Russian air force did a great deal of damage to the Shavl railway station. So began a near 20-mile march to Pajevonys. The weary walkers, dehydrated by the hot sun, spent the night in the sugar factory before boarding a transport train at the nearby station for a long journey to the camp at Stutthof, about 30 miles from modern day Gdansk, in Poland.

One family never reached camp. The Parisers boarded a separate carriage from the rest of the Shavl Jews. At the last station before Gdansk, guards quietly removed their baggage. The family swiftly joined their cases on the platform. They removed their yellow stars and walked out of the station unchallenged by any authority present that day. No doubt, that was a reward for a job well done on behalf of the SS. He did get his come-uppance in 1945 when a former ghetto inmate spotted him walking the streets of Gdansk. The Russians arrested him and jailed him for ten years in Kazakhstan for his treachery. After his release, he joined his family in what was West Germany at the time.

ON SATURDAY, JULY 24, Wulf looked around the reception area of the tiny ghetto hospital. It was so much smaller than the 40-bed hospital next to the Jewish cemetery in the former Kaukazas ghetto area. Nevertheless, he and his colleagues had saved many a life here, only for the Nazis to snatch some of them away in a later abomination.

He feared the 16 patients left there would never see the outside of this place again. He was sure the departing Nazis would simply set it alight and leave as they reportedly did in other ghettos. He must stay with his patients to the end for it would be his end too. He no longer had that wine he had saved "to ease my eventual departure," as he had told Reska Weiss.

The opening of the door disturbed his ruminations. The SS is here, he thought, turning to greet his expected, if uninvited, visitors. Before him were not men in uniforms but two women. He did not know them; perhaps they were from among the recent arrivals.

They began to plead with him: "Doctor, we have come about our mother."

They moved swiftly to the area where the patients rested, pointing to the woman in the last bed. Under any other circumstances, he would have intercepted them before they crossed the threshold. However, what was the point of trying to preserve the privacy of his sick charges, especially if they were family?

"We would like you to give her an injection, doctor," said the speaker for the two.

"She is being taken care of and has the medication she needs," Wulf responded.

"No, you don't understand, we want you to take her life before the Nazis do."

They too had heard the stories of the Nazis putting ghetto hospitals to the torch, most recently in Kovno (Kaunas).

"I can't do that because it would be murder," said Wulf, knowing his declaration would have no impact on the sisters.

The second sister finally spoke up: "We can't force you to but we appeal to you to consider what we have asked. Surely you will not be punished for such an act either on this earth or by God."

Wulf's older brother Chaim, who entered quietly moments before, overheard part of the women's plea. The women turned and were startled to see him standing there. They left the troubled doctor and his sibling to assemble with the remaining inmates to await their evacuation. Chaim was only two years his senior but today he would speak to Wulf as his father might have done had he been alive.

"They are right, Wulf. You cannot leave these poor people to die at the hands of these wretched people. It is obscene."

Wulf dug in and repeated his responsibilities as a doctor.

"I will stay here with them until the end. I will not be marching today."

Chaim saw red and cuffed his honourable yet stubborn brother. He was getting nowhere.

"If you don't join us today, then the rest of the family will remain to share your fate."

Wulf did not move but stared into space. Chaim left, flustered and shaking. The older Peisachowitz and his wife took their places at the back of the line by the ghetto gate. They kept looking towards the hospital for a sign of Wulf acquiescing to their wishes. They prayed that he would show up and not commit them to perish alongside him.

There was activity at the front of the queue among the Germans. This was the moment of decision. Chaim looked at Rachel. They knew they must stand aside and walk to the hospital. Moments later, they were aware of Wulf's presence behind them. He said nothing. He looked contemplative. Dr. Luntz and his wife nodded but there was no reaction from Wulf. Nearby, Riva and Saul Gotz eyed both of the doctors, who were so instrumental in bringing their son Ben safely into this troubled world and ensuring he survived.

As the ghetto emptied, soldiers began searching every house and building. Once satisfied that there were no stragglers, the searchers climbed into a car and headed off to join up with the march. There was no conflagration. The only matches struck were those used to light the cigarettes with which the guards rewarded themselves for a job well done.

Some hours later, a few locals entered the ghetto to see if there was anything of value worth removing. They burst through the doors of the makeshift hospital. Inside they found 16 motionless figures in an area where bodies were prepared for burial when the place functioned as intended. There was no evidence of a struggle. The corpses bore no sign of wounds. It was as though they had all slipped peacefully into eternal rest at the same time, killed by lethal injection.

HUNDREDS OF THE LOCAL population lined the route taken out of town. Most were there to gloat, believing the Jews were finally getting their just deserts. As the march hit the more rural area, the numbers of onlookers decreased.

WULF COULD NOT resist taking a last look at the spot near the family home where he had buried gold and other valuables. His secret stash had served him well in securing goods for himself during the life of the ghetto. More importantly, it had enabled him to bribe the appropriate people to get the medicines he needed to save lives and thus score his own little victories against the Nazis. He would return to dig up what remained when the war was over. However, that would not happen. The only beneficiaries would be some road construction workers who in future years would unearth the treasure while building a crossroads in that location.

AT ONE POINT, near Amaliai, Wulf noticed a familiar little Jewish girl at the roadside holding the hands of her rescuers. He looked around and made eye contact with her, holding her gaze for a few moments and nodding ever so slightly. Ona and Antanas squeezed the hands of Ruta. She knew they had seen Uncle Wulf too. Mama and Papa were not among those people, she told her rescuers on the way home. No, they must have escaped, she was told. She hoped so but was not so sure. One thing she was sure about: she should convert and become an obedient and observant little Catholic girl.

BARBORA RUSHED INTO the house. She put the fear of God into her guests.

"What? What?" asked Meyer, impatiently and loudly, forgetting their vow of silence while in hiding.

Barbora scampered up the ladder and led them to the rear wall when she peered through the cracks to the outside.

"Look, look."

Clearly, Barbora was not going to offer any more information verbally. Three more pairs of eyes joined her at the wall and squinted as they looked out. They could see a long line of people moving slowly along the nearby highway. Meyer could not make out any individuals but he knew this was the last of his fellow ghetto neighbours marching into the unknown. It was the same procession viewed a short time earlier by his surviving daughter, Ruta. At least they had not been shot, as Meyer feared would happen at the ghetto liquidation.

Later that night a train pulled away, its freight cars loaded with the last of Shavl's Jews. It was bound for Stutthof and another concentration camp outside Munich, in Germany, the infamous Dachau.

SHORTLY AFTER, THE WAR front returned to Shavl as the Russians and Germans exchanged heavy bombardment. The city's population began to leave their homes at dusk and head to the fields on the edge of town to spend the night. This development scared the Krons and Reis family. They no longer felt in the least bit secure in their hiding place.

Two days after Barbora delivered the bad news of the ghetto liquidation; it was her brother's turn to show up with some good news. Well, it may have been good news for Pranas but it was dire news for his Jewish guests. He spoke excitedly about how the Germans were pushing back the Red Army. Pranas really did not get it, thought Meyer. The occupation barely touched his simple life, living where he did. He had no concept of what the Jews suffered in the last few years.

No sooner had Pranas finished his news update than there was a knock on the door. The Jews in the household bolted for their hiding places. The knocking became more persistent and louder.

When Pranas opened the door, he was face to face with Jocius, a man he had heard about from the Krons but never encountered. He invited the man in; worried he might be doing the wrong thing. On hearing the distinctive voice of Jocius, Meyer shot down the ladder and embraced him.

Jocius was looking for a place to hide from the Germans. The Germans were drafting able-bodied men to dig trenches at the front to enable them to make a stand against the advancing Russians. However, he was more than willing to help dig trenches around his temporary refuge.

That very night, the Krons caught themselves smiling when the first bombs began falling. A perverse comfort perhaps, but it meant the Russians were not beaten and soon, like Jocius, they would be knocking on the door.

As darkness fell, Jocius left for a location he chose not to reveal. He had his own idea about where the safest place would be for him to spend the night, doubtless somewhere prearranged with his wife. After bidding farewell, the Krons hastened to the zigzag shaped trench close to the rear of the home. They were not alone; among them were villagers they did not really want to see. Maybe the fear factor would keep these simple farming folk from noticing their new neighbours. Even if they did, surely they would think twice about making trouble. They would be more concerned about just keeping their heads down, literally and figuratively.

As the night wore on, the time between the flashes of light and bursts of noise got longer until silence reigned. People became restless and anxious to return to their beds to sleep their day away before again striking out into the night to escape death at Stalin's hands. They became creatures of the night.

As dawn displayed its first light, a young lad jumped out of the trench. Maybe a rat nibbled at his foot made numb by sitting in the same position for hours. Perhaps he just wanted to get out and go home. Suddenly there was a burst of automatic rifle fire. In an instant, he was back in the trench sobbing. Above his cries, now muffled by his mother's hand, the trench dwellers could hear a shout from the near distance, "Stoy!" It was followed by an order to those inhabiting the trench to get out. A translation from Russian was not necessary as its delivery and the brandishing of guns made the meaning of the order clear.

OVER AT THE Kleiba rectory, the priest's guests crept down each night to listen to his radio. He too greeted the imminent arrival of the Russians with some disdain. He knew what it meant for his Jews but the Bolsheviks were a godless lot in the main. He knew them to be tyrants in a different uniform. The Germans were not welcome in his homeland either, so he prayed for the day when Lithuania would regain its independence, something that would not occur for decades, long past his death.

He lived in fear of his Jews' betrayal by the less Christian of his flock, seeking to gain some advantage even in these dying days of the Reich's influence. Kleiba had trained those he sheltered in the ways of the Catholic faithful but he had little faith they would be able to pass themselves off convincingly as members of his flock for very long.

Polina Toker was likely one of the few that could fool others into thinking she was Catholic but she had another problem. She came from a prominent family in Radvilishok and she was a popular dentist. Many of Kleiba's congregation in Kuzh visited there to shop and do their daily business. She could be recognized by one of her former patients and then no mimicry of Catholic practices would save her.

As the front line closed in on Kuzh, the Lithuanian supporters of the Germans became hysterical. Rather than sinking quietly into the background, they roamed the land looking for communists and Jews to kill. They offered rewards for information on the whereabouts of such "vermin" as they called their intended victims. Kleiba's Jews pleaded with him to let them go and find their own new hiding places but he would only shake his head.

"If it is fate to perish, we shall all perish together; but in that case I shall die knowing that I did some good in this or that way," he told them bravely.

In the end, Kleiba left in advance of the Russians' arrival and his whereabouts would remain unknown to his flock until after the war. After a few days secreted in the attic, Polina and the others left their safe house for the last time. Dressed like farmers, they piled on a horse drawn carriage and headed for the home of a teacher they thought might aid them. Along the way, stray German soldiers tried to talk to the rag tag bunch, looking for directions and sources of food. Polina shook her head, shrugged her shoulders, and waved her hands as though she did not understand their questions posed in German.

A teacher let them into her farm home but no sooner was the door closed when the crack of gunfire shook the tiny home. Within seconds, they were in the middle of an inferno. Their stay was short and they ran to the safety of the nearby woods. In abandoned trenches, they laid low for 48 hours until the gunfire was only intermittent.

They took a chance, emerged from their hiding place and then headed towards Kuzh, which they were sure by now the Russians must control. Their war was not quite over. As they crossed a potato field, a German plane roared overhead firing at them as he flew past. They sank into the mud and sought cover beneath large plants. The Luftwaffe pilot soon tired of strafing nothing and took off into the wild blue yonder in search of other potential victims. The Jews got up shakily, brushed themselves off, and once again began to make their way to the safety offered by a Russian controlled Kuzh.

CHAPTER TWENTY-ONE

Liberators

A farmer's field outside Shavl – July 26, 1944.

THE KRONS CLIMBED OUT of the trench at the Russian's command, not wishing to provoke the young man whose finger hovered around the trigger of the automatic rifle he pointed towards them.

Once he was upright above ground, Meyer could see the soldier was one of a dozen or more young soldiers, all similarly attired in blue trousers and green shirts but no protective headwear. They were a fast-moving advance reconnaissance group, picked for their youth.

The young man who issued the order for them to vacate the trench looked to be in his 20s and even at that tender age, perhaps the oldest of the bunch. He was the troop commander and identified himself as Borovick. Meyer greeted him in the man's native tongue. Comrade Borovick stepped forward and helped Papa Shifman out of the trench while Meyer stretched out a hand to his wife and drew her closer.

Borovick looked up and down the three people before him. He was somewhat taken aback to discover a Jewish family among his captives. He was also Jewish and was very aware of the slaughters that took place wherever the Nazis roamed these past few years. How had they survived? In the near future, it would be a question asked of Meyer many times in a most menacing fashion.

The soldier barked orders at his comrades. They immediately lowered their guns and relaxed their stance. Meyer understood what was said but hoped the non-Jewish co-occupants of trench had not comprehended. The officer had identified the Krons to his men as being fellow Jews. Tomorrow, the Germans may be back and he would not put it past some of his fellow trench occupants to betray his family if it meant winning favour.

The dim light of dawn struggled to break through the clouds that swirled above. When the sun did break through, it offered enough light for the Krons to see that the clouds above were not made of droplets of water but smoke created by a thousand explosions.

The hours passed and the trench occupants roamed a little more freely, as they were no longer captives. Most followed the advice of the young Russians and stayed close to their temporary home hewn from the soft earth. Bombs were still falling and periodically a bullet would stray perilously close to them.

An officer previously unseen showed up with shovels commandeered from a nearby farm. His mates set about digging trenches for their own protection. The sound of shelling and gunfire died down shortly after noon but it was to be the calm before another man-made storm. In the late afternoon, Borovick strode over to Meyer after completing a long radio call to his superiors. He spoke respectfully to his elder, advising Meyer to collect his belongings and move his family back a few fields away from town. He was less polite to the others. Meyer regretted the Russian singling him out for such respectful treatment. The young officer said he suspected the ground on which they currently stood would soon become a battleground. Towards sundown, the artillery fire increased and Meyer figured they were the meat in a sandwich. The Germans were still in control of the town centre of Shavl and the main Russian offensive units were moving towards the Krons. It was not a safe spot.

A couple of young Russians escorted the group in the general direction of their advancing comrades. They were still in the middle of the action. For hours, artillery shells flew over their heads from behind towards the city. It is hard to imagine boredom creeping in but it did, or at least that is how Meyer recollected the occasion later.

Meyer and some of the other men in the group began playing cards. They played Blackjack for Ostmarks; next time they were sure it would be for Russian Roubles rather than their currency of choice – Litas. While the men passed their time, Gita chatted to her father, hoping to calm his nerves. He had survived so far, she was not going to let him fail now.

The card game continued until it was too dark to see, and then they moved into a nearby barn. One by one, the group fell asleep on the straw-covered floor. It was a fitful sleep for most, disturbed by shells flying overhead or the mooing of a startled cow in one of the stalls.

The next morning, Meyer came round with a jolt when another occupant of the barn opened the door and bright daylight bathed his bleary eyes. He shook Gita. She squinted as though somebody had turned on an electric light. For a moment, she thought she was back in her own bedroom, but the aroma of the cattle sharing her room soon reminded her of her location.

Through force of habit, she ran the fingers of her right hand through her hair as though to make herself presentable. Papa was already awake. There was not a sound above the twitter of birds in the bushes. The artillery units were silent. Who had won?

Cautiously they went outside and surveyed the scene looking for any sign of men with weapons – from either side. Meyer and another man crawled to the crest of a small hill, which offered an unobstructed view of Shavl. It had taken a serious pounding. Plumes of smoke rose from a dozen or more spots.

"We must stay put until we know who is in charge," Meyer told Gita, who offered no counter-argument.

Some of the others wandered off to see if their homes were intact. Some of the curious would fall victim to crossfire, confirmation of the wisdom of Meyer's words to his wife. Hours passed. Suddenly they became aware of the presence of others. The fields around them were filling with soldiers. Most arrived on foot but some rode aboard small, horse-drawn carriages that were no more than peasant carts. What a contrast to the modern and well-equipped army it was trying to dislodge from the Baltic countries.

The threesome decided it was safe to approach, encouraged by the smell of hot food emanating from the temporary kitchen the soldiers had quickly assembled. As they neared the encampment, a loudspeaker crackled and the air filled with the declaration that the glorious Russians had liberated Shavl.

The Krons did not dance a jig when they heard the news. All they wanted now was food and some uninterrupted sleep. They would ponder what this all meant to them later. Besides, they still feared the tide could turn again. Then they would be in the middle of the fighting not knowing where to go for safety. They went back to their hiding place, planning to remain there until either Pranas or Barbora could ascertain if it were safe to venture into Shavl. Jocius returned at daylight, which was a relief, but he left again, telling Barbora he was going back to his home, as he had nothing to fear from the Russians. Of course, this was no indicator of how safe it was out there for anybody else. He was certainly no stranger to risk taking.

Moshe was prepared to stay indoors until the all clear. However, curiosity got the better of his younger relatives. They set off to see for themselves what had become of their hometown. As they neared what should have been familiar territory, they were shocked to discover that they did not recognize the streets. From a distance, it looked as though somebody had erected a series of columns on both sides of the streets. When they closed in, they realized they were chimneys; the only parts of the structures left. In their retreat, the Germans set fire to the buildings they passed.

Meyer and Gita turned into a road that looked more familiar. Burned out vehicles, dead horses, and corpses littered its length. It was a horrible sight to encounter. They both recoiled as the stench of burnt flesh permeated their nostrils. The heavy bombardment had almost reduced the whole city to ashes. Few buildings remained untouched.

They walked on. Occasionally they would come across others wandering aimlessly. It was as though they were invisible. Not one passerby acknowledged them. Then partisans emerged from the hideouts in the woods and showed up on the streets. They had red bands on their arms and toted automatic rifles. One or two recognized Meyer and did acknowledge him, though not in a friendly way. They urged him to join their ranks immediately. An offer Meyer declined, diplomatically, telling another he would think about it once he had established where his family was hiding. A lie but it seemed to work.

Others looked at the Jewish couple with great suspicion, doubtless asking themselves the same question that crossed the mind of the young Russian soldier hours before. Meyer began to feel threatened. A zealous partisan might take it into his head to arrest them as German spies.

They picked up the pace and entered another street that was lined with the bodies of German soldiers, their boots and watches removed no doubt by the poorly shod Russians. The watches would appear on the black market in the days to come as the soldiers sought cash to buy vodka. They had seen enough and were not going to risk their lives by continuing their sightseeing. They returned to their safe haven and spent the hours before bedtime relating what they saw to Moshe Shifman and their hosts.

MEYER PLANNED TO return to town the next day to seek out whoever was in charge. That became unnecessary, as his whereabouts were known. Shortly after returning from their reconnaissance, there was a knock on the door. The callers summoned him to attend a meeting concerning the reopening of Frenkel's factory. Meyer found it a little scary to know how easily he had been located. However, his thoughts did not linger on that worry for now there was a chance to return to normal life or at least the Russian version of normal. It was not a great prospect but better than living under the heel of a Nazi boot, that threatened to stamp them out of existence on a whim. In the near future, Meyer would have cause to seriously re-evaluate his position that Soviet rule was the lesser of two evils.

Before setting foot in Shavl, the Soviets already had an administration ready to go. There was a mayor, an industrial chief, a police chief and even the factories had directors ready to step in and restart production. In the city government, there were some old friends, who had fled to Russia before the Nazi takeover. He thought that would bode well for the future wellbeing of the Krons. Chaim Hirshovitz was in charge of rebuilding the city. The Russians tasked Dr. Levine with reconstituting medical care for the population and Jacob Shumkauskas became director of the tannery. The director's first job was to reappoint Meyer Kron as chief engineer. Meyer's immediate task was to marshal the resources to rebuild the part of the tannery destroyed by bombs. It was not just a job though; it was likely a lifesaver. If there had been no position for him, the new masters would have outfitted Meyer with a uniform and dispatched him to the front.

THE FIRST FEW days of the re-occupation by the Soviets were much the same as those witnessed during their last visit. They helped themselves to everything that took their fancy, especially vodka and women and in that order. A gang of them burst into the factory warehouse one day and made off with every drum of Amyl acetate they could find. It has a fruit-like smell – pears, apples, perhaps even bananas – and they mistook it for drinkable alcohol. The outcome was a repeat of what happened during the German occupation. This time there were no deaths reported from drinking the faux alcohol but there were some very sick Russians in the infirmary.

Gradually, the Jews who escaped the ghetto liquidation began to return. There were not many, maybe a dozen or so. Some had remained undetected in the tannery and survived the bombing. Kaplan, one of Meyer's co-workers, hid in one of the patent leather department's ovens. Kaplan sought out Meyer on his first day back on the job. Meyer was delighted to see him but became worried by the intelligence his old friend provided. Apparently, a high-ranking Red Army officer was looking for the chief engineer. Kaplan did not know the officer's name because he heard only on the grapevine about the Russian's interest in Meyer.

Meyer need not have panicked because it was Shavdya. He was one of the soldiers who had shared their family's home during the last occupation and become the family's protector. Shavdya had risen to the rank of General in the intervening period and was responsible for the military supplies department.

"My friend, you are alive," Shavdya shouted as he hugged Meyer. The garrulous Russian told him he was some 60 miles away when the news of Shavl's liberation had reached him. He just had to find out for himself what had happened to his dear friends, the Krons.

His smile disappeared when he heard what happened to Tamara, Meyer's mother and other members of the family. The high-ranking officer in Stalin's army broke down and sobbed the tears you would expect only from a family member. It was supposed to be just a lightning visit but he stayed on for a few days to make sure his colleagues looked after the Krons properly. He said the right things in the right places at the right time. He also helped on a much more practical level, diverting hundreds of cans of a variety of foods into the Kron home, which was temporarily in the Kaplan household. However, his role in helping the family's first attempt to return Ruta to the bosom of the family was his most valued gesture.

RUTA'S SCHOOLHOUSE SANCTUARY was still very close to the fighting in what was virtually a no man's land, cut off from Shavl and its immediate surrounding area. It was strictly a no-go zone for the town's citizens, by order of the new Soviet authorities. Nevertheless, Shavdya arranged for the Krons to have an army vehicle at their disposal complete with an armed guard of two of his men.

Despite this protection, it was still a risky adventure. It was a risk all parents would embrace given the opportunity to reunite with their only surviving child.

The resourceful Meyer managed to get a message to Ona and Antanas through channels open to Jocius. When they rolled up in the military vehicle, the only one surprised was Ruta. In fact, she was scared rigid. She heard nothing good from Ona and Antanas about the Russians during her stay. She saw the open truck roll up with her mother standing in the bed at the back, her blonde hair blowing in the breeze caused by the vehicle's forward motion. It floated down to rest on her shoulders as the vehicle ground to a halt. It was then that Ruta saw her father come around the side of the now–stationary vehicle.

Ruta moved away from the window and began to run to the back of the house. Her parents rapped on the door. Ona answered, beckoning the little girl to come with her. Ruta ventured forward a few steps hiding behind Ona's skirts, as she did the day when a succession of Jews showed up at the same door. She peeked at them suspiciously. There was not a trace of a smile. Meyer and Gita had prepared themselves for this kind of reception. Rescued children often rejected their own parents in these circumstances. Meyer and Gita smiled bravely and restrained themselves from scooping up Ruta to give her the hugs and kisses they longed to rain on the little one. Even Meyer, not given to such public shows of affection, wanted to feel the soft skin of his daughter against his unshaven face. She was a little taller and was not as skinny after a year in the care of her rescuers but she was still unmistakably their little girl.

Ruta wanted nothing to do with them. She just stared at them, clinging tightly to Ona. As Meyer shifted his position on the doorstep, Ruta crossed herself; beseeching her new God to save her from these strangers that threatened her safety. It was a peculiar sight for her Jewish parents to behold. They did not flinch or show any sign of distaste. They were just grateful she was alive and healthy.

The sound of artillery drowned out parts of the somewhat stilted conversation with Ona that followed. Everybody at the doorstep flinched with each explosion. This was not to be the day for a reunion. The disappointed couple left, reassuring Ona quietly. They would be back again.

The second time they came, Ruta agreed to go for a walk in the neighbourhood. She spoke little and what she did say was in

Lithuanian only. Her parents quickly realized they should not speak in Russian or Yiddish. Just as they seemed to be winning her confidence, a little dog ran out of a yard and bit Ruta! The distressed little girl screamed as blood gushed from the wound. The severity of the injury did not require hospital care but to Ruta it was as though the dog had ripped a chunk of flesh from her. Her incessant wailing was related more to the shock of the occasion rather than the size of the wound.

Meyer and Gita's gentle persistence paid off on their third visit a few weeks later in mid-August. Ruta agreed to go home with them under certain conditions, which she spelled out. They must not speak Yiddish as somebody might hear and betray them to the men who took Tamara. Meyer bit his lip and resisted telling her that there no longer was such a threat.

Her next demand was that she could go to church whenever she wanted. Gita shook her head in agreement, wondering how she could facilitate that. It turned out not to be a challenge. A cleaner working at Kaplan's place agreed to take Ruta to Mass. In turn, Gita would perform her domestic duties.

Once the negotiations were over, Ruta hugged Ona and Antanas, telling them she would be back to see them soon. She would be back at Ona's forever if her parents did not meet any of her terms and conditions. Gita and Meyer had also discussed the possibility that Ruta might not settle. They resolved that should that be the case, then they would return her to the Ragauskas family. It was a remarkable attitude not shared by many in their unenviable position. Some families would just drag the child away, while in many other cases the rescuers would refuse to give up their charges.

Ruta walked towards the car Meyer borrowed for the occasion. Her father lifted her little bag of clothes into the back seat and returned to the house to thank Ona once again. He could find no words appropriate for what she had done for them.

Ona thrust out her right arm and asked him to take the bag she held. Meyer recognized it as the one he had filled with valuables and given to her for safekeeping during one of his clandestine visits. If Ona needed money for Ruta, she was supposed to sell a trinket or two to meet the needs as they arose.

In the other hand was a dog-eared address book full of Kron family information about who to contact in the event of Meyer and Gita's early demise and where to sell any valuables that remained.

Meyer accepted the book but wanted her to keep the valuables. She would hear none of it. He insisted, giving her more valuables that he had retrieved from elsewhere. There was no point in fighting. She would continue to keep them safe for the Krons. In truth, the most valuable reward he bestowed upon her was the huge box of groceries Shavdya secured from the army supplies warehouse.

Kaplan's house was across the street from the church Ruta attended with her rescuers. The church was badly burned in the last of the fighting, especially the tower. Ruta spent hours at that window praying and crying for her church. Shortly after returning to the family fold, Ruta helped herself to one of the charred bricks in the ruins. It became her security blanket. She would sleep under its protection, placing it beneath her pillow every night before bedtime.

It would be many months before Ruta no longer asked to go to church. Her fascination with Catholicism and the beauty of its churches would last a lifetime. Her return to Jewish practices would not come easily.

❧

IN THE PAST, Meyer had viewed Shumkauskas with some suspicion because he showed him so much hostility during the first Russian occupation. The events of the past four years caused the man to reconsider his attitude to Meyer and Jews in general. He became a good friend to the Krons, helping them resettle.

On August 16, 1944, he was sitting chatting with Meyer and Gita in their home when a messenger arrived to summon him back to headquarters. Before making the dash across town, he warned the Krons that there was word of a German counter offensive and they should thus consider retreating further behind Russian lines.

Meyer borrowed a horse and wagon and made for the Jakubaitis home where Papa Shifman continued to lodge. The closer they got the louder the artillery fire became and on the horizon the glow of fires raging through homes lit the late afternoon sky. One of the buildings set alight was the little schoolhouse Ruta had called home until very recently.

In less than an hour, the whole family was aboard the same cart and they were heading to Ponevezh, where they hoped to secure temporary accommodation with his married sister Tzilia Schatz and her family. Yet again, the Krons were on the run from the Germans, using the same mode of slow transport taken the first time around. They could not afford to return to Shavl, as surely this time a vengeful force would slaughter them.

As they left town they witnessed the bombing of the airport. The countryside appeared to rock under the thunderous explosions. Meyer feared the Germans would overtake them so he urged on the horse as though stepping up the pace would save them from a motorized army. Not likely but he felt better for trying.

It took a solid two days to make the 60-mile journey to Ponevezh. When they finally hit the city limits, they were shocked at how the town had remained untouched. This quiet and peaceful place looked as if no ill had befallen it or its citizens.

The Krons soon learned the Nazis murdered their kin and the rest of the town's Jews shortly after their takeover. The people living in his sister's house described in heartbreaking detail how all the Jews were rounded up and marched to a little valley on the outskirts of town and shot. Only one Jew survived and the Krons met the young man. His Catholic girlfriend saved him and kept him hidden for the entire four-year occupation.

As if that were not enough, the Krons also learned that Meyer's brother Yaakov, wife Eva and son Zali were also murdered in 1941. All 27,800 Jews from the Riga ghetto were marched to the nearby Rumbula Forest between November 30 and December 8, 1941, where they were shot and buried in mass graves.

It was time for the Krons to move on, both figuratively and literally. Together with other refugees, the family climbed onto the flat bed of a rail car bound for Vilna, a much safer place to be. Lady luck smiled on the Krons when they bumped into old friend Chaim Hirshovitz shortly after their arrival in what would become the capital of the new Lithuania. He was in charge of restoring the surviving buildings to their full use. Chaim had an apartment at his disposal and gladly gave the keys to his friends. There was not a stick of furniture inside the four walls. Its Pro-Nazi tenants fled with their belongings as soon as the Russian takeover became inevitable. The Krons were comfortable with their fellow tenants, some of whom had shared their ghetto address. There was some laughter but the adults spent a lot of time discussing lofty topics, such as where was a world in turmoil going to go from here. The battlefronts were moving back and forth but ultimately there was no doubt that the Russians would push the Nazis homeward through Poland. For almost six weeks, the Germans pounded the Russian positions around Shavl, but gradually the force of the offensive petered out. The Americans were also coming in from the west and again there was agreement: it would be better to be in the jurisdiction of the Americans than that controlled by the

Russians. It was a position that events would reinforce for the Krons in the coming months.

With each mile the Germans retreated, the weight of fear lifted a little more from the group's shoulders. Meyer felt like a free man with the world at his feet; a world he would take pride in helping to renew. He was less ebullient when a truck suddenly appeared at the front of the building one day in the early evening. It was full of armed men. His legs wobbled when the leader got out, pointed at him and asked sternly, "Are you Engineer Kron?"

The man could see from the expression on Meyer's face that he had his man. The colour returned to Meyer's cheeks when the man continued:

"You are requested to return to Shavl immediately to rebuild the factory."

Meyer was disturbed again by the ease with which he had been found. Would he have to spend his days looking over his shoulder and watching carefully what he revealed to others? He would come to know just how efficient the Russians were at extracting information from people.

The man waved his rifle as he told Meyer to join him on the truck immediately. This was no mere request to return to Shavl but an order. An outstretched hand pulled him up onto the tailgate and before he had steadied himself, the truck roared off. He did not have time to ask his neighbours to convey that everything would be fine to his family. However, they witnessed the event in its entirety so he felt confident they would reassure Gita that he would come to no harm. The Germans were in retreat but the front was still uncomfortably close and the flashes of artillery fire lit the night sky as they headed to Shavl.

MEYER MOVED INTO one of the small houses within the tannery compound. Ona was the last person Meyer expected to see a couple of days later when he answered the door to a persistent knocker. He smiled broadly but uncharacteristically, she did not reciprocate. The Russians arrested her brother Leonas and accused him of collaborating with the Germans. Of course, nothing could have been further from the truth. Somehow, she thought Meyer would be able to help get him out. He was successful in securing the young man's release but it was not his powers of persuasion. Several pieces of leather did the trick with the guards though.

Ona returned to thank him. Only then did he learn how the Germans destroyed the schoolhouse as they retreated. Ona and Antanas, like many of their neighbours, hid in the woods in a tent for eight weeks before emerging, tired and very hungry.

IT WAS NOT until the middle of November 1944 that the Red Army finally pushed the Germans away from Shavl. By then the Krons had taken up residence in one of the few houses remaining intact. They took the downstairs suite while Shumkauskas lived upstairs.

Gita decided to become a nurse under the guidance of Dr. Goldberg, the new chief doctor in the city. Papa Shifman and Nesia, a cousin who survived the concentration camp but lost her husband and two children in the ghetto, moved in and took over the running of the household.

By then, the Soviet armies were pushing the Nazis back into their homeland and some soldiers were already returning with the booty they pillaged along the way. They marched back with thousands of heads of cattle, truckloads of furniture, radios, carpets and even works of art. The soldiers were hungry for cash, so the Krons made some good deals and the suite was soon furnished. Of course, their currency was leather, which the Russians gratefully accepted because they could easily turn such currency into roubles.

The military unit stationed in Shavl was the so-called 'Lithuanian Division', which was formed inside Russia during the war. It was largely Lithuanian Jews, many of whom enjoyed the hospitality of the Krons, sleeping on the floor for a night or two on their way to the front or home.

Quite often, they also accommodated high officials from Vilna or Moscow. They came with a different hard currency with which to reward their hosts: hard liquor! In the evenings, they would drink real vodka and play poker, losing most of their roubles in the process. Not that it seemed to worry them. Ah, yes, Mother Russia would always provide, especially if you held the right rank in the People's Army. At the end of the game, they would toast each other: "Day boch neposledenyuyu!" which loosely translated means, "Let's hope that this is not the last drink!" For many heading towards the front, it was their last drink.

The secret police assigned to look after the security of the front and find spies and German collaborators were very active. Meyer would soon find out how they worked. Agents called on him looking for information. Each would pointedly comment on how remarkable it was that Meyer and his family had survived the Nazi regime. It was a not so subtle way of telling Meyer they suspected him of collaborating with the Nazis. He should cooperate or find himself becoming the subject of investigation.

They did not necessarily believe that, but making such comments was a way of coercing those reluctant to help them. It was generally the same scenario: Meyer would answer the door to a Russian, more often than not in the middle of the night, who would inform him that his presence was 'requested' immediately for an interview.

However, one memorable encounter started during daylight hours. He had just returned home for lunch one day when a jeep showed up, loaded with armed men. He kissed Gita goodbye, not knowing what he was going to face or whether he would return home. They drove him to the outskirts of the city to a little house. An anxious Meyer was kept waiting for an hour that passed slowly. Finally, he was ushered into another room. Behind the desk was a small man in a general's uniform. He stood abruptly and turned towards Meyer. Are those tears in his eyes, wondered Meyer. Yes, they were.

The man embraced and kissed Meyer, saying in Yiddish, "You are an engineer? A Jew?"

He was overwhelmed because all the time he was progressing with the advancing Red Army he had not seen a Jew alive. The two Jews subsequently became firm friends and the friendly general would prove to be a solid ally.

As the situation calmed, more people began moving back to the Shavl they had fled with the retreating Russians at the outset of Operation Barbarossa. Russian citizens also drifted through town looking for their relatives, mostly unsuccessfully. Some caught at the outbreak of war failed to escape and became prisoners of war. A man called Budyansky was searching for his wife and daughter who arrived in Lithuania just before the war to visit their relatives. He stayed with the Krons for several weeks, scouring every part of town and every neighbouring village for a trace of his women folk. He left with a broken heart.

On New Year's Day, 1945, there was a great celebration at the factory. Meyer was in charge during Shumkauskas's temporary absence so he had the honour of delivering the main speech praising the Red Army and comrade Stalin for the deliverance of him and his fellow compatriot. He nearly choked but he got the words out.

Meyer sensed their newfound freedom would only be temporary. Nevertheless, while things were good the couple decided to enjoy their good fortune. That night the musical entertainment was excellent. There was a singer from the Bolshoi Opera and a guitarist from the Moscow Symphony.

After the great ball, Meyer invited the top musicians and singers to his home as well as the Political Kommissar, who was Professor Slavsky, a professor at the University of Marxism and Leninism in Moscow. Meyer knew how to make the right connections. The friendly Jew was due for release from the army and planned to return to Moscow. Through him, the Krons were able to send a parcel for his sisters – some food and clothing as well as boots and a leather briefcase for Yuly, Meyer's brother-in-law. He found out later that he never used them. The clothes were too luxurious for him to wear before his students. Truthfully, the best gift he sent them after the German withdrawal was the news of his survival.

They stayed in contact with Slavsky. He knew many things unknown to the general population. He told of the hundreds of concentration camps that existed in Russia, especially in the distant east and north. What had happened to Gita's cousins, Ore and Hoda Shifman, was now clear.

It was Slavsky's job to visit the camps and indoctrinate the inmates. These were not prisoners of war but political prisoners and there were millions of them. Stalin was a ruthless tyrant who was suspicious of everybody. He killed millions and sent millions more to Siberia. Those living in the newly liberated areas formerly held by the Germans were starting to feel the grip of this pathological suspicion. The honeymoon period of the liberation was over. Meyer's thoughts would soon turn to how his family might again attempt to flee – this time from their so-called liberators now turned tormentors, the Russians.

CHAPTER TWENTY-TWO

Torment

Shavl – Early 1945.

THE RUSSIANS IN SHAVL inherited a bombed out city from the Germans and the task of restoration fell squarely on the shoulders of the surviving and returning residents.

A few months after the final German retreat in late 1944, the new occupiers became very hard taskmasters, treating the beleaguered Shavl citizens as though they were responsible for the infrastructure's destruction.

Meyer and his team had to rebuild two unrelated operations and combine their activities: his own Frenkel leather factory and the Batas' shoe factory. Time bombs set to explode two days after the Germans' exit destroyed the shoe factory.

Shumkauskas and Meyer could not help feeling they were set up to fail. There was no way they could obtain what was necessary to rebuild and swing into production. Everything required an official permit. Although all plans submitted were for the common good, to fulfill ambitious government targets, it made not one jot of difference to the obstructive bureaucrats. Of course, red tape was not the only barrier to success: the machinery and raw materials were scarce and just not available through legally approved channels.

In the later years of the twentieth century, author Joseph Heller coined the phrase Catch-22, which he used to describe a false dilemma where no real choice existed. That same predicament was the one faced years earlier by the likes of Meyer and Shumkauskas. Using the black market to get what they needed to fulfill targets could land them in jail if caught, as would not meeting Russian expectations!

The two men rolled up their sleeves, figuratively speaking, and immersed themselves in the black market, deciding that failure to satisfy their masters was not an option. In order to secure coal for power generation, they spent considerable time drinking with, and bribing, military officials over at the airport where the Germans left a healthy supply. In fact, that was pretty much the pattern of every transaction whether it was for building materials, machinery or even the raw materials needed to manufacture the products demanded by Moscow.

The factory workers had similar larcenous tendencies, although theirs were purely for their own benefit, which might seem a harsh charge under such awful circumstances. Their wages were paltry and only the selling of scraps of leather enabled them to put food on the family table. It was a risky business also because of the frequent frisking of workers departing at the end of their shift. Of course, those charged with searching were also susceptible to a little bribery.

Leather was currency. Despite having storage centres full of the material, it was not easy for the bosses to lay their hands on it. Informants would notice their entry to the warehouses without good reason. Instead, Shumkauskas and Meyer had to devise acquisition and sales schemes that were more sophisticated. For instance, they would make an under-the-table deal with some distributors and supply more goods to them than were ordered. They split the profit generated by the sale of the surplus between themselves and their partners in crime.

The challenge was to find the raw material to create those ghost products. The light-fingered workforce, most of whom were already helping themselves to the in-house supplies, compounded that difficulty. They knew that if materials were missed, then the spotlight of suspicion would always shine more brightly on management. It worried Meyer but he did not want to become too diligent in stamping out such practices and thus remove the means by which normally honest folks could feed their families.

Thus, he devised a clever system that would not only enable the workers to steal for themselves but also for the greater good! When a shipment of hides arrived in the factory – often thousands at once – a committee of workers checked the quality of the hides. The leaders soon caught on to what their local bosses wanted and falsely downgraded the quality of many perfectly good skins. All was duly recorded and then the documentation was then kept under lock and key for later retrieval should there be any investigation into missing leather dubbed low grade. Two probes failed to find any evidence of malfeasance.

This technique was particularly useful in the shoe factory, where lower grade leather always yielded many fewer pairs of shoes than that of a higher grade. Some so-called low-grade leather thus created many more shoes than expected, which provided the likes of Meyer much more product with which to barter.

The illicit gains made by those on the outside went into their back pockets, whereas those realized by Meyer and Shumkauskas would be used primarily to secure their safe future and that of their workforce. However, if the spy agency unearthed the conspiracy, its investigators would not likely see the good in this strategy. The workers were thankfully unaware of the risks taken on their behalf. If they had known, surely one would have given the game away in exchange for a few roubles.

Such fraud was not unique to Frenkel's. Stealing was a way of life in the new republic of Lithuania, which supposedly took care of its entire people under the benevolent guidance of Moscow.

Sometimes things went wrong. One day, police arrested the entire shaving department of eight workers for theft. One was the husband of the Krons' ex-maid from before the war, Olga. She turned up at the house while Meyer was out. She was holding a live turkey that she handed over to a bemused Papa Shifman, hoping this gesture would encourage his son-in-law to exert some influence on the authorities to free her husband.

Meyer was furious. Acceptance of the fowl compromised him. He had no such influence but the man's release would give the impression he did have close connections with the secret police. That is precisely what happened the next day and there was no persuading the family that Meyer had nothing to do with the man's freedom. From then, the trail to his doorstep was a well-beaten path trodden by people seeking favours and help. Meyer grew more nervous with each visitation. He was sure at least one factory worker was a secret police plant. On the surface, Meyer was revered, but he feared some might think somewhat differently from the way they spoke. The visits from the secret police seemed designed to recruit him as an informant but what if they really did think he collaborated with the Nazis? Alternatively, and just as bad, what if they grew tired of his resistance to recruitment as a spy? Then perhaps he and his family would be just spirited in the night to some far-off gulag.

In April 1945, Meyer's thoughts turned to figuring out how he might visit Moscow to see his sisters. He could not just buy a ticket to fly or take the train. He needed an official reason to travel to receive a permit. The Minister of Light Industry, Teryoshin, would have to approve it. Meyer thought of him as a nice man; when he came to Shavl, he often slept on the floor of the Kron dining room.

Some days later, with permits in hand, Meyer set off with aide Halperin to Vilna where they would pick up the Moscow train. Driver Alexandrovich would escort them to the station and then head back to town. It was more than a half-day's drive along poorly maintained roads often not much better than farm tracks. The chauffeur took along enough rubber and glue to fix the flat tires he just knew they would suffer while travelling the gravel roads.

Seven flats later, there were no materials left to repair the punctured tire they got just 15 miles outside of Vilna. Finally, the men gave up and pushed the car to the side of the road, They then hitchhiked the rest of the way. They called on Teryoshin but he was not in his office because it was a Soviet state holiday.

Meyer knew the only way they were going to get a replacement tire was to visit one of the military transportation units stationed there and barter for one. Once found, they told their story to the officer in charge and offered him a pair of boots for a tire. He became angry at the suggestion of bribery and threatened to call the secret police. They had just not reached his price – three pairs of boots. When they did, he revealed that in order to honour the trade he would have to steal one from his general!

Goodness knows how he was going to explain away to his superior the loss of one of the tires from the luxurious and powerful ZIS-10A limousine. The car, modelled on the U.S. manufactured Packard, was the pride and joy of the senior officer. Meyer handed over two pair of boots and promised to deliver the third when he got back, which was perfectly acceptable to the soldier.

The rail trip passed uneventfully but Meyer later described it as an appalling experience.

"We travelled through the area where the major fighting took place in 1941," he told Gita after his return. "It was a picture of complete devastation. Hour after hour we travelled through the vast spaces where everything was destroyed – homes, farms, whole cities."

Meyer spotted stovepipes popping out of the fields where displaced people had dug themselves shelter below ground. As they steamed towards Moscow and its environs, everything changed. The Russians restored the battle-damaged areas exquisitely, leaving no signs of destruction. There were new buildings, a new university and even a Metro subway system featuring extravagantly and ornately decorated stations.

The station at which Meyer alighted was in complete contrast with his sister's apartment building round the corner. Its structure and general appearance was the same as he remembered, though there were many more cracks on external walls and it was more rundown inside. He learned later from his sister that the Tsar was in power when it was last painted!

Inside suite number four, the greeting awaiting Meyer was as warm as ever, despite the absence of some of his loved ones. His sister Chaytze was at the Far Eastern Front with Japan, so he had no chance to meet her again after his last goodbye back in 1920. Mary was at the ear, nose and throat clinic when he arrived.

Nevertheless, Yuly, Chaytze's husband, and Anne were at home. It was the first time he had met his brother-in-law and 24 years since he had last seen Anne. Back then, she was a lively, happy girl with bright eyes and curly brown hair. By 1945, her hair was grey and her eyes were opaque and unsteady. Throughout Meyer's stay, she appeared to be on edge all the time. Her voice was quiet but not naturally. It was clear she wanted to ensure that neighbours could not hear any of their conversation.

Yuly was a different story. He was a confident, good-looking and well-built man, who wore pince-nez and sported short black hair. Meyer reckoned he looked every inch the professor. He wore a khaki shirt with a high neck and a semi-military suit. After half an hour of exuberant chatting, they hatched a plan for Meyer to show up at Mary's clinic as a surprise patient. After she got over the shock, she leapt at Meyer and almost squeezed the life out of him.

It was an exciting two weeks, full of tears of joy and sadness in equal parts. There was much to be thankful for but the family losses also brought home to all how fragile their grip on survival had been.

Meyer's gifts – a basket of food and wine – were welcomed as warmly as he was. In the days that followed his arrival, all the contents were savoured and consumed slowly, for they knew not when they would sample such delights again, if ever. Muscovites faced severe rationing and lined up for hours to obtain even a piece of bread. Clothing and other necessities were not available at all. Meyer quickly realized just how much of a position of privilege he enjoyed back home in Lithuania, having access to exclusive stores set up for the elite. His sisters could visit the peasant market where fresh produce was available but prohibitively high prices deterred them. Meyer returned from the market one day, laden with the kind of fresh meat and vegetables not enjoyed by his hosts for many years.

There was work to be done. Meyer spent his days meeting with government figures and leather industry representatives. The Ministry of Light Industry bureaucrats warmed to the gregarious Meyer, honouring him as a representative of a "liberated republic"! He delivered several papers concerning the leather industry practices in the West, which was unfamiliar territory to the Russians. He also visited several industrial plants where the shop floor workers were all women.

Though his efforts were appreciated, all anybody wanted to talk about were the glorious advances of the Red Army towards Germany through Hungary, Poland and Bulgaria. Those with whom he conversed were less eager to acknowledge the Allies' progress from the West through France, Belgium and Holland. All agreed, however, that the end of the war with Germany was nigh. The fall of Budapest in February was a great event because the Red Army fought valiantly to take it. That great victory continued to intrigue Russian citizens. Dutifully, the government-controlled press continued to feed an appetite for every detail. The news of Roosevelt's death on April 12 did not make a great impression on them. If the Russian press even bothered to acknowledge American involvement in the war, it was underplayed. All successes were Stalin's and due to the brilliance of the Red Army.

When not talking about old times, the reunited siblings spent their evenings listening to the radio for war news. Meyer's siblings were almost delirious. They had a hard time during the conflict. They evacuated to Kuybyshev, now called Samara, a large city in the southeastern part of European Russia, when the Germans reached the outskirts of Moscow in the winter of 1941. They did not know what to expect when they returned. They just locked the door and left. They came back to discover not one stick of furniture was touched.

· As the stay ended, they anxiously talked about the next time Meyer would visit, this time with Gita. True to his word, Meyer showed up on the doorstep again with his arm around his wife.

It was September 1, 1945, the day that marked the final victory over Germany and its Far Eastern ally, Japan. The streets were alive with celebrations, with crowds dancing, singing and kissing each other with giddy abandon. The biggest impression left on the couple from Lithuania was images of Lenin and Stalin created from fireworks.

It was the perfect welcome for the couple, though there were times on their journey that they did not think they would make it. Gita needed a special permit from the Council of Ministers of the Lithuanian Soviet Republic to accompany her husband. Again, Teryoshin came through and they boarded the train in Vilna. They had separate seats in the same compartment as Meyer thought it unwise to sit together should one run into difficulties. Meyer's name was spelled "Kronas" in Lithuanian and Gita's was spelled "Kroniene" which means "Mrs. Kron." They passed through checkpoints without any problem. Then the railway police made the family connection and began to question the relationship. Trains were for business travel, not joy riders travelling for frivolous means.

Meyer's papers identified him as the chief engineer in a big factory, which seemed to satisfy them. Gita accompanied Meyer as his secretary but was without proof of her occupation. Meyer cursed his oversight. Just outside Moscow, the police ordered her to leave the train at the next stop. Meyer reached for what he called his diplomatic papers – perfectly cut pieces of sole leather packed into his briefcase. He tried to get a quick audience with the train's chief of police – every train included a police carriage. His request was denied so when the train pulled into Vyazma the two of them disembarked.

The ever-resourceful Meyer slipped into the men's washroom and set about creating the papers his spouse needed to continue her journey with him. From his briefcase, he drew a sheaf of the factory stationery he always carried for such emergencies. He carefully penned a note in a different hand from his own that identified Gita as his secretary. It informed the reader that she was travelling with him to Moscow on government business. He signed it Shumkauskas and used the rubber stamps stashed in his case to add to the authenticity of the documentation.

Then he spent a few moments deciding what approach he should take in solving this matter. He decided to play the role of an aggrieved captain of industry, a guest of the government, no less. Armed with the documentation and a thunderous look on his face, he addressed the station chief politely but assertively. He told him of the humiliation he and his secretary suffered at the hands of his uncouth men. They both boarded the next train and left the chief holding a rather fine piece of leather for his 'diplomatic' services.

For the remainder of the journey, Meyer and Gita stared out of the carriage windows lost in their thoughts. They found their tongues when the door to suite four opened at his sisters' dingy old apartment building.

The joy Meyer and his sisters shared on his previous visit multiplied as the Moscow family members enjoyed the company of the feisty Gita for the first time. After a few days, it became apparent to his sisters that there was a side of Gita that caused them great consternation. She was much more open in her conversation than her hosts and did not shy away from criticizing the Russians. She even hinted at a desire she shared with her husband to escape to the West. The sisters were true children of the revolution and their horrified response indicated they were scared even listening to her.

Meyer indulged his love of opera on what he and Gita knew would be their final trip to the Bolshoi. They were thrilled to see and hear the premier mezzo-soprano of the time – Vera Davydova – perform in Bizet's Carmen.

They danced a few a nights away in the Hotel Moscow's elegant ballrooms. While Gita powdered her nose between dances, her enterprising husband took advantage of the black market at the bar, buying gold coins at knockdown prices with roubles. They would be far more useful than roubles.

Acting on a tip he was given back home, Meyer bought lighter flints, which were sold there by the pound rather than by the piece as they were in Lithuania. These profitable transactions would help smooth their passage to the West. Meyer also did some legitimate business, settling a contract with an engineering firm to rebuild the factory back in Shavl.

The train journey experience on the outbound trip persuaded them that taking a plane home would be a wiser choice. They boarded an ex-military plane based on the Douglas DC3; confident they would be home in little more than an hour or so. Both suffered serious flight sickness in a terribly slow and bumpy trip. There was a special compartment at the back of the plane where air sick passengers could hang on to a pole mounted in the centre. It was a crowded place. One day they would laugh about it but then they thought they were about to meet their maker. Gita took some pills and slept, awakening as they landed with her head resting on the knees of an army sergeant!

THE REBUILDING PROJECTS GOT onto the fast track once Meyer returned and the engineer from Moscow was in place. In the New Year, the Krons began a serious project of their own – taking flight. Now there was extra incentive: Gita was in the first trimester of her third pregnancy.

CHAPTER TWENTY-THREE

Final flight

ESCAPE WAS NOT easy for any person, but belonging to a well-known family in the community made it even tougher.

Meyer and Gita were also concerned that if they fled while still living in the same household as Shumkauskas he would stand accused of assisting them. There was no choice. Meyer must quit his current job and move away from Shavl, which was easier said than done. He needed a special order from the Ministry.

Meyer procrastinated for a week or two, kidding himself that things might improve. Then something occurred that pushed him over the edge and he stalled no longer. At one of the regular after- work gatherings, he got a shock. A man known to him as a member of the secret police struck up a conversation with him after a few too many shots of vodka.

"You know, Miron Levovich, if I were you I would not stay very long in this place," he said, addressing him in typically Russian fashion as Meyer, Son of Leo. "Your file is about complete, considering your previous status."

Meyer's drunken informant stumbled back to another table, leaving Meyer white faced and dumbfounded. He knew this meant that the secret police considered him 'the son of an exploiter rather than the son of a worker'. Days later, the new director of Batas quietly offered the same warning. First, he was a collaborator, now an enemy of the people. It all added up to the same thing, a one-way trip to Siberia.

The only way he would get a ministerial order for a transfer to somewhere like Vilna would be for him to find his own replacement. He did not have far to look. When the Nazis ran the show, he had trained a man to do his job. Fortunately, the Germans had never had any confidence in the Lithuanians intended to replace their reliable and skilled workers, or else Meyer would not likely have survived. His name was Jakubauskas. After recommending his ready-made successor, Meyer got the bureaucratic ball rolling. He told Teroshyn he could not stand to live in the city anymore because of the sad memories it held for his family. He was sympathetic and especially cooperative after receiving some of the more desirable contents of Meyer's 'diplomatic' bag.

Meyer took a month's vacation and headed to Vilna to do some groundwork on securing a new position and discreetly finding a way of getting the whole family out of the country. While there, he bumped into Nachman Daitch, a Shavlite well known to Meyer. He had a reputation for being a resourceful man. As Meyer trusted him, he asked for an introduction to somebody who might operate an escape route.

Within minutes, they were sitting at a table in a nearby restaurant. The cafe owner began explaining his operation in barely a whisper as they toyed with mugs of coffee. Just as he was getting to the significant part – how he transported people over the border – in walked the Reises.

Meyer was shocked to see the family, who had shared the Krons' hiding place at Barbora's. Meyer curtailed the conversation swiftly. He got up to go, bidding the owner goodbye and telling him he would get back to him if necessary. He exchanged pleasantries with the Reises, though he did not really feel like doing so after spending such a stressful and thoroughly unpleasant time with them in hiding.

As he walked away, he decided he would not be contacting the people smuggler again, even if the plan did sound like a good one. It was too risky, especially as the Reis family had now seen him in the man's presence. Everybody was suspicious of everybody nowadays, he thought as he walked away.

In the spring of 1946, the Regular Congress of the Communist Party of the Soviet Union met. Every republic had to account for its activities and progress at this large conference. To prepare, Teryoshin called an advance meeting of top technical personnel to give an indication as to whether or not they were meeting the Russian dictated targets. The situation at Frenkel's was not promising to say the least. There was by then a shortage of everything. Meyer was brutally honest with Teryoshin. The Minister led Meyer into another room and shut the door behind him.

"If you want to get your Prikaz to move from Shavl, you better make sure that the plan is fulfilled."

Meyer did not blink. He could have cried. Fulfillment of the plan in terms of producing the leather or shoes in the quantity required was impossible. Both men knew that. Meyer caught on quickly. What the Minister really wanted was a report from Meyer stating that all was well and on track. Subsequently, Meyer, with the cooperation of local planners and some trickery, delivered a wonderfully rosy account of activities and accomplishments and got his permit. It brought a smile to the top bureaucrat's face.

Shumkauskas knew of Meyer's ultimate goal and wished him luck, grateful the Krons were putting some distance between them and him. The fly in the ointment was Papa Shifman, who refused to leave. Nevertheless, he raised no objection to their departure and wished them well.

The Krons moved to Vilna and stayed with Gita's old school friend, Dr. Chezia Savich, and his wife Etale, a dentist. Meyer transferred to the Leather Trust, taking up an important position as planning engineer for the whole industry.

Within days, Meyer found out from some trusted contacts that there were planes that left Vilna and went directly to Bucharest, in Romania. He eagerly sought out the address supplied to him but was not able to locate it. Did he take down the address wrongly? The mistake would have been finding the location, for it was a trap devised by the secret police.

So much for trustworthy contacts, thought Meyer. Nevertheless, he continued to meet people secretly; each person vetted and vouched for by those he trusted the most. On each occasion, before talking business, they would agree on the official topic of the conversation. Thus, if later questioned, they would both tell the same story. It was a simple measure that would later prove its worth.

Finally, in March of 1946, the Krons found a group whose leaders seemed reliable based on verified successes. Meyer made a down payment on their passage in the same way as they would for a family holiday. This would be a permanent holiday, they hoped. The date of departure would be in April chosen by the smugglers later. Shortly thereafter, the Krons received papers identifying them as Polish citizens with permission to leave Lithuania. What they could take with them was severely restricted for obvious reasons. Meyer bought a double-lined suitcase, figuring he would need somewhere to stash the black market gains they would surely need at some point to bribe some official to guarantee safe passage.

Meyer decided to leave for a two-week inspection trip of the leather and shoe factories in mid-April. It was the first day of Passover when Jews celebrate flight from Egypt. He figured nobody would notice his absence for a few days because it was a Jewish Holiday and by then the family would be long gone. The family celebrated the first Seder with their hosts, not telling them that the meal would be the last shared in Lithuania.

The next day Meyer tucked the bogus Polish documents into his pocket and left the office for the last time. He would first pick up his new suitcase from his supplier. He took a circuitous route there, passing along the quiet streets. After a few minutes, he felt sure somebody was following him, so he stopped to let a man behind him pass.

Meyer's heart almost stopped when the man stopped by his side and asked:

"Are you Engineer Kron?"

"Yes."

"Do you work at the Leather Trust?"

"Yes."

"Are you going on a business trip?"

"Yes, I am."

"You are under arrest."

The man produced a card identifying him as an officer of the secret police.

"You have no right to arrest me," Meyer pleaded. "For this you need an order of the Sovnarkom (Council of People's Commissars)."

The man produced it before the words were out of Meyer's mouth. During the exchange, the man kept his right hand in his pocket, indicating that he was holding a gun.

"You walk ahead," he said. "When you meet people you know, greet them, but do not speak. I will show the way."

The man led Meyer to the infamous building that housed the secret police. On the way there, fortune smiled and Meyer met a man from Shavl. He did not recall his name but the other man clearly remembered Meyer and shook his hand vigorously as do long lost friends. Under his breath, Meyer spoke quickly in Hebrew: "Go to my home and tell them that I am in trouble." The old neighbour then followed until he saw Meyer led into the secret police headquarters. It was not easy, but he found where the Krons lived and passed on the message.

Once inside the building, Meyer went directly for questioning. He was surprised to discover his interrogators knew of his every movement for the past couple of months. They knew all about family friends, including Isya Shapiro, who had escaped to Poland previously. They knew the dates of every clandestine meeting

Meyer attended. Thank goodness, Meyer had a cover story for every meeting.

Meyer suddenly remembered the false Polish documents nestled in the inside pocket of his jacket. He would be finished if they were found. During a lull in the examination, he asked to go to the bathroom. A guard escorted him to the toilets. Meyer closed the door and immediately tore the false papers into pieces, popped them in his mouth and chewed them to a pulp before swallowing them.

It was half an hour more into the resumed questioning before it dawned on the main inquisitor that he had not searched his prey. The subsequent search turned up only an innocent letter from Meyer's sisters in Moscow. They questioned Meyer for another two days, his interrogators changing every few hours.

Each inquisitor repeatedly asked Meyer if he had something to confess during the 60-hour grilling. Finally, Meyer decided he had to say something about his visit to the bakery, where the spies spotted him. He revealed that he heard others talk about escape but he was vague and that was of no interest to the man asking the questions

At about four in the morning on the third night, his inquisitors changed their tune. They began to praise him as a good worker and vital cog in the Soviet wheel. Then they got to the point of the charade. They wanted him to cooperate secretly and work with them as an agent to help discover the enemies of the people. Well, it would not be too hard to find Lithuanians who collaborated with the Nazis against the communists, Meyer thought. There were hundreds of them.

However, that is not what interested them. What they wanted him to do was spy on Jewish friends and report to them on people who wanted to leave the country or do anything else deemed anti-social. Meyer figured the only way out of this was to feign cooperation. They gave him the code name 'Match' – was this a sick joke? If it was, they did not smile. Did they expect this Match to burn his friends? They handed him a piece of paper on which was typed the address of a remote little house where he was to report to them at regular intervals.

Satisfied that they had turned him, they sent him on his way with the warning. His would-be controllers informed him that they would shoot him and ship his family to Siberia if he failed to report nefarious activities or, conversely, gave false reports. Meyer could not figure out why they let him go because they had enough proof to show he was not loyal to the state, or at least enough proof that would satisfy one of their kangaroo courts. His taking a new job in Vilna was too transparent for them to believe, or were they just stupid? No, he knew that not to be true.

However, later he discovered he had an ally in high places. The top man of the secret police of the Republic was a frequent visitor to Shavl and shared many a glass of vodka with Meyer, always leaving with all the leather he needed. He had taken an active interest, so to speak, after hearing of the interrogation from a friend of Meyer's. The friend was Irene Schochet, who worked at the factory before the war. The secret police drafted her during the conflagration. After demobilization in 1945, she married Meyer's leather chemist, Sam Barit, and they moved to Vilna. She took a big chance in approaching the chief of the secret police but it paid off.

Meyer arrived home in the early hours. After a prolonged embrace of Gita, he got straight to business:

"Up to now we have tried to escape together. Now we have to find a way for me to escape first, because I will not work as a spy against my friends."

The only alternative would have been suicide, Meyer thought, though he did not share that option with his wife. Gita and Ruta would have to go into hiding until there was an escape plan for them all.

Before releasing him, the police told Meyer to keep his arrest secret and to go about his usual business as if nothing had happened. Some chance of that. In the following days, it seemed to Meyer that everybody in the republic knew not only of his arrest but also of his release. Nobody would take the chance of talking to him about illegal matters again because they would assume he was turned.

Meyer continued with his inspection tour and went on to Shavl. Gita stayed in Vilna to try to make new connections because the original plan was no longer an option.

In Shavl, he stayed with Shumkauskas, who knew the whole story. Meyer sought out Jocius and after the customary bear hug – something Meyer never quite got used to – Jocius revealed that he knew of some escape operations in the Suvalki area. There was a spot along the border where it was easy to cross into Poland. Several days later, he had the names of the contacts. Meyer made some inquiries but his gut instincts told him to pass on that opportunity. A good choice, as a later story about a series of arrests confirmed.

That day in May 1946 was the last time Meyer saw Jocius. He had no chance to wish him well or thank him for his love and devotion to the family. Thanks to him, the Krons were alive. Meyer could not help thinking that Tamara would have survived if they had accepted his offer to take one of the girls in the early days of the German occupation.

A day or two later, a noisy, smoke-belching military truck – a Gazik – showed up at Meyer's lodgings one night. Out jumped two strangers dressed as Polish army officers. They had a simple, short message for him: "Gita sent us to pick you up."

He had to go with them and take a chance that it was not a trick. After all his efforts, Gita had been the one to find an escape route! He awakened Shumkauskas to tell him that he was leaving and asked him to find an acceptable excuse for his sudden departure. His actions would put the Shumkauskas family at risk but the man took the news calmly and wished Meyer the best of luck.

Gita found it desperately difficult to find help because everyone refused to talk to her after Meyer's arrest. Then she came across the two men now driving him back to Vilna and an escape plan was quickly agreed. They would drop Meyer off in the city, where he would wait until they returned with Gita and Ruta and others following the same escape route. They would then proceed eastward towards White Russia.

Not everything went according to plan. The truck kept breaking down. By the time they reached Vilna it was much later than expected. Passing through town, Meyer lay on the floor of the truck covered by a cloth. At the other side of town, because of the late hour, they stopped not at the agreed rendezvous but at some peasant's home. Meyer, dressed in a leather jacket and high leather boots, played the big shot. He sent his two escorts back to Vilna, telling them loudly that he would wait there for their return. The peasant was overawed and agreed to provide shelter for this man of great importance!

In Vilna, the plan was falling apart. Gita, who was by then seven months pregnant, had an additional burden. Ruta had scarlet fever and was not fit to travel. Nevertheless, it was now or never. They showed up in the district of Lipovka as planned during the afternoon. Unfortunately, Gita became lost, as she was unfamiliar with the neighbourhood. They left had Savich's house early with no baggage and without taking any documents with them. She did not want to appear to be leaving for good to anybody that might be watching them. All she took were her valuables.

Savich, who was dressed as a Red Army colonel, left separately and headed in a different direction. Miraculously, they came across each other at the entrance to a movie theatre. They stood side by side, looking at the displayed pictures of scenes from the movie playing that day. Savich secretively removed their identification documents from his pocket and put them in Gita's pocket before walking away without saying a word.

Now Gita and Ruta had to find the group. The only way to get there was to hire an Izvoshchik, a driver with a horse-drawn carriage. When they found one, he refused to take them because he feared they would not pay, especially as Gita was so vague about the destination. Ruta could see her mama was extremely worried and began to whimper.

"Don't worry, we'll find papa," said Gita, trying to comfort her child.

The mother-daughter exchange softened his attitude, if only a little. Now he was prepared to take them as long as they paid his fare up front. Gita handed over the cash, praying she was doing the right thing.

Meanwhile, Meyer watched the evening close in. There was still no sign of the returning Gazik. He left the peasant's house but not before jotting down a message. If anybody came by looking for him, his hosts should tell the visitor he was at the dentist's surgery – Savich's home.

Meyer was now in a very dangerous predicament. He began walking in the direction of central Vilna. When he entered Lipovka, he noticed a carriage across the street. Sitting on it were two familiar figures he could just make out in the failing light. Meyer shook his head in disbelief at his good fortune. Gita, her heart pounding, turned away from the man approaching in the leather jacket, terrified that he might stop them.

Meyer called her name and her head swivelled in an instant. He helped them off the carriage and sent the driver on his way. Their attempt to flee had failed. Meyer consoled Gita, trying not to transmit his anxiety to Ruta. His thoughts turned to considering what they might do next. Only minutes later, the truck with the rest of the group aboard came by and picked them up. It was another day of miracles.

There were ten people including the two leaders. The truck drove in the darkness. They would journey to a railway station and take a train to Brest, a border station between White Russia and Poland. All seemed to be finally going smoothly.

As the sun began to rise the following morning, the truck came to a sudden halt, jerking awake the snoozing passengers. One side or the other had blown up the bridge ahead.

The group was in the middle of nowhere and would look to be a very suspicious lot if discovered by patrolling soldiers. They ran for cover under bushes at the bank of the river, out of sight from the bridge. After catching their breath, they spotted a small boat hidden among the bushes. Their fortuitous find transported them all across the river, three at a time.

They were now in no man's land. After roaming around for nearly half the day, they came across a military station. The leaders bribed a guard to drive the motley crew to the next station. Meyer was relieved that their journey could continue. Ruta dutifully stepped up, accepting the hand of a man who helped her over the raised side of the vehicle. She was now quite adept at clambering on and off trucks.

Then, once again, Meyer helped his tired wife to climb up into the back. Her face was grey and she was scared half to death at the prospect of delivery not to the station but into the hands of the authorities. She need not have fretted, for the young soldier's word was good. They pulled up at the Baranovich railway station a short time later. They were not alone. Thousands of people were lining up for tickets. The escape leaders changed again into Polish uniforms and played the role of senior officers to the hilt. They procured the tickets just in time to board the train.

The next morning, as they approached the border station of Brest, border police took up positions at the door of each car. They led everyone to a field where they would wait until the train to Poland showed up. A good part of the day passed. The wait was nerve wracking for everybody: everybody except the kids who made new friends and played with each other in the field, never straying too far from their parents or guardians. Ruta may have left some of her new playmates with an unexpected gift, scarlet fever! Her parents were not going to worry about such an indiscretion.

The Krons and their fellow travellers received new documents, which identified them as hailing from different families. If the authorities arrested one family member, the others could escape because they went by a different surname. Meyer was now Max Weiss, the surname being his late mother's maiden name, while Gita and Ruta shared the name Wallach.

The leaders assured their charges that they had good relations with the border police and they should not worry. Meyer hoped so because the documents in their hands would not stand up to much scrutiny.

When the train arrived, it took an age to load. Every uniform put the fear of God in Meyer and Gita. Even when every carriage was full, it was several more hours before a wheel turned. On the steps by every door was a Russian border policeman. Was this a trap? That sickening thought entered Meyer's mind and remained there for the duration of the trip. The distance from Brest to the border with Poland was only a few miles but the train moved very slowly. The distance seemed endless and the hours that passed were many.

Finally, the border was crossed and the Russians jumped off the steps. Meyer and Gita both sighed with relief as the soldiers' heads passed their carriage window. There was a search at the border but the Krons carried no luggage, just the paper bags supplied by their protectors containing food for the journey. Ruta clung extra tightly to her bag, for hers was the most valuable. She had a big responsibility.

The wily Meyer decided the food would serve a second purpose aside from the obvious one. Gita worked two gold coins into some toothpaste until they were covered. They also rolled some American dollars in plastic, courtesy of Meyer's black market activities. He tucked that money, a diamond ring, and a couple of other items of jewellery into the bellies of the salted herring.

He handed that bag to Ruta as they boarded the train and just looked at her face to face for a few seconds, without saying a word. She watched him hide the valuables and did not need telling that she should hold on to it and not let it out of her sight. Papa trusted her and that meant a great deal to the little girl still tormented by the belief that she alone was responsible for the loss of her little sister.

A big cheer rose from the whole train as people realized they were across the border and safe at last. Meyer celebrated with a vodka or two provided by the escape team leaders. The train journeyed on to the Polish industrial city of Lodz, where the weary wanderers alighted and slept off their fears in rooms booked as part of the escape package. These boys would have a future in the travel business, said Meyer.

Lodz was bursting at the seams with thousands of people in transit, many just like the Krons with false documents. Many were Russians running away from Stalin's evil empire. The Krons sold some of their stash to get money for food. Gita even met one of her former university professors, who found a way to sell the gold chain that once belonged to Meyer's late mother. They also met Leiba Peisachowitz, another of Gita's cousins. He had just come out of the woods, where he spent the wartime with partisans of Vilna fighting the Germans.

This was not the end of their journey. They were still not in the Western Zone, the only place beyond the reach of the Russians. Meyer left Gita and Ruta in their awful room in Lodz to travel on to Breslau, where he hoped it would be easier to plot the final leg of their journey to freedom. He hated leaving them there but at least it was safe, if unsanitary. It was a middle room, though which other tenants could walk at any time. The bed was half-broken and there was no toilet. They had to go down several flights of stairs to a dirty toilet without a seat situated in a dark corner of a room.

Meyer folded the remaining proceeds of his wheeler dealing and put it into his wallet. He then took a bus to Breslau – now Wroclaw. Breslau had been part of Poland – as it was again – the Kingdom of Bohemia, Austria, Prussia and Germany.

The largely German-speaking city had suffered heavy bombardment and it was impossible to find any address. While walking around Meyer met a Jewish man who kindly helped find a place to stay for a few days. When it came time to pay his rent Meyer reached into his back pocket to discover his wallet was missing. While dozing on the bus somebody helped himself to the last of Meyer's cash. More saddening was it contained the very last picture of Tamara in existence anywhere.

Meyer was close to breaking point. He sobbed. The distressed man poured out his soul to the property owner, a Jew by the name of Kabrovski, who survived the concentration camps. The generous man forgave Meyer the rent due. He went further, offering advice on how Meyer might secure passage to the West.

Transportation to the American zone of Germany was available for Jews who were born in Breslau. The problem now was how to get papers saying they were born there. It could be done but for a price. A price Meyer feared he might not be able to meet even by selling the diamond ring still in his possession. He reported to the friendly innkeeper that the cost was 50,000 zloty. Kabrovski agreed to sell the ring for him. As he took it in his hand, he looked more closely at it, and then held it to the light, admiring the setting of the small stones. Meyer explained it was his father's, passed on for several generations.

"In that case," Kabrovski said, looking Meyer in the eye, "don't sell it."

"It's the only way I can afford those papers," he answered woefully.

"Don't worry. I will lend you the money and you can pay me back later," said Kabrovski, waving off any objections before Meyer even had the chance to make them.

Kabrovski planned to move to Munich eventually. He was a good businessman and, after liberation from the concentration camp, he prospered in Breslau. He sent Meyer on his way with money for the forged documents and enough to get back to Lodz to pick up Gita and Ruta and transport them all to their final destination.

A couple of days later they returned and the amiable landlord greeted them all as if they were long-lost relatives returning to the bosom of the family. The man's money was burning a hole in Meyer's pocket: the next day he went to get the vital documents he needed.

Gita and Ruta stayed behind in the small upper floor room. Gita sat by the window staring out at the busy multitudes below. She welcomed the rest. This child inside her was going to survive and live in freedom. Ruta ran around with boundless energy, occasionally joining her mother at the window. It was a warm spring day and the window was partially open so she could hear the chatter of people below. For the first time she noticed many of them spoke German. She reached for her mother's hand. Gita read her mind.

"It's alright. These people just speak the language. They are not real Germans," she said, patting Ruta's hand. That made sense, thought Ruta, Germans could not possibly have children of their own; they were so cruel that they killed children.

Meyer returned soon after with the new documents. He stuck with his mother's maiden name. It had been lucky for him so far. They successfully registered for transportation the next day and spent a couple more days as non-paying guests of their new benefactor. Much vodka was downed and Meyer vowed to repay the man's generosity in Munich. They parted as dear friends. Their benefactor wished them well.

"See you in Munich, my friends!"

BOARDING THE TRAIN was not without incident. Soldiers repeatedly checked every traveller's papers and tickets. The delays and the rough treatment of the German speaking Polish guards irritated Gita. She boiled over when one prodded her large belly with the business end of a bayonet.

"So, what's in there?" cackled the soldier, with a whiff of vodka on his breath.

Meyer watched in horror as she shoved the soldier's rifle aside and slapped him on the face with a staggering force never witnessed before:

"You have already killed one of my children . . . you are not going to kill another before it has taken its first breath."

The stunned young officer retreated hastily without saying another word, much to Meyer's relief. Ruta was a little confused, as only the day before mama assured her these were not the same kind of Germans.

Minutes later, they were aboard, but it would be another few very tense hours before the wagons were rolling. The British zone would have been a short journey in normal times but it took several days. The train stopped at every station along the way to pick up more refugees. They travelled in rail freight cars without toilet facilities. They were not unlike those in which the children of Shavl, including Tamara, had travelled to their final destination – Auschwitz. Gita sat on a makeshift seat, while Meyer leaned against the walls of the car, changing position when it became uncomfortable. Ruta just squatted on the floor.

Everybody was jittery. Whether they would make it to the West was the foremost question on everybody's mind. There were quarrels between the real German Jews of Breslau and the fake Breslau Jews, who were mostly Polish. The former group was offended 'ineligible' Poles would take valuable space, denying their 'eligible' kin seats on the train. The Krons spoke German well so they never became embroiled in any conflict.

By the time they finally arrived at the Displaced Persons Camp controlled by the British Army, the train was a tinderbox. Another few hours in the oppressive overcrowded conditions and Meyer feared it would have exploded in violence. He heaved a sigh of relief as they disembarked. The train's occupants gathered in a large compound where they awaited screening. All had to appear before the British soldiers and if they satisfied their inquiries then they would be given new identification cards. From there they would proceed along a narrow corridor to where the departing vehicles waited.

Being taller than most of the crowd, Meyer could see that there was a second screening place. There people were sent either to the left or right. A selection technique not unlike that staged at Auschwitz and one with which many around Meyer would have been all too familiar. Instinct would have told them that direction to the right would be desirable because that direction saved them once before. The checkpoint officer asked Meyer to state his birth date. In perfect German, he answered:

"I was born on the seventeenth of March, 1905."

The correct answer but for a reason other than it merely being the truth. Meyer soon discovered it was a trick question. Some of the ethnic German Jews aboard the train told the British authorities that some of those presenting themselves as Germans were Polish and therefore had no right to passage. It was a cruel thing to do to their fellow Jews but they left the British soldiers little choice. Now that they knew of the subterfuge, they had to follow the protocol agreed between the Allies and the Russians no matter what they may have privately wished to do. The trick was that westerners gave their birth date in day, month and year order whereas eastern Europeans generally volunteered only the year.

The Polish Jews whose ruse was uncovered found themselves in a compound waiting for transport back to Poland. While waiting they learned how they were tricked. The mob overcame the guards and rejoined the screening line-up. This time they would give their birthday in the western way. The Brits at the head of the long line quickly learned of the break out and ordered everybody back for a further screening.

This time they did not buy Meyer's story and disqualified him, putting him under guard. He never did figure out what it was that caused them to disqualify him, not that such knowledge would help him out of this plight that threatened to separate him from his family.

They believed Gita, let her out of the holding compound and she went immediately to pick up Ruta from the field where the children were playing peacefully, as though this were just one big, fun game. She had no idea that the two of them and her unborn child faced an uncertain future alone. She would soon discover, once it was too late to go back, that her husband was about to be handed back to the Russians.

He would surely be dispatched to Siberia and never have contact with his family again. He would not be able to watch his third child grow, play with its big sister, and enjoy the fruits of the abundant West. Meyer tried to be more positive and turned away from the sorry group before him, all of whom must have shared similar depressing thoughts.

He looked out of the fenced compound just as trucks began pulling up to pick up the 'legal' passengers to take them to the train to Munich. He saw Gita and Ruta outside set to board a truck. Well, at least they would be able to pay back their Breslau patron. Despite his personal circumstances, he smiled and tried to think positive thoughts. Maybe he could get a message to Kabrovski to pass on to Gita before his expulsion to Lithuania. He was sure that is where he would be, following the inevitable discovery that he spoke not one word of Polish and therefore could not claim citizenship of that country.

Suddenly, a ruckus broke out among some of those unlucky ones waiting for transport in the opposite direction from where they wished to go. The guards rushed in to break up the fight and Meyer saw his chance. He ran faster than he had ever done before towards the low wire fence and leapt over it, tumbling to the soft earth as he landed. He picked himself up and chose the exit to the westbound trucks. He would always have a soft spot for those members of the Polish nation who unwittingly caused such a diversion.

Luckily, his demonstration of athleticism went unnoticed by anybody that threatened his freedom. Though Gita missed the sprint and high jump she saw him, seconds later, dive onto the back of one of the trucks. She pulled Ruta in the direction of that same truck and calmly tossed several packages sitting on the ground onto the truck bed, covering her husband in the process. A smiling Brit soldier helped the heavily pregnant woman up onto the truck.

Once they were safely on their way, Meyer emerged, dusted himself off and the reunited couple roared with laughter. Ruta did not know what all the fuss was about and why her mother hid her father in that way.

Meyer hauled out the cognac Kabrovski gave him for the journey and took a long swig. Unthinkingly, he offered Gita a belt of the hard stuff. She just smiled and patted her belly. She was taking no chances at this stage of her pregnancy. There would be plenty of time for celebratory drinks after the birth of their first son, Leo.

"We're free at last," he yelled.

Gita's smile grew wider.

"Yes, my Mara, we are," was all she said. They were lucky ones, for the nation they left behind would remain under the governance of the Russians for another 44 years.

The laughter of her parents faded as Ruta retreated into the private world of her imagination. She recalled the time when she had missed the ride on the back of the big truck that had taken her little sister Tamara.

Tamara's screams drowned out her parents' celebrations. She could hear her sister's desperate pleas for help. She could see those outstretched stick-like arms waving all over again.

Ruta stared expressionless as the mayhem of the displaced persons camp disappeared into the distance, wishing she could have had another chance to hold on tightly to her sister.

CHAPTER TWENTY-FOUR

Epilogue

Vancouver, Canada – March 2001.

THE SILENCE THAT GREETED Ruta Kron Sigal's closing words was not the polite quiet in which she began to deliver her message to the high school students 20 minutes earlier.

Now it was a stunned silence.

During the first few minutes, one or more of the 60 or so chairs occasionally creaked as its teenaged occupant restlessly shifted position. Less frequently, a stage whisper from the rear was faintly audible as it penetrated the front row of the large room in the Vancouver Holocaust Education Centre.

Nevertheless, Ruta's dramatic story of her family's escape from the clutches of the Nazis and her chilling recollection of how many fellow Jews they murdered during their bloody occupation of her native Lithuania soon glued the youngsters to their seats and tied their tongues.

Brows furrowed while young fingers nervously stroked and tapped chins. At times, there were furtive sideways glances from boys checking to see how their friends were dealing with all this talk of real death and destruction. Strange, given the long hours many had undoubtedly spent unleashing death and destruction via electronic war games on their home computers. They noticed the girls with tears in their eyes and quickly looked away, perhaps fearing an errant droplet of water would leak from their eyes.

A cough or a loud sigh might actually have provided a welcome break in the tension that now filled the room. There had not been a single auditory disturbance since the first five minutes had ticked by. Only the naturally amplified sound of Ruta nervously swallowing to lubricate the lump in her throat punctuated her shaky delivery. As the head of a large university women's program, she had frequently spoken with confidence and directness to much larger audiences. This was different. Her personal story, no matter how many times she told it, never got any easier to tell.

"Just before World War Two, in Siauliai where I lived – which we knew better as Shavli or Shavl – was a thriving, small city in the north of the country. And at that time the Jewish population was 5,360," Ruta informed them in the same straight forward, just-the-facts-manner a social studies teacher might address this same group back at school.

The vivacious grandmother, whose attractive appearance belied her painful past, even smiled as she talked about the richness of Jewish family and cultural life. For her father Meyer Kron, mother Gita and little sister Tamara lived a blessed life prior to the outbreak of the Second World War.

Nevertheless, the sentences she spoke a few minutes later wiped a smile from her face that would not reappear until much later when she spoke lovingly about those who risked their lives to hide her and save her parents.

"The Jewish population grew to 6,500 as Polish refugees and other Jews from elsewhere tried to outrun the advancing Nazis. About 1,000 of them fled into Russia a few days prior to the German takeover of Shavl on June 25, 1941. In the first two weeks of the occupation, 1,000 Jews were murdered by the Nazis and many of our own neighbours."

Almost a month later, the Nazis ordered the remaining Jews to move to two ghettos in the poor part of the city, while that shabby neighbourhood's former residents helped themselves to the homes of the displaced Jews.

"A further 1,000 Jews sent to nearby Zhager were killed there over the last four months of the year and another 750 Jews, who were forced to work in other nearby villages, were also wiped out."

The facial expressions on the young audience matched the speaker's for seriousness and concentration. She paused to give the audience an opportunity to perform some mental arithmetic.

Ruta continued teacher-like: "If you are good at math you will have figured out that by the end of the year more than half of the original Jewish population was murdered."

She told them with a despairing sigh that the story throughout Lithuania was the same. At the beginning of the war, more than 200,000 Jews called Lithuania home. After the cessation of hostilities, around four per cent of them remained and it no longer felt anything like home to those that survived.

Ruta's voice grew a little louder and the words came a little quicker as she recalled:

"My parents' determination to survive grew as members of our family and good friends died or suffered at the hands of the Nazis or the Lithuanian fascist collaborators.

"They became more inventive and daring in their bid to keep our family together. No matter what our tormentors did we were not going to allow them to beat us into submission."

She went on to tell some of the stories of bravery and cowardice recorded in the chapters that precede this one. At this point, many fellow Holocaust survivors would have stepped back and asked if there were any questions. Ruta pressed on. She had something to say about why the young audience before her should care about this piece of history from the last century.

"I'm sure you must think my story is horrific. I do too. It happened many years ago so perhaps you think it means nothing today but if you do you would be wrong."

Her mild rhetorical admonishment hung in the air briefly. There was still no discernible movement among the audience.

"My story was locked away in a mental closet of my own making for many years," she explained, preparing to bare a little more of her soul.

"Our elders told us: 'You did not suffer. You were safe. You were hidden in the homes of rescuers.' We 'the hidden children', as we are known, were left feeling that our stories were not as important as those told by older people who had survived Hitler's concentration camps – Auschwitz, Dachau to name but two of the death camps."

Unfortunately, that suppression of memory made many younger survivors victims again. With no outlet to confront their past, they found themselves unable to deal with life today or relate healthily to their spouses, their children and their grandchildren. That said, many were so emotionally damaged by the experience of being removed from their families and, in some cases, coerced to convert to Christianity it is likely that they would remain silent whether their elders had given them 'permission' to speak or not. Fortunately, today, there are support groups for child survivors and their offspring.

Ruta continued: "A few years ago I reached that age when people often begin to reflect on their life. I needed to come to terms with it and fortunately I had a loving, understanding family that helped me wrestle with my past."

For this trained psychologist and counsellor, the disturbance of old, painful memories long locked away was at first a self-awareness exercise, designed to bring her some peace in her later years. Then events around the world persuaded her she must emerge more publicly from her mental closet to tell her story. This initially self-indulgent exercise had revealed to her that she had a valuable lesson to share with today's youth. If she chose not to tell her story then it would die along with her, because she was among the last living witnesses to this most terrible era of human history. This was an uncomfortable realization for such a private person.

The memories of survivors and witnesses to the Holocaust are sometimes incomplete and accounts may be coloured by the bitterness and trauma of their experience. The Holocaust deniers pounce upon such human failings and the historical inaccuracies they produce as proof that it never happened or is no more than a wild exaggeration. Ruta anticipated that these members of a generation brought up on the wonders of the Internet, where deniers freely spread their hate-filled messages, would raise these doubts about the believability of Jewish claims.

"It happened. I was there," Ruta testified succinctly, adding, "The records of the Nazis prove that it happened. The mountains of Jewish hair in the Auschwitz museum prove it happened. The broken Zyklon B canisters used to gas thousands of Jews before sending them to the ovens also on display prove it happened."

If the students believed that genocide was an aberration of the past, Ruta quickly disabused them of that hopeful notion.

"I saw the sickening TV footage of the genocide in Rwanda and later in the Balkans," she explained. "Ethnic cleansing is the new phrase coined to describe the slaughter of one particular race or tribe of people. The term sounds a little too 'clean' for me. Let us call this form of cold-blooded mass murder by the dirty word it is – genocide.

"It wasn't the Jews that were victimized this time but I have to ask how long will it be before somebody comes after us again?"

A few seconds of silence followed then she walked a couple of steps before answering her own question.

"Anti-Semitism is on the rise again, even here in Canada where we pride ourselves on being liberally minded and tolerant of others."

This was not just a 'feeling' or a pet theory: it was a truth. A year later, news stories independently confirmed her fears when they revealed that Canada had recorded 197 anti-Semitic incidents in just six months.

She politely thanked the youngsters for their attention. There was a loud sniffle from a blonde girl at the back, which triggered more sniffles. Ruta's powerful story always had the same effect on the kids. She took heart in such a reaction, daring to hope that the new generation will learn from history and not be doomed to repeat its errors, to paraphrase an oft-quoted yet frequently unheeded piece of popular wisdom.

One after the other, a dozen youngsters approached Ruta to embrace her as their classmates quietly filed out. They were long, heartfelt hugs. The high school students spoke no words. None seemed necessary, as Ruta had said it all.

A little more than a year later, Ruta thought it was time to open her mental closet doors still wider, to revisit her childhood years when she bore the name Ruta. She decided she must record the Holocaust experience of the Krons of Shavl (Siauliai) and she completed that task just before her passing on December 16, 2008.

A small news item Ruta spotted back in 2002 drove her to complete the task. Two more that followed served only to convince her of the wisdom of that decision.

Siauliai, Lithuania, April 20, 2002: On this anniversary of Hitler's birthday, swastikas were found painted on almost all of the gravestones of Jews in Kristijonas Donelaitis cemetery of this small Lithuanian centre.

Siauliai, Lithuania, January 2003: Neo-Nazis disrupted Hanukah celebrations. On Christmas Eve, somebody pulled down a menorah that was to be lit that evening. Activists from the Lithuanian National Democratic Party, the country's main neo-Nazi party, which has some seats on the local city council, held a rally during the ceremony, holding anti-Semitic signs and shouting insulting slogans.

Vɪʟɴɪᴜs, Lɪᴛʜᴜᴀɴɪᴀ, Fᴇʙʀᴜᴀʀʏ 2004: Lithuanian Poll on Ethnic Tolerance Released. Lithuanians are generally tolerant towards dark-skinned people, extremely intolerant towards Roma (Gypsies) and split on attitudes towards Jews. 30.9% of respondents had positive feelings towards Jews, 20.4% had a negative attitude and 54.8% were neutral. The January 29, 2004 edition of the news magazine Veidas contains an article in which the author argues that if the question about Jews were to include the contentious issue of the restitution of Jewish property lost during the Holocaust, tolerance towards Jews would instantly disappear.

CHAPTER TWENTY-FIVE

After the Holocaust

THE KRONS journeyed to Munich after their flight from Lithuania, following brief stops in displaced persons camps.

There they reunited with the Peisachowitz family, some of whom were liberated from the Dachau Concentration camp. Dr. Wulf Peisachowitz was serving as the chief director of a hospital in Bogenhausen, which served the ever-swelling displaced persons population.

Gita's cousins found Meyer a job as the principal of the Organization for Rehabilitation-Through Training School (CORT) in the small Bavarian town of Feldafing. Gita gave birth to Leo on August 1, 1946, in a nearby hospital.

Soon after, Meyer started a tannery in Diessen with an acquaintance from Lithuania, staying there for almost five years. They then decided to move to Israel to reunite with Gita's sister Bluma. However, Gita developed a heart condition and Meyer feared the desert heat might be deleterious to her health.

On March 11, 1951, the family of four arrived in Halifax, Nova Scotia, in Canada, and travelled on to their destination, Montreal. Meyer spent three months in hospital with infectious hepatitis. An attempt to operate a new tannery fell apart but Gita prepared for a new career as a teacher attending the Jewish Hebrew Teachers' Seminary.

Meyer left Montreal in March 1952 to operate a government-run tannery in Regina and the rest of the family joined him at the end of the school year. The factory burned down in May 1953. A client in Winnipeg offered Meyer work at the J. Leckie Company in New Westminster, near Vancouver, where he stayed until 1964, when he moved to his final job at B.C. Fur before retirement. Gita obtained a teaching post at the Beth Israel Religious School and Talmud Torah Day School in Vancouver. Meyer died October 10, 1986 and Gita on November 10, 1994.

Ruta – known as Ruth in her adopted country – obtained a degree in Bacteriology at the University of B.C. She subsequently married Cecil, a successful dermatologist.

They had three children, Marilee, Elana and Michael, and all live in Vancouver. Marilee married Avihu Nachmani and had Tamara, Benjamin and Naomi. Elana married Dana Prince and had Zachary Meyer (died age 16, leukemia) and Joshua. Michael married Bibi Fishman and had Aaron.

After doing research and social work for 10 years, Ruth went back to UBC, at 39, to gain her second degree in Counselling Psychology. Ruth was the Director of the UBC Women's Resources Centre for 25 years.

Before and after her retirement, she received a number of notable awards, including the YWCA award for lifetime achievement, UBC President's Award and Gold medal, the Canadian Government award for contributions to Canadian society as a Hidden Child Survivor of the Holocaust and the UBC Alma Mater Society Great Trekker Award.

Ruth was also a cofounder of the Vancouver Child Survivors of The Holocaust group.

In 1996, she had a kidney cancer removed. In 2007, she was found to have widespread metastases and died on December 16, 2008.

Ruth's brother Leo graduated medical school at UBC before training to become a child psychiatrist in New York. He lives there with wife Jill Rubin and they have a son, Josh, and a daughter, Emily.

Wulf Peisachowitz moved to New York after the war, where he was affiliated with Mt. Sinai Hospital. He remained unmarried and continued to practice until his retirement and died in 2003, just a month short of his 98th birthday.

Chaim and Rachel Peisachowitz moved to Montreal. Chaim died in 1965. Rachel married Lazar Lapidus and died in 2003.

Dr. Joseph Luntz was liberated from Dachau. Berta (Barbara) Nurok Luntz survived the forced march from Stutthof Concentration Camp but her mother Eugenia died en route.

They reunited by chance in Prague when Joseph spotted his wife on a street corner. They had a son called Eugene in 1947 while in Munich. The family moved to New York in 1950, where he practiced medicine and rekindled his friendship with Wulf Peisachowitz. Joseph died of cancer in 1958, aged 59, and his wife died just six years later, aged 48.

Simcha Brudno survived Dachau Concentration Camp and became a noted professor of mathematics at MIT in Chicago.

Zava and Riva Gotz survived Stutthof and Dachau and reunited in Rome, Italy in 1948. In 1949, they had their second son Amos. In 1950, they moved to the United States and in 1957, they reunited with their 14-year-old son Ben. Riva died in 1990 and Zava in 2000.

Ben is now a retired engineer living in New Jersey with his wife Bernice. He has three children and five (6 in December) grandchildren.

Yankl Ton and Esther Ziv were married after the war and lived in Kaunas, where in addition to Ben and Haviva Ziv (Esther's daughter - born 1940 - and a child survivor of the Shavl Ghetto), they had two additional children. In 1972, Yakov, Esther and their extended family immigrated to Israel, where they have nine grandchildren and ten great grandchildren. Yakov died in 2008.

Misha Shabsels – the Living Corpse – also made New York his home. He married, raised a family and reintroduced himself to his saviour – Wulf Peisachowitz – when the doctor attended a reception for the arrival of Ben Gotz from Lithuania. His whereabouts after that occasion are unknown.

Nathan Katz escaped the ghetto with his young wife Sima and after the war moved to New York, where he headed a successful real estate business until his death in 2005. In 1999, he published his autobiography, 'Teach Us to Count Our Days'. He was instrumental in placing memorials to the Jews executed by the Nazis and their collaborators.

William (Wulf) Levin, the ghetto policeman who helped Ruta off the truck during the Kinderaktion, survived Dachau. He also immigrated to New York, where he now lives in retirement with his wife Manya. They have two sons, eight grandchildren and six great-grandchildren.

Polina Toker reunited with her husband Chaim when he returned from the Eastern Front and they immigrated to Israel.

Joseph and Felya Zilberman survived the concentration camps and made a home after the war in Paris. They had a second daughter, Sonia (Wasserman), who lives in Rehovat in Israel.

The Rescuers

RUTH'S RESCUERS ONA and Antanas Ragauskas remained in Lithuania for the rest of their lives, though daughter Grazina eventually immigrated to Canada and now lives near the Sigals in Vancouver. Ruth visited her rescuers four times over the years. Ona received recognition as one of the Righteous among the Nations by the Yad Vashem Holocaust Martyrs' and Heroes' Remembrance Authority in Israel. Antanas died in 1998 and Ona in 2004.

Dr. Domas Jasaitis fled in 1944 and ended up in Tubingen, Germany. He became head of the Lithuanian Red Cross and worked for a relief agency. He and his wife Sofija landed in New York aboard a Liberty Ship in 1950. After passing the American medical boards examinations, Domas practiced until 1968. He died in 1977 and his wife in 1981.

In 2001, the Lithuanian government recognized each of them posthumously for their rescue of dozens of Jews, including the Judenrat scribe Eliezer Yerushalmi and his family.

Jonas Jocius remained in Shavl and died in the 1980s. He remained in touch with the Krons for years.

Father Adolfas Kleiba returned to Lithuania after the war and served as a priest in Ligum. He died of kidney cancer on an unknown date. Father Justinus Lapis and Father Vincas Byla also continued to serve their flocks in Lithuania until their deaths.

Pranas and Barbora Jakubaitis remained in Lithuania until their passing some years ago.

The Nazis

LIMITED ACCESS TO THE personnel records of the key Nazis featured in Ruta's Closet and the natural inclination of these individuals to disappear without trace have made it difficult to ascertain exactly what happened to them after the war.

SS Hauptsturmführer Heinrich Forster showed up in Dachau Concentration Camp and sought out the Shavl Jews. He tried to maintain the ruse that the children taken in the Kinderaktion were safe in a children's camp. There was a post-war investigation into his conduct but no charges resulted and he died in a bicycle accident in 1955.

Gebietskommissar Hans Gewecke received a four-year jail sentence for his role in the hanging of Mazovetsky. What happened to Hermann Schlöf after the war is unknown to the authors.

Bibliography & recommended reading

The books listed were among those most frequently consulted in preparation for the writing of Ruta's Closet. The names may refer either to authors or in some cases compilers or editors. The current publishers and ISBN catalogue numbers also appear in the cases of widely published books.

Annihilation of Lithuanian Jewry:
Oshry, Rabbi Ephraim; Judaica Press 1995. 1-880582-18-X.

The Routledge Atlas of the Holocaust:
4TH EDITION: GILBERT, ROUTLEDGE, ISBN-10: 9780415484862

Auschwitz: Nazi Death Camp:
PIPER, F & SWIEBOCKA; T, AUSCHWITZBIRKENAU MUS., 83-85047-74-3.

Barbarosa: Hitler's invasion of Russia 1941: GLANTZ, DAVID M.; TEMPUS 2001, 0-7524-1979-X.

Barbarossa: The first 7 days, FOWLER, WILL; AMBER 2004, 0-9544356-8-0.

Black Cross, Red Star: Air war over the Eastern Front Volume 2 Resurgence: BERSTROM, C & MIKHAILOV, A; PACIFICA MILITARY HISTORY 2001, 0-935553-51-7.

Conscience & courage: Rescuers of Jews during the Holocaust: FOGELMAN, EVA; ANCHOR BOOKS 1995, 0-385-42028-5.

Death Dealer: Memoirs of the SS Kommandant of Auschwitz: HOSS, RUDOLPH; DA CAPO PRESS 1992, 0-306-80698-3.

Destruction of the European Jews: HILBERG, RAUL;
HOLMES & MERCER 1985, 0-8419-0910-5

Einsatzgruppen Reports: ARAD, Y; KRAKOWSKI, S;
SPECTOR, S; YAD VASHEM 1989, 0-89604-058-5.

Essays on Hitler's Europe: DEAK, ISTVAN; U. OF
NEBRASKA PRESS 2001, 0-8032-6630-8.

Eyewitness Auschwitz: Three years in the gas chambers:
MULLER, FILIP; IVAN R. DEE 1979, 1-56663-271-4.

**Good old days, The: Holocaust as seen by its
perpetrators and Bystanders:** VARIOUS; KONECKY
& KONECKY 1988, 1-56852-133-2.

Hidden Children: Forgotten survivors of the Holocaust:
STEIN, ANDRE; PENGUIN 1994, 0-1401-7051-0.

Historical Dictionary of Lithuania: SUZIEDELIS,
SAULIUS; SCARECROW PRESS 1997, 0-8108-3335-2.

Hitler 1936-1945 Nemesis: KERSHAW, IAN;
NORTON 2001, 0-393-32252-1.

Hitler: 1889-1936 Hubris: KERSHAW, IAN;
PENGUIN 1998, 0-14-013363-1.

Hitler's Police Battalions: WESTERMAN,
EDWARD B.; KANSAS 2005,0-7006-1371-4.

Holocaust Chronicle, The: VARIOUS;
PUBLICATIONS INTL. 2000, 0-7853-2963-3.

Holocaust in history: MARRUS, MICHAEL;
KEY PORTER 2000, 1-55263-120-6.

Holocaust, The: GILBERT, MARTIN; HENRY
HOLT & CO. 1985, 0-8050-0348-7.

I escaped from Auschwitz: VRBA, RUDOLF;
BARRICADE BOOKS 2002, 1-56980-232-7.

Jews of east central Europe between the world
wars: MENDELSOHN, EZRA; INDIANA
UNIVERSITY PRESS, 0-253-33160-9.

Jews of Lithuania, The: GREENBAUM, MASHA;
GEFEN 1995, 965-229-132-3 Jews,

Lithuanians and the Holocaust: EIDINTAS, ALFONSAS;
VERSUS AUREUS 2003, 9955-9613-8-4.

Journey through hell: WEISS, RESKA; OUT OF PRINT.

Judenrat: TRUNK, ISAIAH; U. OF NEBRASKA
PRESS 1996, 0-8032-9428-X.

Kollaboration und Massenmord: STANG, KNUT;
PETER LANG 1996, 3-631-30895-7.

Kristallnacht: Prelude to Destruction: GILBERT,
MARTIN; HARPER COLLINS, 0-06-057083-0

Litvaks, The - A short history of the Jews in Lithuania:
LEVIN, DON; YAD VASHEM 2000, 9653080849.

Masters of Death: The SS Einsatzgruppen and the
invention of the Holocaust; RHODES, RICHARD;
ALFRED A. KNOPF 2002, 0-375-40900-9.

Mein Kampf: Hitler, Adolf; VALORE
BOOKS & OTHERS, 395951054

National Socialist extermination policies: HERBERT,
ULRICH; BERGHAHN BOOKS 2000, 1-57181-751-4.

Operation Babarossa 1941 (2) Army Group North:
KIRCHUBEL, ROBERT; OSPREY 2005, 1-84176-857-X.

Pinkas Shavli: A diary from a Lithuanian ghetto (1941-1944):
YERUSHALMI, ELIEZER; YAD VASHEM 1958, UNAVAILABLE.

Righteous, The: GILBERT, MARTIN;
DOUBLEDAY 2002. 0385-60200-X.

Siauliai Ghetto, The: lists of prisoners: VILNA JEWISH MUSEUM, 9955-9556-0-0.

SS: Hitler's Foreign Divisions: BISHOP, CHRIS; AMBER 2005, 1-904687-37-7.

Sword and the Cross: History of the Church in Lithuania: SUZIEDELIS, SAULIUS; OUR SUNDAY VISITOR, 0-87973-416-7

Teach us to count our days: KATZ; NATHAN; CORNWALL BOOKS 1999,0-8453-4874-4

Vanished World of Lithuanian Jews, The: NIKZENTAITIS, A ET AL; RODOPI 2004, 90-420-0850-4.

Villa, the Lake, the Meeting, The: Wannsee and the Final Solution: ROSEMAN, MARK; ALLEN LANE PENGUIN, 0-71--399570-X.

War of annihilation: Combat and genocide on the Eastern Front 1941: MEGARGEE, GEOFREY P.; ROWMAN & LITTLEFIELD 2006,   0-7425-4482-6.

Wartime experiences in Lithuania: BOGOMOLNAYA; RIVKA LOZANSKY; VALLENTINE MITCHELL, 0-85303-406-0.

Years of Extermination, The: Nazi Germany and Jews 1939-1945: FRIEDLANDER, SAUL; HARPER PERENNIAL, 978-0-06-093048-6.

Index